THE DISCOVERY OF LANGUAGE

THE DISCOVERY
OF LANGUAGE

Linguistic Science in the
Nineteenth Century

HOLGER PEDERSEN
translated by
JOHN WEBSTER SPARGO

INDIANA UNIVERSITY PRESS
BLOOMINGTON

TRANSLATOR'S PREFACE

FOR the most part this work is a translation of Professor Pedersen's *Sprogvidenskaben i det Nittende Aarhundrede: Metoder og
Resultater*, Copenhagen, Gyldendalske Boghandel, 1924, which appeared as Volume XV of *Det Nittende Aarhundrede*, an imposing
series edited by Aage Friis and designed to present the cultural history of the nineteenth century in all its aspects. The relatively un-
important deviations from the original have been made either by the
author or with his advice and consent. Scholarly works which have
appeared since 1924, and are of such a nature as to affect the conclusions expressed in the original text, have been mentioned by the
author in the translation; other changes include occasional amplifica-
tion of a statement or the use of different examples. Word-forms
thoroughly familiar to the Scandinavian reader might not be illuminating to the reader of an English translation, and therefore
more appropriate examples have been selected in place of those on
page 272, the first paragraph of page 273, and most of the first paragraph of page 274 of the Danish text.

The way of the translator is hard, as any one knows who has gone
that way; especially hard when a work of a scholarly nature is involved, where extreme fidelity in translation is imperative. That
way would not have been trod in the present instance if the translator had not thought he saw in the original certain cardinal virtues
which would make the book a desirable addition to the English
literature of linguistics. The problems, as well as the accomplishments, of the study of linguistics during this most important of
centuries are faithfully and clearly recorded. Before each step in
advance is described, the need for this step is pointed out, so that we
have not merely a dry recital of events, but a story which gives us a
series of living pictures of these pioneering intellects actually at work
wrestling with problems the solution of which constitutes one chapter
of the most stirring history we know, the history of the achievements
of the human spirit in winning new knowledge.

In spite of the tremendous advance in knowledge of the past
century and a quarter, the results have not been incorporated in our
general culture. The average cultivated person of today can be
expected to know less than nothing of linguistics. One reason is that

these results have not been easily accessible to any save specialists, and another is that this remarkable story has never before been told as Professor Pedersen tells it. Perhaps the most important reason of all is the terror of language study so prevalent in America, a terror which would be comical if it were not so far-reaching in its effects, culturally and spiritually. It is the hope of the translator that this book will help to dispel some of that feeling by showing how really interesting and relatively simple the study of languages is.

Finally, one important feature of the work which should be mentioned is the striking rôle assigned to the study of phonetics in increasing our knowledge of linguistics. It is shown clearly that every important advance during the last century and a quarter was made by a scholar who attacked his problem from the phonetic side. Surely this fact has its importance for the future of linguistic study, and suggests that the indifference to phonetics in many of the graduate schools in the United States is an evil presage for future progress.

In translating the Danish words *sprogvidenskab* and *filologi*, the English words *linguistics* and *philology* have been used, respectively. Present usage is quite distinctly tending toward a differentiation of terms for the activities formerly combined under the one word *philology*. Certainly the work of scholars like Skeat and Pollard, or Sweet and Wyld, is sufficiently different to warrant calling the specialty of the latter two *linguistics*, while the field of the former two remains *philology*. This usage detracts in no way from the scope of the old usage of *philology*, and in addition introduces a precision desirable for the more highly specialized field.

Two of my colleagues, Professors W. F. Bryan and A. W. Smith, have kindly read portions of the manuscript, and the former has helped with the proof-reading. Professor George Lyman Kittredge has examined the entire work, and has made innumerable suggestions for improvement. Without his interest and encouragement, and without the practical assistance of my wife, the translation would never have been printed.

JOHN W. SPARGO

NORTHWESTERN UNIVERSITY
EVANSTON, ILLINOIS
August 1, 1930

CONTENTS

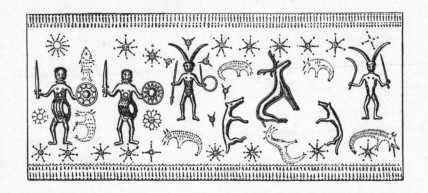

INTRODUCTION

UNTIL the close of the eighteenth century, European linguistic science had advanced but little beyond the knowledge of linguistics achieved by the Greeks and Romans. It is true that little by little some of the elements had appeared which were necessary for development beyond the limitations and errors of the ancients, but as yet they had no influence. The soil was prepared, but it was not until the nineteenth century that growth was destined to spring from it.

PAGAN ANTIQUITY

The characteristic striving of the Greeks toward an understanding of existence in all its aspects naturally led them to philosophize about language. From their starting-point in philosophy they passed on to a description of language, which was further developed by the careful study of their ancient literature. What the Greeks created the Romans took over. The Greek names for the sounds and parts of speech and for inflectional endings were translated into Latin, and were handed on from the Romans to medieval and modern Europe as a living testimony of Hellas's contribution to linguistic science.

But when the Greeks — or the Romans — ventured on inquiry concerning the origin of words or the relationship of languages, they necessarily went astray.

They could not possibly have clear ideas on the relationship of languages, since they had no material for comparison. Although there were several different dialects in Greek literature, the differences among them were too slight to provoke deep speculation; and the study of foreign languages was not a matter of concern to the ancients. Certainly the Romans studied Greek assiduously, bowing as they did before the superior culture of Greece; but the study of the "barbarian" languages, which were without literature for the most part, belonged to the culture of neither Greek nor Roman. It was purely accidental if an individual Greek or Roman had any knowledge of one or another of these languages, and his knowledge in this respect had to remain necessarily his own private property under the conditions of book publishing in ancient times. When the poet Ovid was banished from Rome to the province south of the mouth of the Danube, where the city of Costanza is now, he had an opportunity — which he certainly did not desire — to learn the speech of the inhabitants. These were the Getæ, a Thracian tribe, of whose language modern scholarship would gladly have more exact knowledge which would help to solve many problems concerning the linguistic transition between the Balkan Peninsula and Asia Minor. Ovid displayed his ability as a linguist when he wrote a poem eulogizing the Emperor Augustus in the language of the Getæ. We deplore the disappearance of this poem, but its loss was inevitable. Who was there to preserve or copy it? No Roman could read it, and of the Getæ nobody would bother with it. Antiquity did, however, produce men who by virtue of unusual linguistic talents mastered a number of different tongues. Just as the nineteenth century had its Cardinal Mezzofanti, who could converse with every traveller to Rome in his native language, but who nevertheless produced nothing of value to linguistic science, so the last century before Christ had its admired linguist in King Mithridates the Great of Pontus, who is said to have known twenty-five languages. His kingdom was in Asia Minor, which must have been in ancient times a land of the most varied dialects; and Caucasia, which also felt his power, is to this day famous for its Babel of tongues. But such stores of knowledge could neither be made publicly accessible through the book trade nor be employed in the interests of linguistic science. Antiquity may have had its Mezzofanti, but it had no Rask or Bopp.

It is therefore no great wonder that the comments of ancient authors on speech-kinship are extremely naïve. When they hit upon the type of similarity between two languages which we have learned to explain on the ground of common descent from a primitive language long since extinct, they knew of no better expedient than to assume borrowing or to regard the one language as the source of the other. Thus, Latin passed for a corrupt form of Greek, and certain superficial observations gave rise to the supposition that it was descended from one particular Greek dialect, Æolic, spoken in the coast regions near Troy, whence legend claimed that Æneas, progenitor of the Romans, had wandered. Moreover, antiquity saw no objection to the idea that a single language still living at that time might have been the source of all other languages. It was a problem of discovering merely which of the living languages was the oldest. Very characteristic is the story in Herodotus of the method used by an Egyptian king in his attempt to solve the problem. He had two new-born infants reared out of all hearing of human speech, in order to find out what they would first say after they had passed the stage of unintelligible cries. After two years the children were heard to cry *bekos*. The king asked in which language this word had a meaning. He learned that in Phrygian — spoken in the province of Phrygia, in Asia Minor — it meant "bread," and thereafter Phrygian was regarded as the oldest language: so easy was it to establish the naïve conviction that the first and most primitive language still existed as a contemporary tongue. Such a view leaves no possibility of any idea of linguistic development; it permits only the conception of linguistic corruption.

The lack of a clear conception of the reciprocal relationship of languages does not in itself preclude an intelligent grasp of the relationship among words in the same language. We shall see below that the people of India, aided by the great clearness of their language, had carried very far the analysis of the component parts of a word which convey meaning, and the investigation of word-formation. But Greek and Latin were far from the transparency of Sanskrit, and the Greeks and Romans did not attain anything like the Indian mastery of word-analysis. Hence etymological science could gain no foothold among them. In so far as etymology was concerned, they lacked any sort of method, either in the analysis of forms and the determination of semasiological development, or in the investigation of phonetic changes. To their eyes a word seemed a formless mass. They made no serious effort to determine what was the stem and what was the inflectional ending, what the root and what the derivatory element. Therefore a Roman could imagine that *vulpēs* "fox," genitive *vulp-is*, really was "fly-foot," compounded of *volō*

"I fly" and *pēs* "foot," genitive *ped-is*; and that *lepus* "hare," genitive *lepor-is*, really was "lightfoot," from *levis* "light" and *pēs* "foot."
It did not occur to the Roman that the stems were entirely different
in these words. And he would not have understood that there could
be any objection to this procedure. Dropping the *d* in the oblique
cases of *pēs* and changing it to *r* in the genitive *leporis* occasioned
him no scruples. He tampered with sound-changes at will, and
never in his wildest dreams would it have occurred to him that proof
was necessary or could be applied. Much less would he have considered necessary any proof for a superficially plausible development of
meaning. Everything was permissible, even the idea that things
could be named from qualities which were their opposites. *Bellum*
"war" came from *bellus* "beautiful," because war is *not* beautiful;
foedus "alliance, peace" came from *foedus* "ugly," because peace
is not an ugly thing.

A few scattered instances of false etymologies such as these make
no very strong impression; but they can be multiplied until the head
swims. It is significant that nobody knows whether Plato was in
jest or earnest when he put a series of astonishing etymologies in
the mouth of Socrates. If it really was Plato's intention to make fun,
he was sadly misunderstood, for his etymologies found acceptance,
and he himself was regarded in ancient times as the founder of
etymology.

The ancient world bequeathed to Europe a legacy heavy with misunderstanding of the history of language; and European linguistic
science continued to labor under it until the range of linguistic
knowledge had been extended beyond the dreams of the ancients.

CHRISTIANITY. THE MIDDLE AGES

The spread of Christianity marks one of the stages in the history
of European linguistic science. It brought with it the first great
expansion of the linguistic horizon. Christianity broke down the
barriers between the Græco-Roman civilized world and the barbarians, and created literature among many peoples where none
existed before.

None of the numerous peoples who had close relations with the
Greeks and Romans was awakened to an enduring national life by
the pagan culture of ancient times. Practically all of their languages
disappeared (Albanian is almost the only exception), and left behind

them at most a few brief inscriptions which stimulate rather than satisfy the curiosity of our time. But when the doctrines of Christianity were proclaimed in the native tongue of a people, a native literature developed which often very quickly produced worthy results even in secular literature.

The tremendous significance of this new literature for our knowledge of linguistics hardly requires emphasis.[1] But these new creations of Christianity brought with them no immediate progress in method, since conditions of book publishing and bookselling remained the same as before, and made impossible any extensive survey of the European linguistic world which was now accessible through literature. Instead of one small Græco-Roman linguistic circle, there developed a series of circles, all equally small. In the Middle Ages a scholar knew his own language, that of his nearest neighbors, and Latin. But even if he could add a little Greek, like the scholars of Ireland, he had no trustworthy foundation for the study of comparative linguistics. Investigation could be carried out only on the old lines. Here and there valuable work was actually done within these limitations. One example is the four grammatical treatises from the twelfth, thirteenth, and fourteenth centuries which are to be found in Snorri's *Edda*. The first and oldest of these is, under the guise of a proposal for spelling reform, an excellent bit of phonetics — a description of Old Norse pronunciation, which is highly significant for us today. Some grammars of individual languages, too, were written during the Middle Ages. But in the weakest point of the ancients, the Middle Ages made no progress. The etymologies put forward in all seriousness were, if possible, even worse than those propounded by the ancients: Latin *barbarus* "barbarian," genitive *barbarī*, was thought to be a compound of *barba* "beard" and *rūs* "country," genitive *rūr-is*, "because those who dwell in the country have coarse beards"; *barbarus*, then, was "country-beard," a meaning which errs in the same way as the ancient etymologies, but even more seriously, because it is obvious that Latin *barbarus* is simply a loan-word from Greek, and therefore cannot be explained as a compound of two Latin words.

[1] Similarly, modern linguistic science owes much to Buddhism (see, for example, p. 192, below, on Tokharian). On the other hand, we have nothing to thank Mohammedanism for in this respect: it proselyted not so much in the language of the conquered people as in the Volapük of the sword. The *Koran* was not translated, but had to be read in Arabic, and the Mohammedan invaders put a complete stop to many national developments which we should gladly have seen continued to the present day.

THE SIXTEENTH AND SEVENTEENTH CENTURIES

At last the invention of printing put an end to this fatal standstill in method, and rendered possible the more comprehensive survey which was the first requisite for advance in the recognition of kinship among languages and among individual words. From this point of view, the beginning of the modern period is a turning-point in the history of linguistic science. The resumption of the study of Greek, which had been almost completely forgotten in Western Europe during the Middle Ages, and the unexpected expansion of the linguistic horizon with the discovery of America, increase considerably the contrast with the preceding periods.

The effects of this increase of material together with the expansion of horizon quickly became apparent. As early as the sixteenth century, grammatical sketches of the languages useful in practical life had become common, and notes on remote and little-known languages were printed. A case in point is that of the Fleming Busbecq, whose notes on the remnants of Gothic in the Crimea were printed in 1589. During the second half of the sixteenth century attempts were made to survey all the languages then known. The Swiss scholar Gesner published a *Mithridates* in 1555, and in 1592 Hieronymus Megiser of Stuttgart printed *Specimens of Forty Languages*; in the second edition of 1603 the number was increased to fifty. In 1599 Joseph Justus Scaliger divided the languages of Europe into four major and seven minor classes. The four major classes he designated according to their words for "God": *deus-*, *theos-*, *gott-*, and *bog-*languages; that is, Latin and the Romance languages, Greek, Germanic, Slavonic. But he adduced hardly any linguistic material to support the correctness of his divisions, and he included only those languages whose interrelationships must force themselves upon any investigator. Where research was necessary to discover a relationship, he missed the relationship. He even declared in downright terms that there is no reciprocal relationship among the eleven classes. If he observed some of the resemblances — which he could hardly help doing — he must have explained them as due to borrowing, by Latin from Greek, by the modern languages from Latin — that is, in the same direction as the progress of civilization. Thus he did not advance beyond the ancients' unhistorical conception of language.

In general, Scaliger's attitude is typical of the whole period of the sixteenth and seventeenth centuries. Some observers made discoveries in the field of linguistic relationship, but they did not know how to draw the correct conclusions from them. The Lithuanian Michalon pointed out in 1615 the relationship between Lithuanian and Latin. But he concluded that the Lithuanians were Italians and of Latin blood; and on the other hand, he rejected the relationship between Lithuanian and Russian. He felt instinctively that Lithuanian was not, as foreigners have thought, a Slavonic language. This feeling he expressed, quite in Scaliger's vein, by denying categorically all relationship between it and Russian. And from its resemblances to Latin he concluded that Lithuanian was a sort of Latin. The correct conception of a series of coördinated languages which descend from one and the same language no longer existent did not occur to Michalon.

In the same spirit, scholars were ready to consider Persian a Germanic language. We find the first mention of this idea in a work on the language of the Goths, written in 1597 by Bonaventura Vulcanius. He cites several points of agreement in vocabulary (twenty-two instances in all) which a brother scholar had found in an edition of the Books of Moses in four languages, Persian among them. Most of the agreements noticed are correct, but several are wrong, e.g. the comparison of Persian *xudā* [1] "God" with German *Gott* and its cognates. This conception of a special kinship between Persian and Germanic haunted the minds of scholars for more than two hundred years. It was much easier, in view of the linguistic ideas of that day, to adhere to this conclusion than to make the new discovery the starting-point for a complete revision of the conceptions in force regarding the "reciprocally unrelated" linguistic families of Europe. Typical, moreover, is the accidental way in which attention was directed to Persian; nobody worked through all the accessible material in order to investigate the mutual kinship of languages: scholars were content with what they stumbled upon accidentally.

They were not always content, however, with the conception of a number of "reciprocally unrelated" languages. On the contrary, they often dreamed of deriving all existing languages from one and the same source. Usually they attempted to establish Hebrew as the parent language of all the rest. When one realizes that Hebrew has, practically speaking, no resemblance to the European lan-

[1] In this word *x* should be pronounced like German *ch*.

guages, it is not surprising that extraordinarily high-handed methods were necessary to "prove" this theory, such as adding or dropping sounds at will, and every kind of transposition and displacement. One of the principal advocates of the theory explained these discrepancies by the fact that Hebrew is written from right to left, whereas the European languages are written from left to right! It is not impossible that the worst follies committed in the name of the Hebraic theory may have called forth some scepticism in one or another of the more enlightened intellects of the time; but even then scepticism sprang from a certain native common sense. Reasoned objections to this theory were necessarily out of the question at this period. The method followed was still approximately that which had been inherited from the ancients, though it was applied to new material. Even the almost incredible failure to differentiate between writing and speaking, which betrays itself in the reference to the direction of writing, can be paralleled by citations from the ancients. And whatever might have been thought of this or that etymology, the hypothesis as a whole enjoyed wide acceptance. The excellent Danish grammarian Peder Syv in his *Remarks on the Cimbric*[1] *Language*, 1663, explained Danish *barn* "child," "in Jutland *ban*," as from Hebrew *ben* "son," and so on. Thus he was prepared to stand linguistic history on its head for the sake of the theory, and to explain the most recent Scandinavian form as the most ancient.

In these mistaken speculations there is the same fortuitous quality as in the linguistic discoveries mentioned above. No one had actually worked through the material and observed that any language has an older appearance than the others. A scholar selected some familiar language, explained it as the oldest on some basis which had nothing whatever to do with linguistic observation, and then sought to prove his assertion by means of all the wrong-headed methods he had inherited. Hebrew was usually chosen, on supposed Biblical evidence. But others chose their native tongue. Goropius Becanus made Dutch the original language, and so on; and by means of the methods then current, it goes without saying that the truth of any such theory was demonstrable.

[1] By "Cimbric" Syv means "Danish."

THE EIGHTEENTH CENTURY

In the eighteenth century we meet with a new spirit. For the first time, scholars rise superior to accidental circumstances, and are no longer satisfied with patching together at haphazard the materials put into their hand by chance. For the first time, real inquiry starts. The problem of the relationship of languages is formulated in full, and the systematic collection of material begins.

The famous philosopher G. W. Leibniz is the foremost figure in the new development. He inveighed vociferously against the Hebraic hypothesis and every other variety of "Goropianism"; but he did not fall back on Scaliger's hypothesis of a series of "reciprocally unrelated" families of languages. On the basis of material available at that time, though he does not cite the sources of his knowledge, he tried to construct a comprehensive system of linguistic genealogy. This system is set forth in a dissertation in the first volume of the memoirs of the Berlin Academy which appeared in 1710 with the title *Miscellanea Berolinensia*. Leibniz assumes here that the languages in most of Europe and Asia, as well as in Egypt, are descended from one and the same original language. The huge territory which he regards as a unit we now divide among from five to eight linguistic families. Even though there may be some relationship among these various families (see below, pp. 335, 336, ff.), it is nevertheless clear that Leibniz's grouping rests upon no thorough-going analysis, but only upon some sort of inspired intuition. His is not acquired knowledge, but a kind of divination. On the subject of the classification of this immense territory, Leibniz makes several interesting observations. He places Persian at a proper distance from Germanic, and says distinctly that, with the single exception of the word for *God* (compare above, p. 6), he has been unable to find in Persian any more Germanic elements than can be found in Greek. But on the other hand, Leibniz is guilty of many errors, which indicate that either he or the sources upon which he depended could not distinguish between the resemblances due merely to borrowing and those due to deeper causes.

But men's minds were now open to a better understanding of the kinship between languages, and a systematic collection of materials was begun, partly on the initiative of Leibniz, who tried to interest his many correspondents: travellers, missionaries, even Peter the Great of Russia. Catherine II was more interested in linguistic

science than Peter the Great, and as the result of her active interest, a great survey of more than two hundred languages of Europe
and Asia appeared in 1786–87, edited by the famous German traveller, and natural scientist P. S. Pallas. A later edition included also
African and American languages. A similar work was edited by the
Spanish Jesuit Lorenzo Hervas y Panduro in 1800–05; it included
three hundred languages of Asia and Europe, and of America, where
Hervas had labored as a missionary. The last great work of this
kind, *Mithridates*, we owe to the German scholar Johann Christoph
Adelung. Publication was begun in the year of Adelung's death,
1806. The later parts were published by Johann Severin Vater, the
last volume appearing in 1817, by which time a new day was beginning to dawn, too late to affect this work. Certain of the weaknesses
in Adelung's *Mithridates* must be ascribed to its author: the material
is far from being as correct as one might wish. Even with languages
as near at hand as the Scandinavian, comical errors appear, and
several discoveries which had already been made failed to receive
due attention. But on the whole, *Mithridates* may be regarded as
representing the state of knowledge immediately before the dawn
of the new period. By examining it, we can best estimate the tremendous progress in our knowledge of living languages which is due
to the labor of the nineteenth century. Not least instructive is the
treatment of those languages which we have now learned to group
as the Indo-European family. Adelung has no suspicion of its existence. The individual languages of the family are discussed according
to their geographical position — Southern Asia, Western Asia,
Europe — in fraternal association with the alien languages in the
same regions; and the information given on mutual relationships
consists partly of old, partly of new errors. We are regaled with the
old wives' tale about Persian and Germanic, which Leibniz had tried
to kill; and by a curious error Adelung attributes to Leibniz himself
the assertion that entire verses may be written in Persian which a
German can understand. Such a wild statement had actually been
made, but not by Leibniz. From classical antiquity Adelung took
over the idea of special kinship between Latin and Greek. To this
he added a mass of pretended learning on a whole series of ancient
languages now extinct, of which he really knew nothing. With the
help of these, he constructed a "Thracian-Pelasgian-Græco-Latin
family of languages." [1]

[1] On Thracian, compare below, p. 223, where it appears that the language was Indo-Euro-

Thus the eighteenth century outlined a comprehensive programme for linguistic science, and undertook the great labor of
collection. It would be unjust not to mention the completion of
several works treating scientifically and in detail various limited
linguistic fields: Job Ludolf compared all the then known Semitic
languages in 1702; Lhuyd treated the living Celtic languages in
1707; the Swedish scholar Ihre published in 1769 his *Glossarium
Suio-Gothicum* — an attempt at a great Swedish etymological
dictionary; Gyármathi produced grammatical proof of the kinship
between Hungarian and Finnish in 1799.

All this activity presaged the new day which was to dawn in the
nineteenth century.

pean, but that it stood, in spite of its geographical proximity, none too close to Greek. The Pe-
lasgians are often spoken of by Greek authors, but the conceptions which the Greeks associated
with this name were rather indefinite. The name was given to several peoples who dwelt or had
dwelt in Greece or its immediate vicinity, among others, to the people of Lemnos (see below,
p. 215). To judge from these facts, Pelasgian was not an Indo-European language. On the relationship between Latin and Greek, see below, p. 78.

THE NINETEENTH CENTURY

IN the Introduction we have seen how the opportunities of surveying a greater and greater linguistic territory increased from one period to the next, until, in recent times, after the resumption of the study of Greek, the linguistic horizon of the ancients was combined with that of the Middle Ages in one great survey. This survey produced in itself the need for method, the need for a principle of rational classification of this vast material.

In spite of its very different appearance, the linguistic science of the nineteenth century carries on logically from the earlier development: the butterfly bursts forth from its cocoon as the result of the growth it has experienced within its winter shelter.

The nineteenth century created the method which the previous development called for, and still further increased the material available for study. This new material was not the least important factor in revolutionizing the whole conception of language. The knowledge of the language of ancient India was a genuine revelation, not only because of its great age and transparent morphology, which unexpectedly cast new light upon the related European languages, but also because European scholars here became acquainted with a highly developed linguistic science which had other points of departure and another evolution than the linguistic science of the Greeks. Moreover, it was distinguished by the very thing so lacking in Greek linguistics — systematic, rational analysis of the forms of speech. But this was not the only addition to previous knowledge. Everywhere linguistic material from older times was brought to light which made an historical treatment of language possible — in distant Iran as well as in the regions of Europe known in ancient times, among the Slavs, the Germans, the Celts. Thus in every way the study of the Indo-European family of languages was broadened. Of this family, whose existence was first recognized at the beginning of the century, even the least-known members were drawn into the circle of investigation: first Lithuanian, the great age of whose forms became evident in the new light of linguistic comparison, and attracted attention early; then, much later, Albanian and Armenian, which required a more mature scholarship to penetrate their secrets, because of their less perfectly preserved forms. Contemporaneously, knowledge of the non-Indo-European families was increased to a degree previously unknown, although the thorough-going comparative study devoted to the Indo-European group was only occasionally extended to them. The discovery and interpretation of inscriptions and archæological discoveries, for the most part written in unknown script and composed in extinct and forgotten languages, played an especially important part throughout the century. They have brought us message after message from civilizations long since vanished, and apart from their great significance for linguistic science itself, have made possible a conception of the history of writing which earlier times never dreamed of.

Evolution of method and expansion of material went on side by side, with constant reciprocal influence. But in the following treatment, the two sides of the growth of our science will be considered separately. First the broadening of the horizon will be treated; then the evolution of method; and finally we shall comment on the pre-history of our family of languages, from the vantage-point of the present day.

I

THE ANCIENT LITERARY LANGUAGES OF INDIA AND IRAN BECOME KNOWN

INDIAN

IN very ancient times the Indians had already developed a literature. Its oldest monuments are religious in content. The *Vedas* (*vēda-* = "knowledge") are collections of ritualistic hymns, the oldest being the so-called *Rig-Veda*. The oldest prose works are what might be called theological dissertations. To determine exactly the age of the most ancient literature is very difficult, as the Indians did not interest themselves in history or chronology. One's conclusions must be drawn from internal evidence. The geographical area of the *Rigveda* is the region about the Indus, and its hymns apparently date from a period before the spread of the incoming people of Indo-European race throughout India was complete. Thus they reflect a stage of society and of civilization very different from that of later periods. With these facts in view, it is customary to date the oldest Vedic literature about 1500 B.C. One scholar, alleging astronomical observations, would place the date at least a thousand years earlier. To what extent reminiscences of so ancient a time are actually to be found in the hymns of the *Rigveda* does not concern us here; but it is incredible that the *Rigveda* as an organic whole can date from such a period. It is difficult enough to explain how Vedic literature could have survived from 1500 B.C. to the time when the Indians created their own delicate script on the basis of the Semitic alphabet, apparently about 800 B.C.[1] The explanation is to be found in the constant care with which the Indians watched over the correctness of the sacred words, even down to the finest shades of pronunciation, in the belief that otherwise their religious sacrifices would fail to produce a beneficial effect, or might even work harm. This solicitude for the sacred texts gave the first impulse to the study of grammar, which subsequently was applied to secular literature. This secular literature, written in a form of the language to which the name

---

[1] Very recently certain scholars have assigned a considerably later date to Indian literature, but no doubt they have exaggerated their point.

Sanskrit is given in a narrower sense, because it varies slightly from Vedic, comprises great epic poems, lyrical and dramatic works (the most famous of which is the Sākuntala of Kālidāsa), fables, and philosophical treatises. It is a rich and varied literature.

Sanskrit quickly became a learned tongue, like Latin in Europe, and has maintained itself as such among the Brahmins to the

CHRISTIAN LASSEN
Norwegian scholar, one of the founders of Indo-Iranian philology in Germany
[After *Skilling-Magazin*, Christiania, 1875]

present day. It has been victorious time after time in struggles for existence against later (middle Indian) literary languages. The moment at which it ceased to be a living language is hard to determine. It survived longest among the higher castes. As late as the time of the famous Indian grammarian Pāṇini, probably about 300 B.C., Sanskrit must have been current among certain castes. But among the people in general at that time, and even earlier, the language had changed considerably. Thus the Buddhist king Aśoka about 250 B.C. used in his numerous inscriptions, which are the oldest Indian inscriptions we have, not Sanskrit, but a more recent form, Prakrit. And in Indian drama it is the general rule that only men of the higher castes speak Sanskrit, while members of the lower castes and women speak Prakrit.

The latest stage in the evolution of the language of India is that of recent times, modern Indian. The date of the rise of modern Indian as a spoken language is uncertain. It first begins to appear in literature in the twelfth century of our era. Today there are about twenty-five different languages in India, all descended from

N. L. WESTERGAARD

Sanskrit. In 1901 they were spoken by some 221,000,000 people. The most widely known dialects are Bengalese and Hindustani. But the Indo-European peoples of India did not succeed in extending their language throughout the Indian peninsula; approximately one-fourth of the population speak non-Indo-European languages. (See below, pp. 127–131.)

A very remarkable modern Indian language is that of the Gypsies, a language whose dialects are spoken by wandering tribes the world over. It is not to be confused with the artificial thieves' jargon employed by sundry other 'travellers' of uncertain origin. A study of the language of the Gypsies shows easily enough that their home is in India, and we can locate it even more definitely:

the European Gypsies must have come from northwestern India. In the course of their distant wanderings they accumulated a number of loan-words which indicate the direction in which they travelled. It is interesting to notice that all of the European Gypsy dialects contain loan-words from Greek, among others the numerals *seven*, *eight*, and *nine*, which throughout Europe have forms agreeing very well with those of modern Greek. They contrast strangely with the other numerals, whose Indian character is striking, as for instance *five* and *ten*. Greece was evidently the common home of the European Gypsies for a considerable period. These nomads first appeared in Western Europe in the fifteenth century.

As early as the sixteenth century, we find the first notices by European scholars of the Gypsy language; e.g. by Bonaventura Vulcanius in his book (mentioned above) on the language of the Goths. This was Europe's first acquaintance with the languages of India, which thus early were as unhappily represented as possible; but no one suspected that these troublesome roaming visitors hailed from India. They were supposed to have originated in Egypt, and it was not until the end of the eighteenth century that observation of the resemblance between Gypsy and Hindustani put European scholars on the right track. During the nineteenth century, Pott, Miklosich, and F. N. Finck, not to mention others, thoroughly investigated the Gypsy dialects.

On the other hand, the ancient and precious linguistic tradition of India remained completely unknown in Europe. In ancient times, Europeans had no knowledge of Sanskrit, in spite of the domination of the Greeks in India during the period after Alexander the Great. The whole spirit of antiquity was obstructive. Not only did the Greeks look upon the Indians as barbarians; the Indians in their turn would have as little as possible to do with the Greeks. And even for modern Europe Sanskrit remained practically an unknown tongue until the beginning of the nineteenth century. Occasionally a European had had occasion to acquire a more or less thorough knowledge of Sanskrit, but the results of this knowledge had not been published.

It was English rule in India which gradually brought about more direct contact, and English scholarship first spread the knowledge of Sanskrit in Europe. The impression the language made on English scholars is best seen in an often quoted statement of Sir

William Jones in 1786, to the effect that Sanskrit in relation to Greek and Latin "bears a stronger affinity, both in the roots of verbs and in the forms of grammar, than could possibly have been produced by accident; so strong, indeed, that no philologer could examine them all three without believing them to have sprung from some common source, which, perhaps, no longer exists; there is a similar reason, though not quite so forcible, for supposing that

THEODOR BENFEY
[After Benfey, *Kleinere Schriften*]

both the Gothick and the Celtick, though blended with a very different idiom, had the same origin with the Sanskrit." This pronouncement is extraordinarily clear, and it recalls the old ways of thinking only in that it holds the possibility open that the original language may still exist, and in the belief that the more divergent appearance of Gothic and Celtic must be due to speech mixture. But it was not until the first decade of the nineteenth century that Sanskrit grammars by English authors began to appear; and because of Napoleon's continental blockade these books were not obtainable on the mainland. Dictionaries and texts were lacking. Yet the library in Paris possessed a number of Indian manuscripts, so that the study of Sanskrit could be pursued there. This Friedrich von Schlegel did during his stay in Paris beginning in 1803. As the result of his studies he published a book *Über die Sprache und Weisheit der Indier* (Heidelberg, 1808). Its great importance was the awakening of a lively interest in and enthusiasm for Indian culture; but it also expressed certain correct ideas on language. We find here for the first time the expression *comparative grammar*. A whole

OTTO BÖHTLINGK

programme is outlined in the words: "Comparative grammar will give us entirely new information on the genealogy of languages, in exactly the same way in which comparative anatomy has thrown light upon natural history." Sanskrit had its influence upon Friedrich von Schlegel as well as upon William Jones!

But the first to introduce the real study of Sanskrit philology on the Continent was Friedrich von Schlegel's brother, August Wilhelm von Schlegel, who became Professor of Sanskrit in Bonn, where his pupil, the Norwegian Christian Lassen, also worked. The first to begin the comparative linguistic analysis of Sanskrit was Franz Bopp, in his work *Über das Conjugationssystem der Sanskritsprache in Vergleichung mit jenem der griechischen, persischen und germanischen*

Sprache (Frankfurt-am-Main, 1816). The significance of this work for the foundation of the study of comparative linguistics will be discussed in a following chapter.

From this time on, the study of Sanskrit struck fast root in Europe, where there is hardly a university of any importance which has not a chair in the subject. In America it is taught in at least twelve universities. Space prohibits a complete discussion of the progress

WILLIAM DWIGHT WHITNEY
Author of *A Sanskrit Grammar* (1879)
[After Lanman, *The Whitney Memorial Meeting*]

of this new philology during the century. What men like Niels Ludvig Westergaard, Theodor Benfey, Otto Böhtlingk (who with Rudolph Roth produced a Sanskrit dictionary in seven large volumes, St. Petersburg, 1855–75), Hermann Grassmann, William Dwight Whitney, Jakob Wackernagel, Charles Rockwell Lanman, each in his own field produced by industrious and inspired research must be passed over here. A summary of the results of investigation appeared toward the close of the century in G. Bühler's *Grundriss der indoarischen Philologie und Altertumskunde.*

relieve du Perron of military duties and to pay his passage to India. After all manner of difficulties he reached Surat, where at first he met with one rebuff after another, but at last overcame apparently insurmountable obstacles and won the confidence and favor of the priests. Having mastered modern Persian, he induced the priests, little by little, to teach him the ancient sacred language and to initiate him into some of their religious rites and ceremonies, and to turn over to him some manuscripts. After a stay of seven years among the Parsees, he returned home in 1761, and visited Oxford in order to compare his manuscripts with the one which had started him on his travels. He wished to convince himself that he had not been deceived. Then he spent ten years more studying manuscripts and preparing a translation, and finally in 1771 he published his three-volume translation of the sacred writings of the Parsees, under the title *Zend-Avesta*,[1] *ouvrage de Zoroastre*.

But Anquetil du Perron's troubles did not end here. Enthusiasm over the new acquisitions was quickly dissipated in scepticism and disappointment. This scepticism was partly unjustifiable; and among many the disappointment was due to the fact that the philosophical ideas they had hoped to find were not there. But criticism was aroused largely because of shortcomings in du Perron's work. He had solved bravely and cleverly the practical side of the problem. Equipped with his knowledge of modern Persian, he had compelled the priests to give over all efforts to deceive him. He had done what no one before him had been able to do. But his schooling in linguistic science was too slight, and he had no special capacity for following out linguistic clues. Hence he not only made mistakes of his own, but failed to rise above the priests' understanding of the texts. And the priests' understanding of forms of speech which had died out more than two thousand years previously was naturally somewhat inexact. So voices were heard to assert that Anquetil du Perron had been humbugged, and that his *Avesta* was modern patchwork. These assertions were made, shortly after the appearance of the translation, by no less a person than Sir William Jones (see above, p. 18), and although Anquetil du Perron had his defenders, the adverse critics continued to hold the upper hand until Anquetil's death in 1805, and for a score of years afterward.

---

[1] The appellation *Zend-Avesta* is due to a misunderstanding; *Avesta* alone is the name of the ancient work. Because of this misunderstanding, the Avesta language was wrongly called Zend.

In 1826 Rasmus Rask caused a change in opinion by his article *On the Age and Authenticity of the Zend Language and of the Zend-avesta*. Rask refers only in passing to Sir William Jones's article of 1771, which he calls "a libel full of venom and gall and quite unworthy of its author's name," and restricts himself otherwise to the more recent expressions of doubt. The strong resemblances between the *Avesta* language and Sanskrit could not have passed unobserved; they are so marked that at times they call to mind the relationship between modern Danish and Swedish. Whole verses in the *Avesta* can be translated into Sanskrit simply by observing the sound-changes. On the other hand it was obvious that the *Avesta* tongue differed widely from modern Persian — more widely than the language of *Béowulf* differs from modern English. With the hazy ideas on the relationship of languages which were a heritage from the ancients, scholars might easily be led astray. The great conception of a linguistic family spreading from India to the Atlantic Ocean had not yet been attained, and the resemblances between Avesta and Sanskrit would lead only to a false hypothesis similar to that which had been applied earlier to the much less striking similarities between Lithuanian and Latin (see above, p. 7). The Avesta language was believed to be a dialect of Sanskrit which had been adopted for use as a sacred language but had never been spoken by the people in any part of Persia. Rask, who long since had attained a true conception of the Indo-European linguistic family, and who had the sure eye of genius for linguistic relationship — no one has surpassed him in this respect; in fact, no one has even equalled him, — refuted with masterful clearness these erroneous conclusions, and assigned to the Avesta language its proper place as coördinate with Sanskrit. Its agreement with modern Persian (and with Ossetic) still appears clearly in its most indispensable words. Rask pointed out, moreover, that the language whose relationship he had thus determined must be that in which Zoroaster's teachings were originally written, since all the special religious terms had developed from that language and from that language alone: there were no words which were derived from foreign sources, like our *angel*, *devil*, *priest*, *dean*, *bishop*.

Rask also rendered great service to Avesta studies when in the course of a long journey he stayed for two months in Bombay, and brought away with him a store of manuscripts which are for the most part the originals of which Anquetil du Perron had obtained only copies. In short, Rask made a collection of the oldest and best manuscripts. Even if he had accomplished nothing else on his journey, Denmark's investment in his travelling expenses would have been repaid over and over again.

Subsequent research developed rapidly beyond the insecure foundation laid by Anquetil du Perron. Two different methods have yielded results: on the one hand a careful study of the old texts

EUGÈNE BURNOUF
[After *La science française*, 1915]

themselves, partly aided by comparing the language with Sanskrit; on the other a more complete utilization of the traditions of the Parsees in the oldest forms accessible to us. It is impossible to go into details regarding the progress of scholarship. The first steps were taken by the famous French Sanskritist Eugène Burnouf, who used among other means a Sanskrit translation dating from the fifteenth century of our era. I shall not treat in greater detail the question of the transmission of the *Avesta*. There is a problem here, as even Rask realized: the alphabet in which the *Avesta* survives is much later than the text itself.

I shall not pass over, however, the two chief editions of the *Avesta*. The first we owe to Niels Ludvig Westergaard, who published it at Copenhagen in 1852–54. Westergaard, naturally, used Rask's manuscripts. His labors as editor were carried out with such philological mastery that the next editor, the German Karl F. Geldner, explains in the preface to his edition (Stuttgart, 1895) that there would have been nothing left for him to do but for the fact that there still existed in India a number of manuscripts which he (Geldner) had been able to use. Geldner's pupil, the American A. V. Williams Jackson, wrote the first really modern Avesta grammar, published in Stuttgart in 1892, and the German scholar Christian

CHRISTIAN BARTHOLOMAE

Bartholomae prepared his *Altiranisches Wörterbuch* (Strassburg, 1904), a large volume of two thousand pages, where there is given in dictionary form a complete interpretation of the texts.

How we have achieved an understanding of the other ancient language, Old Persian, in which there was the problem of discovering the meaning of the characters themselves, can best be shown in a later chapter as a part of the history of epigraphy. There, too, it will be convenient to discuss the means by which we have gained a knowledge, quite recently, of Middle Parthian, of Middle Sogdian, and of Middle Sakian. The only Iranian people which has an uninterrupted tradition from the Middle Iranian period to the present is the Persian people. But the study of Middle Persian, which is of great importance, since Middle Persian literature contains the oldest native interpretation of the *Avesta*, is extraordinarily difficult because of the almost undecipherable Pehlavi alphabet.

Even in the case of modern Iranian we have had no beaten track. The greater part of our knowledge of the languages and dialects was discovered during the nineteenth century by European travellers and investigators, and much remains to be done. For example, we owe most of our knowledge of Ossetic to Klaproth (1814), to Sjögren (1844), and to Vsevolod Miller (1881-82).

A summary of the results of previous investigation is contained in the *Grundriss der iranischen Philologie*, published by Wilhelm Geiger and Ernst Kuhn beginning in 1895.

II

THE GREAT LINGUISTIC GROUPS OF MODERN EUROPE: GERMANIC, SLAVONIC, CELTIC

THE new light from India cast its rays upon the more familiar languages, and a systematic study of their older stages was begun. In the case of the Germanic and Slavonic tongues this occurred early in the century, so that the historical study of Germanic in particular contributed substantially to the foundations of the new comparative linguistics. Celtic, on the other hand, remained throughout the first half of the century a happy hunting ground for the visionary. It was only toward the middle of the century that its historical study was undertaken.

GERMANIC

The group of languages to which our own belongs is best called Germanic. This is the designation the Romans used for all the tribes included in the group. In English the Roman name has been applied especially to one country and one people (Germany, German), so that some English scholars have tried to find another term for the group as a whole; but since all the names proposed (Teutonic, etc.) are open to still graver objections, it seems preferable to keep to the term Germanic, which after all has no ambiguity.

The Germanic group of languages includes the following divisions:

A. East and North Germanic
    1. Gothic
    2. Scandinavian
        a) Gotlandic, Swedish, Danish
        b) Norwegian, Icelandic, Faroese

B. West Germanic
    1. Coast and Islands:
        a) English
        b) Frisian
    2. Mainland:
        a) Low German
        b) Dutch
        c) High German[1]

---

[1] The division of the Germanic languages in two main groups, East Germanic and West Germanic, is that advocated by Scherer and other great German scholars. The most important of the common Gothic-Scandinavian developments is the change of *ww* and *jj* to *ggw* and *ggj* (which later in Gothic became *ddj*): Gothic *triggw-s* "faithful," Old Norse *trygg-r*, accusative *tryggvan*, but Old High German *gi-triuwi*, Old English *ge-tréowe* (Modern English *true*); — Old Norse *tveggja*, genitive plural of the numeral 2, Gothic *twaddjē*, but Old High German *zweiio*; — Old Norse *egg* "egg," Crimea-Gothic *ada*, but Old High German and Middle English *ei* (Mod-

Gothic was spoken by a number of tribes known from the period of migrations: West Goths, East Goths, Vandals, Burgundians, and so on; but the language of the West Goths is the only one of which we have any exact knowledge, since we have a large part of the Biblical translation prepared by their bishop, Ulfilas, in the fourth century, when the Goths were living in the region about the Danube. Ulfilas constructed for the purposes of this translation a special alphabet on the basis of runes and Greek letters. The translation became the common property of the Goths, for our manuscripts are the work of East Gothic copyists. That Gothic language which von Busbecq (see above, p. 6) met with in the Crimea, but which was completely extinct by the beginning of the nineteenth century, appears to have belonged to the East Gothic branch.

It was the destiny of the Gothic peoples to disappear, linguistically speaking, as one consequence of the vast expenditure of energy attendant upon the migrations. A West Germanic tribe who shared their fate were the Langobards. Originally they dwelt far to the north, near Lüneburg, but they migrated thence and after many vicissitudes, having dwelt in northwestern Hungary and in Pannonia, south of the Danube, they finally reached Italy in 568. Here they preserved their own language for a surprisingly long time, even after Charlemagne in 774 ended the empire of the Langobards; and it finally died out about the year 1000. We know this language through names and through scattered words in Latin writings such as the laws of the Langobards. Through these we can determine that Langobardian participated in the consonant shift which is one of the principal characteristics of High German.

ern English "egg" is a Scandinavian loan-word). The most characteristic common West-Germanic development is the loss of a final z: Gothic *gast-s* "guest," Runic *Hlewa-gasti-R*, i.e. *Hlewa-gasti-z*, Old Norse *gest-r*, but Old High German *gast*, Old English *giest*; — Gothic *sunjus* "sons," Old Norse *synir*, Danish *sönner*, but Old High German *suni*. According to Bremer, *Festskrift tillägnad Hugo Pipping* (Helsingfors, 1924), p. 42 f., the West Germanic loss of final -z (Indo-European -s) had occurred already in the first century after Christ (cf. Marcomannian *Catualda*, Batavian *Chariovalda*). As for the vocabulary, one may emphasize such Common West-Germanic words as "to do," "to be," and the preposition English "to," etc.; compare also Old High German *wazzar* "water," Old English *wœter*, but Gothic *watō*, genitive *watin-s*, Old Norse *vatn*. Thus the linguistic facts agree very well with the doubtless ethnological connection of Goths and Scandinavians. But of course the division of the Germanic languages into these two great groups does not imply a denial of the fact that there are some later special similarities between Scandinavian and West Germanic. Scandinavian does not for this reason cease to belong to the East Germanic group. It is commonly admitted, also, that English and Frisian within the West-Germanic group are nearest to Scandinavian; but they do not for this reason cease to belong to the West Germanic group. The division of the Germanic languages into three coördinate groups, East Germanic, North Germanic, and West Germanic, is misleading.

MANNE SNMS AIHTA TYANS SNNNNS
GAH AISAAIAIAA ÏMMA SYES SEIN GAH
AFAK NI MANAᴦANS AAᴦANS BKAHTA
SAMANA AAAATA SA GNHIZA SNNNS GAH
AFAAIΨ ÏN AANA FAIKKA YISANAᴑ...GAH
NSSTANAANAS UAM. AT ATTIN SEINAMMA
NANHΨANNH ΨAN FAIKKA YISANAAN ᴦASAᴑ
ÏNA ATTA ÏS...UAΨ ΨAN SA ATTA AN SKAAKAM
SEINAIM SNKANTᴑ BKIᴦᴦIΨ YASTGA Ψᴑ
FKNMISTᴑN GAH ᴦAYASGIΨ ÏNA

manně	sums	aihta	twans	sununs...	jah	disdailida
of men	a certain one	had	two	sons...	and	he divided

imma	swēs	sein	jah	afar	ni	managans	dagans
between them	property	his;	and	after	not	many	days

brahta	samana	allata	sa	juhiza	sunus	jah	aflaiþ
brought	together	everything	the	younger	son	and	went away

in	land	fairra	wisandō...	jah	usstandands	kwam
into	a country	distant	being...	and	arising	he came

at	attin	seinamma	nauhþanuh	þan	fairra	wisandan
to	father	his;		still	far	being

gasaƕ	ina	atta	is..	kwaþ	þan	sa	atta	du
saw	him	father	his...	said	then	the	father	to

skalkam	seinaim	sprautō	bringiþ	wastja	þō
servants	his:	quickly	bring ye	clothing	the

frumistōn	jah	gawasjiþ	ina.
best	and	array	him.

(Excerpt from Luke xv, 11–22.)

SPECIMEN OF THE GOTHIC ALPHABET

All of the other Germanic races named in the above survey have
not only maintained their languages to the present day, but also
possess ancient linguistic remains.

Scandinavian has the oldest remains, in the form of runic inscriptions, which are at least as old as the Gothic translation of the Bible; in phonology and morphology the language of these inscriptions is even more primitive than Gothic. But the earliest literature dates from a much later period: in Norway and Iceland from the twelfth, in Denmark and Sweden from the thirteenth, in Gotland from the fourteenth century. Gotlandic varies in such a distinctive way from other Swedish dialects that it requires a separate place in any account of the Scandinavian languages.

West Germanic possesses no inscriptions so old as those of Scandinavia, but literature begins both in the north and in the south several centuries earlier; only the Frisians and the Dutch began later than the Scandinavians.

English literature, already illustrious in its older stages, goes back to the eighth century. It is committed to writing in a variety of dialects which correspond to the original tribes of the invaders: toward the north, the Anglian dialects in Northumbria and Mercia; south of them the Saxon dialects, among which that of Wessex is the most important; and, finally, in the southeast a third tribe, the Jutes, is represented by the dialect of Kent.

The names *Angles* and *Jutes* were very early connected with the provinces of Angeln and Jutland (as by Bede in the eighth century). The significance of this connection is uncertain; there are several possibilities to choose from. So much, however, is certain: the Angles and Jutes in England did not speak the language of Angeln and Jutland, but one much like that of their fellows, the Saxons.

The Frisians remained in their old homes and did not enjoy the splendid destiny of their English brethren. Our earliest Frisian document dates from 1300; at present the language seems doomed to extinction. Of the old dialects, West Frisian and East Frisian, the former is still the popular language of West Friesland; but East Frisian is spoken by only a few thousand people in some districts of Oldenburg, while North Frisian is used in the islands from Helgoland to Sild and on the corresponding section of the Schleswig coast.

Low German, which in its oldest period is called Old Saxon, possesses literature from the ninth century; one specimen is a great religious poem, *Heliand*, "The Saviour." At present this language is widely used, being spoken throughout northern Germany, north of a slightly crooked line drawn between Elberfeld and Thorn, and east of a similar line drawn north from Elberfeld, including a strip of the kingdom of Holland. But from about 1650 it has yielded place to High German as a literary language, and has thus taken lower rank. The use of the language in literature by such men as Klaus Groth and Fritz Reuter has not materially altered its position.

The literature of the Netherlands first began to flourish in the thirteenth century, the older form of the language being called Old Low Franconian. Certainly the Netherlands can boast of having the most ancient West Germanic documents, in the form of glosses to the Salic Laws, which were written in Latin during the sixth century. Dutch dialects extend today throughout Holland, northern Belgium, and French Flanders, and toward the south as far as Aix-la-Chapelle and Düsseldorf, where they meet the dialects of High German. The Flemish literary language of Belgium differs but slightly from that of Holland. The language of the Boers in South Africa has sometimes preserved older features.

Old High German literature can compete with Old English in respect to age, but only in that respect. It begins with the eighth century and is found in three principal dialects: Alemannic, Bavarian and Upper Franconian. A treatment of the modern dialects would naturally require many more divisions. Alemannic (Switzerland and the region immediately north: Western Bavaria, Würtemberg, Baden, Alsace) and Bavarian (with which Austrian is included) compose together the South (Upper) German region; while in the Middle German divisions fall, besides the various Franconian dialects north of Alemannic extending as far as the Dutch and Low German districts, a number of eastern dialects in what was formerly

Slavonic territory. One of this last group, Saxon, or "Upper Saxon," is in the main the foundation of the modern High German literary language.

It is almost superfluous to urge that linguistic inferences must be drawn very cautiously from the names *Saxon* and *Frank*, which occur in several West Germanic regions (*Saxon* in English and Low German, and in High German also, as we have just seen; *Frank* in Dutch and High German). These are old political designations, not linguistic terms. But the same thing holds good for *German* as it is ordinarily used. It can be used for an actual linguistic unit only when it is restricted to High German. High German and Low German are two distinct languages, and are not the two West Germanic continental languages which have the closest relationship, although their relationship has been sufficiently close to permit the successful use of a common literary language within the politically united countries. The relationship among the three continental West Germanic languages has no small resemblance to that among the three Scandinavian languages, Danish, Swedish, and Norwegian. In both cases it is true that the political boundaries — and with them the boundaries of the literary languages — do not coincide exactly with the dialectal boundaries, and in both cases the two languages which are the most widely separated have developed a common literary language as a result of political events. To use the term *German* to designate all three continental West Germanic languages is no more correct than to use the term *Danish* for all three Scandinavian languages.

The ancient monuments of the various Germanic languages have never been entirely forgotten. Though perhaps continuity with the past was fully maintained only in Iceland, it was not completely lost among any of the Germanic peoples; and even that literature which had no direct heirs, Gothic, did not remain unnoticed by collectors and scholars in the course of the centuries. Toward the beginning of the modern period, the Abbey of Werden, near the river Ruhr, was found to possess a splendid manuscript of the Four Gospels in the translation of Ulfilas (the *Codex Argenteus*). We can determine that its original home was Italy, where it was written about the year 500; but how it came to Werden, directly, or indirectly, whether by peaceful acquisition or conquest, we do not know; and neither can we be sure whether it was the contents of the manuscript or its rich ornamentation — purple parchment with large initial letters in gold and silver — that first attracted attention. But we have many witnesses to the fact that German and Dutch scholars during the sixteenth century (Gesner, Goropius Becanus, Bonaventura Vulcanius) interested themselves in the manuscript, and made extracts from it. Thereafter it led a wandering existence for many years. During the Thirty Years' War it was seized and sent from Prague to Queen Christina of Sweden, but in one way or another made its way back to the mainland. The Swedish Count de la Gardie finally bought it back from Holland, had it bound in silver, and presented it to the University Library at Upsala, where it is now preserved and where presumably it has found a place of

ANDERS UPPSTRÖM

[After W. Uppström, *Miscellanea*, ı]

repose. While it was in Holland it was examined by Francis Junius, who published the first edition (Dordrecht, 1665), followed shortly by Stiernhielm's (Stockholm, 1671).

Thus the most famous and most important Gothic monument was well enough known before the nineteenth century. Yet modern times, which in almost all fields of linguistics have brought to light fresh material from hitherto unknown sources, have also added considerably to the materials available for the study of Gothic. In the middle of the eighteenth and during the nineteenth century, fragments of various other Biblical writings, among them a Gothic commentary on the Gospel of St. John, were discovered in palimpsests. The *Codex Argenteus* had to be reëdited by Anders Uppström (Upsala, 1854). In like manner our material for the other Germanic languages has been increased almost up to the present day through new discoveries.

But the chief undertaking of the nineteenth century was the scholarly treatment of the older Germanic languages, which previously had been scarcely begun. For Old Norse and Old English the

JACOB GRIMM
[After Oncken, *Allgemeine Geschichte*, iv, 2]

first usable grammars were written by Rask, in 1811 and 1817 respectively. And it was the German scholar Jacob Grimm who laid the foundation for the comparative [1] treatment of the Germanic languages as a whole, within which class Gothic plays a rôle similar to that of Sanskrit in the Indo-European family. The foundation work was Grimm's *Deutsche Grammatik*, a comparative account of all the Germanic languages, principally of their older stages, including, in all, fifteen different languages and stages of languages. The first volume appeared in 1819; it contains no phonology, but begins at once with the morphology, which it completes. But as

[1] Grimm himself uses the term *historical*.

early as 1822 the first volume of a new edition appeared, which
shows much more clearly the creative power of Grimm. It was continued by the second, third, and fourth volumes, in 1826, 1831, and
1837. Preceding the morphology in this edition there is a detailed
phonology of 595 pages, an advance in method wherein Grimm is
not uninfluenced by Rask. Grimm's strength lies not so much in
the phonetic description of sounds as in the determination of their
etymological value and in the exact statement how the sounds of the
various dialects correspond to one another. But in these very things
students caught a glimpse of an entirely new linguistic world. Grimm
revealed an unsuspected regularity when he pointed out that certain
vowels were short and certain others were long in the older Germanic
languages, and that they were precisely the same in Greek and
Latin; for instance, if *a* — in spite of the modern pronunciation in
all the principal Germanic languages — was short in Old Norse
faðir, so it was in Latin *pater*; and if *o* was long in Old English *mōdor*,
so the corresponding *a* was long in Latin *māter*. In addition, Grimm
explained accurately and clearly the changes in sounds which we
now know by the name he used, *umlaut*.

Umlaut is the changing of a vowel under the influence of the vowel in a
following syllable, especially under the influence of *i* or *j*, *u* or *w*. The non-
umlauted vowel is always preserved in Gothic, which shows the causes of
umlaut, whereas those causes have usually been obliterated in the languages
where umlaut has developed.

Gothic	*sunus* son	plural *sunjus*
Modern High German	*sohn*	*söhne*
Swedish	*son*	*söner*

Umlaut may be present in some form of a word which from its meaning
one might suspect to be the original form, while, on the other hand, it may
not occur in another form which is apparently derived:

Compare {Old English *sellan*   to give, sell, preterite *sealde* sold
        {Gothic   *saljan*   to give

and   {Old English *bycgean* to buy   preterite *bohte*
        {Gothic   *bugjan*

In many cases umlaut can be established by comparing related words:
full shows that the *i* in "to fill" is an umlaut. Umlaut is present also in
Old Norse *fylla*, Modern High German *füllen*, but it takes the Gothic form,
fulljan, to show us the cause of the umlaut. Often it is only by means of
a comparison of the different languages that we can determine whether
umlaut has occurred; the non-umlauted vowel is found in Gothic. The
vowel in English "berry," Modern High German *Beere* is an umlaut of *a*:
cf. Gothic *basi*; but the vowel in *to bear*, Modern High German *gebären* is

an old non-umlauted vowel (and the two words *berry* and *to bear* have nothing to do with each other).

Gothic casts a clear light on umlaut in all the other Germanic languages, as well as on several other points in the vowel system. For this reason Grimm was led to conclude that the Gothic vowel system is in all respects older than that of any other Germanic language. Gothic has only three short vowels, *a*, *i*, and *u*; this Grimm regarded as the original Common Germanic condition. That was an error; for we cannot assume that there were less than four vowels in the Common Germanic language: in addition to the *a*, *i* and *u* there was an original *e*. In a case like Old Norse *eta* "to eat," Old English and Old Saxon *etan*, Modern High German *essen*, Gothic *itan*, it is not the *i* of the Gothic form which is the original, but the *e* of the other languages. The slip Grimm made here was not of a particularly serious nature; but he made matters worse by citing Sanskrit, which likewise has but three short vowels, *a*, *i*, and *u*. As a matter of fact the Sanskrit system of three strengthens in no way the Gothic system of three; for the two systems do not correspond etymologically. On the contrary, the relationship is essentially as follows:

Sanskrit	*a*		*i*	*u*
Gothic	*a i*		*i*	*u*
Old Norse, etc.	*a e*		*i*	*u*

Sanskrit *ad-mi* "I eat," shows that the *i* in Gothic *itan* is not original. Grimm's misinterpretation was possible only because comparative linguistics was in its infancy. Yet his conception remained current for some time. He went a step farther and referred to the fact that in Semitic also (e.g. in Arabic) there are only three original vowels, *a*, *i*, and *u*. Since Grimm did not postulate any relationship between Indo-European and Semitic, it must be inferred that he regarded the *a*, *i*, *u* system as the common basis for human language.

And it is precisely this conception which Grimm applies to those old alternations of vowels in the Germanic languages which he calls *ablaut*. In contrast with umlaut, ablaut is present in the Germanic languages from the most ancient period. While the cause of umlaut was clear enough to Grimm, nobody at that time could have discovered any phonetic reason for ablaut, either within or without the circle of the Germanic languages. Ablaut is the alternation of vowels which we have in the verb forms *begin*, *began*, *begun*, Gothic *du-ginnan*, *du-gann*, *du-gunnans*. This type of alternation occurs throughout the whole Germanic group, but it is most plainly seen in the inflection of the so-called strong verbs (so named by Grimm). It is one of Grimm's great services that he made such alternation a subject for thorough study. But at the same time his is the responsibility for the fundamentally false conception that ablaut from the first indicated differences in meaning. In one place he says that it is the consonants which constitute the nucleus of the word, while the vowels determine and explain it; therefore all internal word formation depends upon vowels. His meaning is this: the vowels were in a sense superfluous, since it was the consonants which "constituted" the word; hence the vowels, the three basic vowels admitted by Grimm, are used to express shades of meaning under inflection and word-formation. Here lies more than one profound misunderstanding. What Grimm says about the differing functions of vowels and consonants has very little to do with observation and experience. Certain misunderstood recollections of Semitic may have been in his mind. On the whole, it may be doubted whether vowels were ever changed voluntarily in a word for the purpose of expressing a shade of meaning; and, at least as long as language has been the inherited property of humanity, such a thing has never been known to occur. Often enough we see alternations of vowels arise, and we see them also serve the purposes of meaning. But they arise invariably under the influence of certain phonetic conditions, and become only indirectly a means of expressing semasiological differences. So it has been with umlaut in Germanic, and so it has been with other alternations which have developed in historical times. The phonetic conditions may be of many sorts, but no one has ever observed that any alternation of vowels came into existence independently of phonetic conditions, merely for the purpose of expressing a different meaning. If this could be imagined at all, it must at least be conceived as having taken place in the dim ages when language was first created. And in truth, Grimm is more or less consciously involved in the belief that the comparative linguistics of which Gothic and Sanskrit are the foundations leads us back to the very beginnings of language. But this is a monumental error. In the last analysis it represents a lack of historical perspective quite similar to that which made it possible for the Greeks to believe that Phrygian was the first language, or for Goropius Becanus to believe that Dutch was. Hence Grimm's conception of ablaut has long since been abandoned. That ablaut does not consist of a mere alternation of the vowels *a*, *i*, and *u* was tolerably clear. The belief that it does could exist only as long as observation was restricted to the Germanic languages, and especially restricted to Gothic. But ablaut is not peculiarly Germanic: it is Common Indo-European.[1] Grimm was clear-sighted enough to recognize the connection between the Germanic ablaut and the alternations of vowels in Sanskrit and Greek (cf. above, p. 23); and as soon as the

AXEL KOCK

system of these languages was examined seriously, scholars gave up the idea of juggling with the *a*, *i*, *u* formula. And it was not long before they began to perceive that, in spite of its great age, ablaut was dependent upon certain phonetic causes which could still be traced: causes lying in the original Indo-European accent. But much labor was necessary before the correct methods were learned for comparing the ablaut stages of the various languages, and for drawing the proper inferences as to ablaut in the primitive Indo-European language. And by that time linguistic theory had pro-

[1] In this book a word or a grammatical phenomenon is called "Common Indo-European" when it is supposed to have existed in the original or primitive Indo-European language. — Translator's note.

gressed far from Grimm's language-creating ablaut. For us today ablaut is a result of phonetic laws; it is no longer a sign that our spade has reached the bottom in linguistic excavation, but on the contrary it is an indication that, however deep we may have penetrated, there are many strata below. In ablaut we do not see, as Grimm did, the result of a special linguistic process different from those which are taking place today, but merely alternations of a

ADOLF NOREEN

special antiquity. Ablaut is what we might call, by a longer but clearer name, Indo-European vowel alternation.

Grimm's *Deutsche Grammatik* opened an entirely new world to its contemporaries. Even where it erred it exerted inspiring influence.

In his treatment of consonants Grimm included a detailed exposition of the Germanic consonant-shift (*Lautverschiebung*, as Grimm named it); but here he built on Rask. The structure was finished later by Verner. This point belongs more to Indo-European than to Germanic comparative linguistics and will be discussed in another connection.

Among the most important extensions of the field of Germanic studies belong the interpretation of the oldest Norse runic inscriptions by Sophus Bugge and Ludvig Wimmer, and the investigation of ancient Gothic and Norse loan-words in Finnish by Vilhelm Thomsen. But work has been unceasing in all the far-flung ramifications of Germanic linguistics, from the most ancient languages to the modern dialects. A series of periodicals helped to organize the field: among many others, the *Beiträge zur Geschichte der deutschen Sprache und Literatur*, edited by H. Paul, W. Braune, and E. Sievers, and the *Arkiv för nordisk Filologi*, edited by Axel Kock. The summing up of results is cared for in many ways: there are dictionaries for the individual languages, ancient and modern — the *Oxford English Dictionary* being a distinguished representative; etymological dictionaries, such as Friedrich Kluge's German etymological dictionary, which has appeared in many editions, the English etymological dictionaries by Skeat, various works of the Norwegian scholars Hjalmar Falk and Alf Torp, and so on. There are treatments of the older languages by Paul, Braune, Sievers, F. Holthausen, W. Heuser, Theodor Siebs, J. H. Gallée, J. Franck, Henry Sweet, Wimmer, Adolf Noreen. A *Grundriss der germanischen Philologie*, edited by H. Paul, first began to appear in 1889, and has already had three editions.

SLAVONIC

One of the reasons for the great influence of Grimm's *Deutsche Grammatik* is that it threw light on native material. The native tongues of a whole series of nations which participated in scholarly work were here the subject of a discussion which revealed a past of unsuspected age; and this discussion came just at the time when the waves of sentiment aroused by the Romantic Movement were sweeping over Europe. A comparative treatment of, say, the Romance languages at that time would not have exerted an effect in any way corresponding. It would not have directed attention to an unsuspected past, but simply to the familiar Roman highways; and such a work, carried out with the tools wielded by students of language at the dawn of the century, could not have added so much new knowledge as Grimm's undertaking. Only one great group of European languages — the Slavonic — enjoyed in any degree conditions similar to those of the Germanic group. And here we see national awakening and the beginnings of linguistic science going hand in hand, just as they did with the Germanic peoples.

The Slavonic languages may be divided as follows:

A. East Slavonic
  1) Russian
  2) Little Russian

B. South Slavonic
  1) Bulgarian
  2) Serbo-Croatian and Slovenian

C. West Slavonic
  1) Slovakian and Czech
  2) Sorbian (in Upper and
     Lower Lausitz)
  3) Polish, with Kashubish
     and Slovintzish
  4) Polabian (Elbe-Slavonic;
     now extinct)

The dissemination and linguistic division of the Slavic peoples took place later than was the case with the Germanic peoples. During the first centuries of the Christian era they still dwelt together in the region between the Vistula, the Carpathian Mountains, and the Dnieper. Expansion toward the south and west took place substantially during the fifth and sixth centuries of our era; it was carried out with great vigor, but came to a halt proportionately soon. Expansion toward the east was not so sudden, but has continued to the present time.

The tribes which wandered toward the south came into permanent possession of the northern part of the Balkan peninsula. A Turkish people — that people to whom the name "Bulgarian" originally belonged — followed at their heels, and founded a kingdom there in the seventh century. But these Turkish Bulgars blended quickly with their Slavic subjects, and, so far as language is concerned, virtually disappeared, since beyond the name of the people only a few loan-words were retained. Some Turkish chronological indications which are added to an old list of the first princes of the Bulgars (deciphered by J. J. Mikkola) are a clear testimony of their nationality. Into the southern part of the Balkan peninsula (Albania and Greece) the power of the Slavs penetrated only temporarily, and the Balko-Slavs preserved few connections with their older home. These connections were cut short for the Slavic Bulgarians by the migrations and disturbances which took place after the Slavic migrations, particularly by an Ugro-Finnish people, the Hungarians, in their migration to their present home about A.D. 900. At present, only place-names like *Pest*, which in Bulgarian, and only in Bulgarian, means "oven," testify how far northwest the Bulgaro-Slavic tongue was once spoken. Toward the northwest the different Slovenian dialects spoken in Carniola (with offshoots in Italian Friuli) and in Carinthia and Styria, are closely related to Serbian and Croatian. But Slovenian has had a hard battle with German, and in the mountain regions has become half foreign to its southeastern relatives. Hence Slovenian did not participate in the remarkable linguistic rejuvenation which occurred among the Serbs and Croats in the nineteenth century.

Vuk reformed the Serbian literary language, freed it from the bonds of ecclesiastical language, established a standard orthography, collected folk-songs, tales and proverbs, wrote a dictionary with an exact indication of the shifting musical accent, and a grammar which was translated into German in 1824 by no less a person than Jacob Grimm. And among the Croats there arose a movement for national unity which led to the rejection of the local dialect of Agram (Zagreb), though it was the literary capital, and to the establishment of a southern dialect as the literary language; with the result that thenceforward the Serbian and Croatian literary languages differ only in the alphabets employed, the Greek Catholic Serbs using the Slavic alphabet, the Roman Catholic Serbs using the Latin alphabet. In this movement for national unity the Slovenians did not share, with the exception of a single author. Slovenian literature went its own way, and will probably continue to do so during the present condition of political unity with the Croats and Serbs.

The West Slavs spread northward all the way to the Baltic Sea and westward to the Elbe, and for a time they were dangerous neighbors of Denmark. But most of their territory was afterwards lost. At the close of the twelfth century the Slavs of the northwest were under German or Danish domination, which led quickly to the decline of Slavic nationality in these regions. There remained only the pitiful fragments named in the table on page 44, whose existence is not even suspected by many.

Sorbian is now spoken by 150,000 people in Lower and Upper Lausitz, on both banks of the river Spree, from Lübbenau in Spreewald to within five miles south of the town of Bautzen in Saxony. To their own disadvantage, the Sorbians have two literary languages, one in Upper and one in Lower Lausitz. Kashubish and Slovintzish are spoken between Danzig and Stolp. Polabian is now extinct; it belonged in the region about Lüneburg, and is known through records which date from about 1700.

Of the several West Slavonic languages, only Polish and Czech have remained vigorous. After the defeat of the Czech Protestants in the Battle of White Mountain, near Prague, in 1620, it looked as if Czech also were doomed; the national spirit was broken, and literature declined. But the nineteenth century brought a wonderful awakening, for a literary language was re-created and a new literature developed. The new life brought with it, however, the elements of new dissension. The Slovakians, in the northwestern part of what was then Hungary, who hitherto had had a common literary language with the Czechs, now began to go their own way, and developed a special Slovakian literary language.

Toward the east, in Russia, the Slavs had to fight for centuries against the Turkish tribes who had dwelt there earlier. The most powerful Turkish people were the Kazarians, whose capital, in the neighborhood of present-day Astrakhan, first fell before the Slavs in 969. While those wars were going on, a new enemy appeared to plague the Russians when the Scandinavian Warings crossed the sea and demanded tribute. But this foreign element in the end functioned like a homeopathic medicine, for the tribe of Warings who bore the name *Rus* settled in the country, and founded the kingdom which led the Slavs to victory and gave the country the name Russia.

The ancient Russian chronicle ascribed to Nestor relates naïvely that the Slavs and Finns, after having repulsed the attack of the Warings, decided of their own accord to put an end to internal strife by calling in a prince from Rus. Exhibiting all his learning, the chronicler brings the Waring folk of Rus into association with "Swedes, Northmen, Angles and Goths," and he makes the messenger of the Finns and Slavs speak the winged words, "Our country is broad and fruitful, but therein is no order; come then and rule over us!" So three brothers were chosen, and they took all Rus with them, and came. The Russian rule was established in Novgorod, near the Ilmen Sea, but soon the capital was moved to Kiev. For a century from 862 the Rus princes have Scandinavian names: Rurik (=Hrœrikr), Olég (=Helge), Igor (=Ingvarr), Olga (=Helga); but Olga's son, the suppressor of the Kazarians, bears the Slavic name Svjatoslav, and after him there are no more Scandinavian names in the royal family. In later times it has been the tendency in certain Russian quarters to explain away the whole tradition which makes Scandinavians the founders of the Russian empire. This cannot be done, however, as, in addition to proper names, we have some remnants of the old language of the Rus people. In a work of the Greek emperor Constantine Porphyrogennetos (*ca.* 950) there are cited two sets of names of waterfalls on the river Dnieper, the waterway to the Greek empire. The one set is designated as "Russian," the other as "Slavic": and the "Russian" names are unmistakably Scandinavian, as was best pointed out by Vilhelm Thomsen in *Ryska rikets grundläggning genom Skandinaverna* (Stockholm, 1882, "The Foundation of the Russian Empire by the Scandinavians"). The name "Rus" is identical with the name which the Finns today call Sweden — "Ruotsi" — and is related to an old Swedish name for the parts of Sweden bordering on the sea north and south of the present capital.

The collective name which we use for the Slavic people as a whole, after the example of the Greeks and Romans, goes back to the Slavic tribal name Slověne (plural). Like many other Slavic tribal names (for instance, that of the *Serbs*, which is the same as *Sorbs*) it occurs in several different places. We meet the name in a Russian tribe near Novgorod; among the Slovintzians in Pomerania, and, far to the west, among the Slavs about the Elbe; among the Slovakians in the Carpathian Mountains, and among the Slovenians in the Alps. Even the Bulgarians seem to have called themselves by the same name originally. But as a common designation for the whole group of languages it was first used by foreigners. A second name, Wends, which was used, e.g. by the Scandinavians and Germans, to designate all the Slavs·with whom they came in contact, is not used by the Slavs themselves.

1) Oldest scrolled form of the Old Slavic alphabet:

ⰀⰞⰕⰅ ⰍⰔⰑ ⰔⰖⰁⰎⰩⰄⰅⰕⰟ ⰔⰎⰑⰂⰑ ⰏⰑⰅ, ⰔⰟⰏⰓⰠⰕⰉ ⰐⰅ ⰉⰏⰀⰕⰠ
ⰂⰋⰄⰡⰕⰉ ⰂⰟ ⰂⰡⰍⰟ.

ašte	kto	sŭbljudetŭ	slovo moje,	sŭmr̥ti ne	imatĭ
if	anyone	keep	word my,	death not shall	he

viděti	vŭ	věkŭ.
see	in	eternity.

(John VIII, 51.)

2) The dominant form of the old Slavic alphabet, revised to agree more closely with the parent Greek alphabet:

Іисоѵсъ же видѣвъ матєрє и оѵченника стоѧща,
єгоже люблѣше, глагола матєри· жєно, сє сынъ твоі.

Iisusŭ	že	viděvŭ	matere	i	učenika	stoješta
Jesus	but	having seen	(his) mother	and	(the) disciple	standing

jegože	ljubljaše,	glagola	materi:	ženo,	se	synŭ	tvojĭ.
whom	he loved,	said to	(his) mother:	woman,	this (is)	son	thy.

(John XIX, 26.)

3) The modern form of the alphabet. Two Russian proverbs:

Свёкоръ—гроза, а свекровь выѣстъ глаза.
Тесть любитъ честь, зять любитъ взять, а шуринъ глаза щуритъ.

Svjokor		— groza,	
The father-in-law (the husband's father)		(is) severity,	

a	svekrov'		vyjěst	glaza.
but	the mother-in-law (the husband's mother)		eats out	the eyes.

Test'		ljubit	čest',	zjat'
The father-in-law (wife's father)		loves	honor,	the son-in-law

ljubit	vzjat',	a	šurin
loves	taking (getting)	and	the brother-in-law (wife's brother)

	glaza	ščurit.
	(with his) eyes	blinks.

No Slavonic literary monuments of any sort are to be found before the introduction of Christianity. Literature began only in the ninth century, when the Prince of Mähren called two brothers, Kyrillos and Methodios, from Saloniki to preach in his country in order to counterbalance German influence. With this aim in view, they used a translation of the Scriptures, written in an alphabet specially constructed by themselves on the basis of the Greek alphabet with necessary additions, and set forth in their own native Bulgarian dialect, which at that time was easily understood even by the West Slavs. But the Slavic type of worship quickly disappeared among the West Slavs, and with it disappeared the Old Slavic (Old Bulgarian) church language and the Slavic alphabet. Both were preserved by the Greek Catholic Slavs (Russians, Bulgarians, Serbs), though their later national languages have broken away little by little from the sway of the church language.

Since Old Slavic has been in constant use down to our own day, there might seem to be no necessity for its rediscovery by students of language at the beginning of the nineteenth century. But the necessity was real. In the first place, the use of a language — especially when that use has been restricted to the church — is not the same as scientific study of it; and in the second place, the continued use of a language in a subsequent period is likely to obliterate its original characteristics. Just as medieval Latin is very different from the language the Romans spoke in classical times, so the church language used today by the Greek Catholic Slavs is very different from the genuine old Macedonian tongue of Kyrillos and Methodios. The language had to be traced back to its original form before it could be used as the basis for a comparison of the Slavonic languages now in existence. For this purpose it was necessary to discover and study the old manuscripts and to undertake much grammatical research. Often matters as elementary as the meaning of the letters had to be determined, because in the course of time pronunciation had changed: sounds originally distinct had fallen together, sounds originally pronounced had become mute, and so on. A virtual rediscovery of the old language had to be made, and that was an undertaking beyond the powers of any one man.

A beginning was made by the Bohemian Joseph Dobrovský, whose principal work, *Institutiones linguae Slavicae* ("Laws of the Slavic Language"), appeared at Vienna in 1822. Dobrovský was a scholar of high rank, one of those who early anticipated the correct methods

of modern linguistic science. He was quiet, sober, critical, and con-
scientious. His labors were inspired by a deep and warm sympathy
for all Slavic peoples, but he remained aloof from some of the movements which characterize the beginning of the nineteenth century.
He did not come under the influence of romanticism; Vuk's efforts,
and the Serbian folk-poetry which inspired Jacob Grimm's enthusiasm, made no special impression upon him; and his sceptical nature
had no particular faith that the Bohemian language could rise again

JOSEPH DOBROVSKÝ
[After J. Ritter von Rittersberg, *Joseph Dobrowsky*]

from its profound degradation after the Battle of White Mountain.
Nevertheless, his labors awoke the slumbering national spirit of the
Bohemians. By strengthening their connection with the past he
strengthened national self-confidence also, and called forth a series
of champions who led the cause of the Bohemian language to victory.
Dobrovský is honored now as the father of Bohemian literature, but
first and foremost he is the founder of Slavonic linguistic science.

Various important discoveries were reserved for others, and all
of the most ancient manuscripts exclusively in Old Bulgarian were
found or edited after Dobrovský's death. Some of these had been

preserved from ancient times within the boundaries of Austria or Russia, but were edited relatively late — the first in 1836. One manuscript was taken to Rome from Jerusalem as early as 1736, but was not edited until 1865. The two most important manuscripts of all were discovered in 1843 in two monasteries on the famous Macedonian promontory, Mount Athos. Two others, found in 1850 on Mount Sinai, are a memorial of the numerous pilgrimages made by the Slavs to the Holy Land.

F. MIKLOSICH

The Slovenian F. Miklosich [1] produced the first comprehensive treatment of more advanced Slavonic·linguistics. He came to the task fully equipped with a knowledge of general Indo-European linguistics, and with astounding industry produced a whole series of indispensable works: a comparative grammar of the Slavonic languages in four volumes (1852–75), an Old Slavic dictionary (1862–65), and a Slavonic etymological dictionary (1886). He also threw light on the neighboring languages which have influenced Slavonic or been influenced by it.

One characteristic of the most recent period of Slavonic linguistics

[1] Pronounce *s* like English *sh*, *ch* like English *ch*.

is the increasing participation of non-Slavs, and the growing recognition of the significance of the group for comparison with the other Indo-European languages. The great German scholar August Schleicher produced an admirable book in his *Laut- und Formenlehre der polabischen Sprache* (St. Petersburg, 1871). He was compelled to work with the scanty records left to us, the best of which we owe to Christian Hennig, priest in Wustrow, 1679–1719. But Schleicher investigated most thoroughly the phonetic value of the awkward

AUGUST LESKIEN
[After *Indogermanisches Jahrbuch*, 1]

and capricious spelling of the records, transcribed them in a consistent phonetic system, and extorted from this refractory material a comparative treatment of the phonology and morphology. The sources abounded in misunderstandings, which it was Schleicher's task to straighten out. For example, when one of the old collectors asked what were the words for *yesterday*, *today*, and *tomorrow*, he was answered with the words which really meant *Friday*, *Saturday*, and *Sunday*, and he credulously accepted what he heard. When one of the Elbe Slavs was asked about the word *Stahl* "steel," he thought the verb-form *stahl* "stole" was meant, and the inquirer did not notice the mistake. Schleicher's work is one of the most striking examples of what a masterly treatment can educe from apparently desperate material, and it is a pity that the best manuscript of all escaped him. His labor was by no means in vain, as the language is of the greatest interest, and has played no inconspicuous rôle in modern investigation of the Slavonic accent.

In a later period the German August Leskien rendered great services to Slavonic studies, not only by means of most meritorious

V. JAGIĆ
[After *Archiv f. slav. Phil.*, xxv]

monographs, but also by publishing his excellent *Handbuch der altbulgarischen Sprache*. The second edition of this book (1886) and a series of later editions give us the best existing descriptions of the genuine old Slavonic literary language.

By degrees Slavonic studies branched out so widely that the need for an encyclopedic survey was felt. Such a work began to appear in 1910 in St. Petersburg: *Enciklopedija slavjanskoj filologiji* ("Encyclopedia of Slavonic Philology"), edited by the most comprehensive Slavonic philologist of our times, the Serb Vatroslav Jagić. But his death and the post-war fortunes of Russia prevented its completion, and in 1925 Reinhold Trautmann and Max Vasmer began to publish another survey, the *Grundriss der slavischen Philologie und Kultur-geschichte*. Jagić also edited the first periodical for Slavonic studies, the *Archiv für slavische Philologie* (vols. 1–37, 1875–1920), which is now being continued by Erich Berneker.

CELTIC

Conditions quite different from those prevailing in Germanic and Slavonic were the lot of Celtic. The Celts made their appearance on the stage of history much earlier than the Germans and Slavs. Their power had reached its height when we first begin to hear of the Germans, and before the Slavs had yet emerged in history. Yet, while the two thousand years after Christ are a saga of the steadily growing expansion of the Germans and Slavs, they relate only the uninterrupted decline of the Celts. At the beginning of the nine-teenth century there was no talk of a Celtic revival. No native scholar produced a work on the unity of the Celts and their relation-ship to the whole Indo-European family. The undertakings which Grimm and Dobrovský had begun for their own groups of languages were not attempted in the field of Celtic until foreign investigators set to work. Thus Celtic did not take any serious part in compara-tive Indo-European linguistics until the middle of the century.

The following Celtic languages, living or dead, are known:

A. Gaelic
    1) Irish
    2) Manx
    3) Scotch-Gaelic

B. Brythonic
    [1] Pictish]
    2) Welsh (Wales)
    3) Cornish (Cornwall)
    4) Breton (Brittany)

C. Gaulish

The greatest expansion of the Celts falls in the centuries before Christ. The Celtic languages were then spoken throughout Ireland and Great Britain, and were even more widespread on the Conti-nent. Here the Celts ruled the greater part of Gaul (now France), with the exception of the corner between the river Garonne and the Pyrenees, where a foreign people, the Aquitanians, dwelt. The Celts also played an important part in Spain, where the original popula-tion, the Iberians, racially related to the Aquitanians, were for the most part compelled to submit to the Celtic yoke. And, finally, the habitations of the Celts (Gauls) reached from Gaul far eastward

through the lands about the Danube and the Alps. How wide the
belt was, and how far it extended eastward, it is difficult to say
definitely, partly because the Celts apparently pushed into the territories of other peoples, or ruled only temporarily over other races.
But Celtic place-names are found all the way to the Black Sea:
farthest east, probably, is *Noviodunum*, "the new town," now
Isaktcha in Dobrudzha, about sixty-five miles from the mouth of
the Danube. It is well known, also, that the Gauls made their way
over the Alps and conquered Northern Italy, whence their thrust
southward in the year 390 B.C. mastered Rome. But this mastery
had no lasting influence, and it is only in the western part of the
country about the Po that we can assume from the testimony of
inscriptions the existence of a compact Gaulish-speaking population.
About the year 280 B.C., a hundred years or so after the expedition
to Rome, the Gauls began a series of thrusts toward the Balkan
peninsula. They threatened the sacred oracle of the Greeks at
Delphi, but in vain. During the years immediately following, they
turned to Asia Minor, where at last they settled down in the province which is called *Galatia* after them. *Galatai* was, indeed, one
of the names which the Greeks gave to the Continental Celts, while
the Romans used the term *Galli*.

But as early as the end of classical times the Celtic language had
disappeared on the Continent. It seems to have maintained itself
for about the same length of time in Galatia and in Gaul, but it was
seriously checked in both places at an early date. In the course of
the first century after Christ, the Galatians ceased to use Celtic
proper names; but remnants of the language must have lasted much
longer. St. Jerome (A.D. 331–420), who had been in both Trèves and
the town of Ankyra (now Angora) in Galatia, asserts that the Galatians spoke, in addition to Greek, which was the current language
throughout the Orient, a language of their own which was almost
identical with the language spoken in Trèves. But by that time
the language, in Trèves as well as in Ankyra, must have been at its
last gasp.

The Celts in Britain enjoyed circumstances different from those
on the Continent. They did not lose their national language under
Roman domination. They received a considerable number of Latin
loan-words, many of which spread to Ireland, although Ireland was
never under Roman rule; but the vigor of the Celtic language did
not diminish. Thus the Britons were able to give a new Celtic-

speaking population to a part of Latinized Gaul. From the fourth century on, migration took place from southern Britain, especially from Cornwall, to the old Gaulish province of Armorica, which in this way took over the Brythonic language and received the name it now bears, Brittany. Hence the Celtic language spoken today in Brittany is by no means a descendant of the language of the ancient Gauls. But about the same time that this migration occurred, the Brythonic language in Britain itself met with new competition. The Irish or the Scots — Scottus meant at first simply "Irishman" — established themselves in the northern part of the island. The ancient Brythonic people dwelling there, the Picts, gradually gave up their language, and the land was called Scotia, Scotland. At the present time only place-names give evidence of the ancient Brythonic population. Aber in Aberdeen and in some other place-names is undoubtedly — although this theory has been questioned — the Brythonic aber, "rivermouth," the corresponding Gaelic word being inver as in Inverness. Of the Pictish language nothing has been preserved save a few glosses which give so little information that some investigators have found it possible to deny the Brythonic nationality of the Picts. Irish emigrants settled also in Wales and Cornwall, but played no important part there, as they were absorbed gradually in the British population. The greatest check to the Brythonic language came from the immigration of Germanic tribes from the opposite shore (see above, p. 33), which converted southern Britain into England. It was only in Wales and Cornwall that the old Celtic language maintained itself. Wales has an interesting literature in both the medieval and the modern periods. The modern literature is comparable in scope to the literatures of other small cultivated nations. However widespread the knowledge of English may be in Wales, all talk of the extinction of the national language is at present absurd. Cornwall, on the other hand, is represented late and scantily in literature, and the language itself became extinct during the eighteenth century. Dolly Pentreath, who died in 1777 at the age of one hundred and two, was the last person to speak Cornish.

In contrast not only with the mainland, but also with Britain, Ireland was for a long time the place where Celtic maintained itself undisturbed. The power of Rome did not reach the Emerald Isle, but its studious inhabitants took the opportunity to appropriate Roman culture freely and independently. They continued to speak

Irish, but enriched the language with loan-words from Latin. They accepted Christianity and classical culture and became zealous apostles of both. In Irish monasteries Greek was cultivated at a time when that study was in decay on the Continent. During the years 600–900 the Irish were the representatives of classical culture in the whole Frankish empire, and numerous Irish monasteries were founded on the Continent. The movement reached as far as St. Gall, in the Alps, and Bobbio, in the northern foothills of the Apennines, both of which became famous centers of culture. A heavy time came upon Ireland with the onslaughts of the Vikings. But the "white and black heathens" (Norsemen and Danes), the men from Loch-lann (whatever that name originally meant), were in no position to exercise any influence on the language. The only linguistic traces of their presence are some Norse loan-words in Irish. The Scandi-navians themselves were quickly absorbed, linguistically speaking, after their settlement in Ireland, as was the case also with the English conquerors in Ireland from 1170 to the days of Elizabeth and Cromwell. And all the cruelty exercised by the English from then until the close of the eighteenth century, when brighter days began to dawn, succeeded only in ruining the higher culture and scholarly life of Ireland, not in eradicating the language of the people. At the beginning of the nineteenth century Irish was still spoken by four-fifths of the population. But while the nineteenth century brought about national and linguistic rejuvenation in many places, in Ireland it brought such a decline that at present Irish is spoken by only a half-million people in the westernmost part of the island. The Irish language is no longer a mark of distinction for the Irish nation, and connections with the Isle of Man, where Gaelic is now on the way to extinction, and with Scotland, where Gaelic is also in a decline, are practically severed. Such connections had already been weakened by the fact that each of the three countries — which really spoke dialects of one and the same language, and which to this day call their languages by the same name, *Gaelic*, (originally *Goidelic*) — had settled upon its own individual method of writing.

The Celtic languages have older inscriptions than the Germanic, and the indirect sources, such as names and glosses in the works of foreign authors, are older and richer than those of the Germanic peoples. But the literature itself is contemporary with English and German.

SPECIMENS OF THE MODERN GAELIC LITERARY LANGUAGE

Modern Irish

Ɖo ċáalabaip ʒo
ɲorḃaḋ, Ʒ̊páɾꝺeoċɲ̊ʒ́ cɾ́
ꝺo ċoṁaɲɾa, ⁊ bɾaḋ ꝼáċ
aʒaꝺ ꝺoꝺ ɲáṁaɾꝺ.

Scotch Gaelic

Chuala sibh gu'n
dubhradh, Gràdhaichidh tu
do choimhearsnach, agus bithidh
fuath agad do d' nàmhaid.

The modern Irish text in Latin letters (Matthew v, 43):

Do chúalabhair	*go*	*ndubhradh,*	*Gráidheochuigh*	*tú*	*do*	*chomharsa,*
You have heard	that	it was said,	love shalt	thou	thy	neighbor,

agus	*bíadh*	*fúath*	*agad*	*dcd*	*námhaid.*
and	there should be	hate	with you	against thine	enemy.

The modern Celtic languages have a very different appearance from the old Indo-European type, and their morphology in particular seems very unfamiliar. For these reasons it was doubted, at the beginning of the nineteenth century, whether Celtic belonged to the Indo-European family at all. The numerous similarities in vocabulary certainly could not be overlooked, but, in view of the apparently non-Indo-European system of inflection, scholars leaned toward the idea of borrowing. In his famous prize essay on the origin of Old Norse, Rask maintained precisely this conception. But his own principles forced him soon to relinquish it, and in 1817, the year before the delayed publication of his prize essay, we find him unreservedly referring to Celtic as one of the branches of the Indo-European family.[1] The great German scholar Bopp printed in 1838 a special treatise *Über die celtischen Sprachen vom Gesichts-punkte der vergleichenden Sprachforschung*. Here he succeeded in explaining one of the queerest-looking characteristics of Celtic morphology, the remarkable change in the initial sounds of a word used in sentence combinations. We have in modern Irish, for example:

a cara	her friend ($c = k$)	*a tál*	her adze	
a chara	his friend (*ch* as in German)	*a thál*	his adze ($th = h$)	
a gcara	their friend ($gc = g$)	*a dtál*	their adze ($dt = d$)	

Bopp pointed out that this change depended upon the sound in which the preceding word ended at some time in the distant past. The explanation for the examples cited above is easily seen when we compare Irish *a* "her, his, their," with Sanskrit *asyās* "her," *asya* "his," *ēšām* "their." Other examples show, just as these do, that

[1] *Samlede Afhandlinger*, II, 281.

ch and *th* occur after words which in Indo-European originally ended in a vowel, *gc* and *dt* after words which ended in a nasal. It was thus proved that Celtic once had the Indo-European inflectional endings, and was therefore an Indo-European language. The strange shift of initial sounds no longer served as a proof against kinship with Indo-European, but on the contrary became a conclusive proof for such kinship. However, Bopp did not succeed in explaining the inflectional forms of Celtic then known. He could not, because at that time only modern worn and remodelled forms were accessible.

In the hands of undisciplined dilettantes these modern forms could be used for anything. During the first half of the nineteenth century the Celtic language was a stalking-ground for the ghosts which Leibniz had exorcised. Where the clear daylight of modern linguistic science extended, they dared no longer show themselves, but the Celtic field was sufficiently darkling still to have its "Goropianism"[1] or Celtomania. The Celtic Academy, founded in France in 1805, set itself the task, over which Rask rightly makes merry, "of studying and publishing the etymology of all the languages of Europe by the help of Breton, Welsh, and Irish."[2] Germany, also, had her Celtomaniacs.

The sovereign remedy against Celtomania was to be sought only in a systematic comparative investigation of the Celtic languages on the basis of the oldest documents. And that work was finally accomplished. A Bavarian grammar-school master, Johann Kaspar Zeuss, applied his leisure hours, his holidays, his savings, and his splendid scientific talents and knowledge, in searching for and investigating the surviving remains in Continental libraries of the much-travelled Irish scholars of the early Middle Ages. He found them and understood how to use them. They were merely glosses and explanatory remarks in Irish between the lines of Latin, the three most important manuscripts being from Würzburg, Milan (originally from Bobbio), and St. Gall; but they contained the ancient Irish language in greater purity and clearness than any other documents, and they provided the key for a scientific understanding of the Celtic languages in general. The Bavarian schoolmaster — who had sought a position in Bavarian universities in vain, receiving refusal after refusal — read them (which was an

[1] See above, p. 8.

[2] "D'étudier et de publier l'étymologie de toutes les langues de l'Europe à l'aide du celto-breton, du gallois et de la langue erse."

undertaking in itself), interpreted them, and studied them grammatically. He compared them with the still scarcer sources of Old Brythonic and with the oldest literary monuments of Wales, Cornwall, and Brittany, and with Gaulish names and the other scanty remnants of the language of the Gauls. He completed all this in a masterly manner, and, with no preliminary publications as an indication of what was to come, there appeared, like Athena springing

JOHANN KASPAR ZEUSS
[After *Zeitschrift f. Celt. Phil.*, vi]

fully armed from Zeus's brow, his great achievement, *Grammatica Celtica* (Leipzig, 1853, in Latin). By this work the foundations of Celtic linguistics were laid, and to this day it is the starting-point for all scholarly investigation in the Celtic languages.

But the term "fully armed" must not be misunderstood. There was ample work left for successors. In the first place, the material had to be augmented and made more accessible. Native literature in Irish, which is rich and individual but is some centuries later than the glosses, was not a suitable foundation for the study of grammatical forms, as both language and spelling were in a stage of transition. But after the ground had been broken by the *Gram-*

matica Celtica, the study of these monuments also could be undertaken, and during the latter half of the nineteenth century the work of editing and interpreting this literature was carried on industriously by both native and foreign scholars. The results lie before us in heavy folios of facsimile-editions, and whole shelves full of the usual sort of printed texts, most of them equipped with glossaries. Individual editors like Whitley Stokes, who was indefatigable in

HEINRICH ZIMMER
[After *Journal of the Welsh Bibliographical Society*, 1]

every field of Celtic, have filled shelves single-handed. But the editing of the Old Irish glosses which Zeuss had tracked down and used was also an important undertaking. Here, besides Stokes, the famous Italian scholar Ascoli took a prominent part. The Welsh material required its share of attention and attracted workers. And finally Alfred Holder published, in three stately volumes, beginning in the year 1891, an extraordinarily useful collection of all the Celtic names and glosses to be found in the writings of the ancient Greeks and Romans.

Even the grammatical structure which Zeuss erected showed gaps. Zeuss had not solved the many riddles of Old Irish verbs. They merge with prepositions and pronouns into unrecognizable units in the most perplexing way. Thus, whereas in a language as rich in forms as Latin there is but one form for the third singular present indicative *dicit* "he says," which can be freely connected with independent pronouns, we have in Irish at least twelve different unresolvable forms. In this maze Zeuss found no clue. In many cases he perceived nothing more than a meaningless variation in sound.

RUDOLF THURNEYSEN

Ni ceil and *ni cheil, bermi* and *berme* meant for him one and the same thing, and they are actually used indiscriminately in later Irish; but in Old Irish *ni ceil* means "he does not hide," while *ni cheil* means "he does not hide it"; *bermi* "we carry," but *berme* "which we carry." In other cases the difference could not be overlooked, but Zeuss had to content himself with citing the forms together, because he did not perceive the rules for separating them. Take, for instance, *as-beir* "he says" and *epir* "he says": we know now that the latter form is used in certain definite connections, such as in the compound *ni epir* "he does not say." And yet in other cases the variation was so great that Zeuss failed to discover that the same root was present; as for example in *do-sluindi* "he denies," *ni díltai* "he does not deny," or in *ad-fiadam* "we relate," *ad-cuaid* "he has related," *con écius* "so that I may relate." But the complicated Old Irish system of verbs has revealed its secrets gradually. The beginning was a dis-

JOSEPH LOTH

covery which Heinrich Zimmer and Rudolf Thurneysen made independently in 1884; but it was only during the last few years of the century that a series of discoveries completed the work. These had hardly been made when the investigation of the oldest Welsh poems by John Strachan and J. Loth brought to light the fact that the Brythonic languages at one time possessed most of the finer points of Irish. But Brythonic freed itself from irregularity much earlier. The intricacy of the whole system may be guessed from the fact that the most recent comprehensive treatment of Celtic grammar devotes two hundred and forty pages to an account of the irregular verbs alone.[1]

For comparative Indo-European linguistics Celtic has great significance not only because of the light it throws on many details, but also (and this is not least important) because it shows us a

[1] Holger Pedersen, *Vergleichende Grammatik der keltischen Sprachen*, two volumes (Göttingen, 1909-13). — Translator's note.

strongly divergent type of linguistic structure developed in Indo-European territory, a structure which is astonishing both in the individuality of its final development and in the remarkable fidelity

HOLGER PEDERSEN

with which its peculiar forms often preserve traces of their origin. These features make it possible to draw sound inferences concerning phenomena which have long since disappeared.

III

LITHUANIAN, ALBANIAN, ARMENIAN

TWO of the European branches of Indo-European, Lithuanian-Lettish and Albanian, cannot boast of any ancient literature. But modern Lithuanian itself looks like an ancient language, and hence it promptly took its place in the comparative field. It was only toward the close of the century that a use for Albanian was discovered. A contrast with Lithuanian is presented by Armenian, which is an ancient language, but looks almost like a decayed modern language. Armenian therefore had to wait as long as Albanian before it was thoroughly investigated from the comparative point of view. The dim light from these two languages could not be perceived until the eye which had been dazzled by the new floods of light derived from Sanskrit, Germanic, Celtic, and Slavonic learned to catch the more subdued shades.[1]

LITHUANIAN

After long centuries of subjection, the state of Lithuania (Lietuvà) has become independent; but the Lithuanian language extends a little beyond the boundaries of the new state. If all Lithuanian-speaking people had been united, the town of Kovno (Lithuanian *Kaunas*) would be about the center of the country. Closely related to Lithuanian is Lettish, spoken in what is now Latvia, which corresponds to the old province of Kurland and the southern part of Livonia.

The literatures of Lithuanian and Lettish begin in the sixteenth century. From about the same time there are linguistic documents from a third related tongue, Prussian, in which we have a vocabulary comprising about eight hundred words, and three translations of the Catechism which bear witness rather to the good intentions of the translator than to any profound knowledge of the language. The language became extinct in the seventeenth century.

Lithuanian, Lettish, and Prussian together make up a branch of

---

[1] Poetry discovered the two languages before linguistics did. Lord Byron, who made a visit to Ali Pasha, and who included in his notes to *Childe Harold* a few fragments of Albanian folk-songs in a slightly distorted form, stayed for a time in the Armenian monastery in Venice in order to study Armenian.

languages which we are accustomed to call Baltic, a purely geo-graphical designation used because the three peoples dwelt on the Baltic Sea.

The Baltic languages, especially Lithuanian, have preserved to this day a most ancient appearance. There is no other living Indo-European language which can be compared with Lithuanian in this respect. The forms to be heard today from the lips of the Lithuanian peasants can in general be matched in primitiveness only by the languages of antiquity, such as Sanskrit. For instance, the nomi-native, accusative, and genitive forms of the word *son* in Lithuanian, Gothic, and Sanskrit are:

Lithuanian	sūnùs	sū́nų	sūnaũs
Gothic	sunus	sunn	sunaus
Sanskrit	sūnúš	sūnúm	sunóš

The forms which we attribute to the primitive language of the whole family, after a comparison of the forms in all the Indo-European languages, are:

* sūnús * sūnúm * sūnous

Until the end of the eighteenth century, however, no attention was paid to the extremely primitive state of Lithuanian. As late as Adelung's *Mithridates*, the Baltic languages were regarded as a sort of mixture of Germanic and Slavonic. Rask (*Prize Essay*, p. 144 ff.) put an end to this unreasonable state of affairs and gave to the Bal-tic languages their proper place as a special and very old branch of our family. And since that time Lithuanian has not ceased to play a conspicuous rôle in Indo-European linguistics. The famous German scholar Schleicher travelled to Lithuania in order to study the language in the huts of the poorest peasants, under "privations and hardships," as he expresses it, "of which the cultivated gentle-man of our days has hardly a suspicion"; but he adds that "the joy of hearing the splendid forms of this language in living use" en-abled him to endure all privations lightly. On the basis of the ma-terial thus collected, Schleicher wrote his masterly *Handbuch der Litauischen Sprache* (1856–57). It is the first scientific description of the language.

Yet it was not Schleicher, but a native Lithuanian priest and en-lightener of the people named Friedrich Kurschat (in Lithuanian Pridrikis Kuršatis), who first studied a very important phenomenon in the structure of Lithuanian — the accent. In a work which appeared in 1849 he gave rules for the position of the accent, which in Lithuanian shifts under inflection in a very striking way, and he described two different pitch movements in accented syllables. They may have either a regular sinking pitch (´) or a more irregular rising pitch (˜), the latter of which may be compared with our inflection of voice when asking a question. Schleicher valued Kurschat's work highly for its rules on accent; he calls it "a splendid little work in its way," and explains that he has learned it almost by heart. Without the guidance it gave, he would probably have fumbled in the dark for a long time. But Kurschat's (´) and (˜) he could not in most cases differentiate, and he was therefore inconsiderate enough to say that Kurschat had probably been too subtle.

Meanwhile Kurschat further developed his studies on pitch, and printed the results in his most serviceable works, a dictionary and a grammar, applying them also in an edition of the New Testament and in a popular weekly journal, *Keleīvis* ("The Wanderer"), which he edited from 1849 to 1880. Kurschat's teaching has not only proved to be correct, but the stone which Schleicher rejected has become the corner-stone of Lithuanian linguistic study. Several investigations have thrown light on the history of intonation (pitch): Karl Verner in *Afhandlinger og Breve* (1876, p. 323), the Russian scholar Fortunatov, the German scholars August Leskien (1881), and Adalbert Bezzenberger (1883 and 1887), and the Swiss genius, Ferdinand de Saussure (1889 and 1896). As a result it has been established that the two Lithuanian intonations are a survival from the primitive Indo-European, and that they are the key to the understanding of a great many phenomena in Lithuanian and Slavonic which would otherwise be a complete riddle. It is impossible to go into details here; it must suffice to quote one of Bezzenberger's examples of the agreement between the Lithuanian intonation and the intonations which the ancient Greek grammarians have described for us, but which have disappeared completely in modern Greek. The example is the nominative and genitive of an adjective in the feminine singular:

Lithuanian *geró-ji* the good   Greek *hē mikrā́*
      gerõs-ios   *tēs mikrãs*

The study of intonations, and of the vagaries of the accent, of which Saussure gave an excellent explanation, shows incontrovertibly that there exists some special connection between the Baltic and Slavonic languages. At some distant prehistoric time these two branches, now so widely differing, must have made up a unit within the already divided Indo-European family. And because of its ancient appearance Lithuanian can to some extent be regarded as an older stage of Slavonic. Recently certain modern scholars have wrongly denied this old connection.

A study of the principal dialect of Lithuanian does not cover the whole field of Baltic linguistics. The other dialects and Lettish also have something to teach us. But this side of the question has been studied mainly by native Lithuanian and Lettish scholars. Both peoples have recently begun to contribute in a distinguished manner to linguistic scholarship, a fact which may well be regarded as an augury rich in promise.

Prussian has been industriously investigated. The first significant work was done by the Prussian Nesselmann, who published his results in 1845 and 1873. Since that time investigators of various nationalities have succeeded in extracting much information from the scanty remaining material.

ALBANIAN

Many a storm has raged over the land where the Albanians dwell. Southern Albania is the Epirus of the ancients, where the Greeks had a famous oracle. Northern Albania is a part of the Illyria of the ancients, whence Queen Teuta and King Genthios bade the Romans defiance in the third and second centuries before Christ. Their effort was unsuccessful, and from then on Illyria remained under the sway of Rome. When the empire was divided, Illyria naturally went with the eastern half, and during the Middle Ages it shared the shifting fortunes of the Balkan peninsula. The Goths ruled in Illyria for one hundred and thirty years, to 535. Afterwards all Albania came under Slavic rule, as many place-names testify: for instance, *Berat*, which in the Middle Ages was called *Belgrade*, is a name found in different Slavic countries, identical with the name of the capital city of Servia, and means etymologically "the white town." But the western nations in turn did not leave the land in peace. Durazzo, the *Dyrrhachium* of the ancienst (Albanian *Durresi*), was taken by the Norman chieftain Robert Guiscard, and later was ruled by the house of Anjou in Naples. But most significant for Albania was the commercial influence of Venice,

which began at the latest in the tenth century and culminated in
the fifteenth in a firm political rule over part of the coast. Against
the onward-surging Turks the Albanians defended themselves
bravely under George Kastriota (Skanderbeg). But after his death
in 1468 they were quickly defeated, in spite of help from Venice.
The twentieth century brought freedom from the Turks, but new
storms from other quarters.

Has one and the same people dwelt here during all these vicissitudes? Are the Albanians descendants of the Illyrians, or of some of
the races in Illyria? The question is debatable, and perhaps the
Albanians have no claim on Teuta and Genthios. In any case, the
ancestors of the Albanians lived somewhere in the Balkan peninsula; and in trying to determine their old home, we must not omit
from consideration the fact that their language has been subjected
to very strong Roman influence. Hearing Latin spoken must have
been a daily experience of the Albanians at one time. Their language
is full of loan-words from Latin: they borrowed not only the words
for newly introduced cultural conceptions, with technical, legal, and
political expressions, but also words of everyday use, such as *heaven*,
hundred, cheek, to come. These loan-words were received in times
long past, and have undergone so many Albanian sound-changes
that they do not differ markedly from the genuine Albanian vocabulary. Only the experienced scholar can tell the Latin from the
native words with any certainty. On the other hand, Greek apparently had no influence in classical times, or, if it had any at all, it
was of the very slightest. Albanian has preserved no recollection
of the rule of the Goths; and the numerous loan-words from Slavonic,
Italian, Modern Greek, and Turkish are of no interest here, as they
date from periods when there is no longer any doubt of the dwelling-
place of the Albanian people.

Albanopolis, a town in Macedonia, is mentioned by the Greek
geographer Ptolemy in the second century after Christ. In some
way or other it may be connected with the name *Albanian*, given to
the people by all their neighbors and used by some of the Albanians
themselves in the form *Arbɛr*. In Modern Greek pronunciation *b*
was changed to *v*; hence the Greek form *Arvan-itis*, distorted by the
Turks to *Arnaut*.[1]

The territory in which Albanian is spoken extends considerably

---

[1] The usual native name of the Albanian people is *Shqipɛtar*, derived from *shqipe* or *shqype*,
"the Albanian language" (*Sh* = English *sh*; *q* = *k* mouillé).

SPECIMENS OF ALBANIAN ORTHOGRAPHY

1) From the period of confusion:

Fragment (after Legrand, *Bibliographie albanaise*) of an "entirely new spelling-book," which appeared in 1845 — one of the attempts made by the Albanians to escape from the difficulties of spelling by an entirely new alphabet; it is based on modern Greek. Rewritten in modern form the text reads:

mbi	malet	e	mɛ tɛ	lartɛra.	Ashtu	gjithɛ	gjetɛ	e
over	mountains	the	most	high.	Thus	all	beings	the

gjalla	vdiqnɛ	e	ngordhɛ,	e	gjɛ	tjetɛr	s	mbet	veç
living	died	and	deceased,	and	being	another	not	remained	except

Noes	e	fɛmijes	ti	edhe	ç	kish	mbrenda	ndɛ	koritɛ
Noah	and	family	his	and	what	he had	within	in	the ark

marɛ,	qɛ ata	me	kohɛ	mbushnɛ	dhenɛ	tyke	shtuar.
taken,	which	with	time	replenished	the earth	under	increase.

2) The two modern systems of spelling.

Sami Bey's alphabet	*The Latin alphabet*
Çum' e barðɛ kjo ditɛ	Shum' e bardhɛ kjo ditɛ
Pɛr ɡiðɛ Cqipɛtarɛt,	Pɛr gjithɛ Shqipɛtarɛt,
Do na sjeλɛ ŋɛ dritɛ,	Do na sjellɛ njɛ dritɛ,
Qɛ s' e kiɕin tɛ parɛt.	Qɛ s'e kishin tɛ parɛt.
Kjo dritɛ do na bjerɛ	Kjo dritɛ do na bjerɛ
Tɛ ɡiða mirɛsitɛ,	Tɛ gjitha mirɛsitɛ,
Бe ɡiðɛ dot' i ngrerɛ	Dhe gjithɛ dot' i ngrerɛ
Dɛmet' e marrɛzitɛ.	Dɛmet' e marrɛzitɛ.

Very happy (is) this day
For all Albanians;
It will bring us a light, [2][1]
such as the earlier (races) had not. [3][4][2][1]
This light will bring us [2][1]
All blessings,
And (it)/will/make up for/ all [2][3][1]
Damages and follies.

beyond the Albanian state itself, especially to the east and south. But even beyond this territory there are many Albanian colonies. The Greek capital, Athens, lies in the midst of a fairly large Albanian-speaking district, and colonies are scattered in various parts of Greece. There are Albanian colonies also in southern Italy and in Sicily, whither great numbers of Albanians fled to escape Turkish tyranny after Skanderbeg's death. There is an Albanian colony called Borgo Erizzo far up near Zara, in Dalmatia. One in the county of Syrmia is now losing its national character. Here the Albanians dwell in two villages near Mitrovitza and the river Save. This colony dates from the wars of the eighteenth century.

A people originally closely related to the Albanians are the Ru-manians. They yielded completely to Roman influence, however, and have kept only a few words from their old language, which other-wise was supplanted by Latin. It may be considered certain that originally they dwelt not in their present home but in some district south of the Danube.

The oldest Albanian documents date from the fifteenth century. Literary life first awakened in northern Albania, where there were missionaries from Rome, and in the colonies in southern Italy and Sicily. Southern Albania did not follow until late in the eighteenth century. In the first eighty years of the nineteenth century Albanian literature still remained very inconsiderable, and suffered under the orthographical confusion which arose from the difficulty of repre-senting a language so rich in sounds by means of the Latin or Greek alphabet. In the year 1879 the Albanian patriot and poet Sami bey Frashсri created a national alphabet with thirty-six characters. Thus the Albanians were presented with a gift similar to that which Ulfilas gave to the Goths in the fourth century, and Kyrillos gave to the Slavs in the ninth. The alphabet fitted the language perfectly, reflecting all the sounds with masterly precision and ease. There was no overlapping, no letters with diacritic marks over them; every sound had its special symbol. The Latin alphabet was used as far as it would go. The symbols it lacked were taken from the Greek and Slavic alphabets, without regard to their Greek or Slavic sound-values, but with great care that they should harmonize with the Latin symbols. But the Albanians were forced to recognize that they were not living in the age of national alphabets, but in an international age. To escape molestation by the Turks, the Alba-nian books which now began to appear in steadily increasing num-

bers had to be printed outside Albania — in Egypt, Rumania,
Bulgaria, Western Europe, America — where the new national
alphabet was a handicap. Hence the confusion continued, until in
1908 a spelling commission in Monastir brought about some sort
of order. They were compelled to abandon part of Frasheri's work,
and to recognize certain combinations of Latin letters (sh = *s*, and
so on) in place of the uncompounded signs of the national alphabet.

The Albanian language, much decayed, abounding in loan-words,
and known only from books which were for the most part difficult
to procure, played no part in linguistic investigation during the first
part of the nineteenth century. The greatest desideratum of comparative linguistics at the outset was evidence of the original Common Indo-European system of inflections. This evidence, practically speaking, was not to be found in Albanian. The old endings
are so violently changed that they betray their origin only when
they are examined by modern methods of linguistics. Albanian was
regarded by some scholars even in the nineteenth century as a
foreign, non-Indo-European language. Rask, as well as Pott, expressed himself to this effect; but we find the correct view in one of
Rask's essays,[1] where he relies for proof of the Indo-European character of the language on a point which is valid to this day: the three
genders in Albanian. Rask gave no examples. I shall cite here only
masculine, feminine and neuter words with the suffixed article, and
for comparison the corresponding German words:

Alb. *ulk-u* the wolf   *nat-a* the night   *miell-tɛ* the meal, flour
Mod. H.G. *der Wolf*   *die Nacht*   *das Mehl*

In his work *Die Sprachen Europas* (1850) Schleicher studies Albanian
in considerable detail, employing fresh material, and concludes
likewise that the language is Indo-European. But both Rask and
Schleicher err in placing Albanian in an especially close relationship
with Latin and Greek. In 1854, Bopp printed an essay on Albanian
in which he advanced beyond Rask and Schleicher, for he assumed
that Albanian stands in close relationship to no other Indo-European
language, and hence is not closely related to Greek or Latin.

Much later a scholar appeared who undertook the study of Albanian as his main work. On the basis of the greatly augmented
material which was partly due to the industry of foreigners, Gustav
Meyer determined the sound-laws of Albanian in 1883 and 1892,

[1] *Samlede Afhandlinger*, I, 156.

and undertook to differentiate accurately the native from the foreign
vocabulary. The latter he accomplished in his etymological dictionary of the Albanian language, which appeared in 1891. Here he
collected with tolerable completeness the Albanian vocabulary
known up to that time (this in itself was a great piece of work, because of the many scattered sources); and he also threw light on the
origin of the words, a no less difficult task, especially for loan-words,

GUSTAV MEYER
[After *Kalendari i maleve*, Brussels, 1900]

since it called for a thorough knowledge of all the languages and
dialects of the Balkan peninsula, most of which had been but incompletely described, as well as a knowledge of the Italian dialects.
In addition, he published in 1888 a concise Albanian grammar, thus
providing students with an easy means of access to the language,
and encouraging them to bring this stepchild of Indo-European
linguistics within the scope of their studies. Since that time interest
in Albanian has not abated. The work of Gustav Meyer on the development of Albanian from primitive Indo-European has been
followed up and completed, and the results have thrown light on
other Indo-European languages.

ARMENIAN

The Armenian language is spoken in a much wider territory than that granted to the state of Armenia after the World War. It is difficult to define the boundaries, because Armenian and Turkish are much intermingled with each other throughout the district involved. In general, it may be said that a line northward through Asia Minor, continuing the coast of Syria, is approximately the western boundary of the fairly homogeneous territory where the Armenians played a conspicuous rôle — at least before the latest Turkish cleaning-out process. Outside this territory there are larger or smaller Armenian colonies; as in northwestern Syria (here separated from the central body of Armenians by only a small wedge of Turks); in the provinces of Smyrna, Constantinople, Ismid; near Rodosto on the northern coast of the Sea of Marmora; in Sutchava (Bukowina) and Kuty (Galicia) — both colonies founded by Armenian fugitives in the eleventh century and later; in Rostov on the Don (whither the Armenians came from the Crimea); in Astrakhan; in New Djulfa south of Ispahan, and so on.

From cuneiform inscriptions found near Lake Van, we know that at first an entirely different population of non-Indo-European race dwelt in Armenia. After the Armenians settled there, the country was subjugated by King Cyaxares of the Medes about 600 B.C., and thereafter remained under the domination first of the Medes and later of the Persians. After the fall of the Persian empire, Armenia enjoyed partial or complete independence until it became a bone of contention between the Parthians and the Romans, from the last centuries before Christ onwards. Parthian influence predominated until it was broken by the power of Persia under the Sassanid dynasty, A.D. 226–652. At the fall of the Sassanid empire Armenia passed to the Arabs, and remained under Mohammedan rule with brief interruptions until the World War. But the Armenians, who were the first people to accept Christianity, held fast to their religion and nationality through all these troubled centuries, when so many others succumbed.

Armenian literature begins in the fifth century after Christ. It is written in a special alphabet of thirty-six (later thirty-eight) characters, whose inventor is said to have been Mesrop. It is based on the Greek alphabet, with many additions, but its symbols have been largely remodelled. As soon as Armenian came into use as a literary language and developed a rich literature, its written forms became

fixed, and were retained for a long time in spite of all changes in the
spoken language. As a learned tongue "classical" Armenian is used
to this day. But beside it, later stages have also been used for literature. We have a middle Armenian literature, and two modern
Armenian literary languages, one eastern and one western, each with
its own literature.

SPECIMEN OF ARMENIAN WRITING

> Եւ առաքէ երկուս յաշակերտաց անտի
> եւ ասէ ցնոսա. երթայք ի քաղաք, եւ իբրեւ մտա-
> նիցէք ի քաղաքն՝ պատահեսցէ ձեզ այր մի որ սա-
> փոր ջրոյ յուս ունիցի, երթայք զհետ նորա ։

Ew	*aṙak'ē*	*erkus*	*y-ašakertac'*	*anti*	*ew*	*asē*	*c'*	*-nosa:*
and	he sends	two	of disciples	the	and	says	to	them:

ert'ayk'	*i*	*k'ałak'*,	*ew*	*ibrew*	*mtanic'ēk'*	*i*	*k'ałak'-n,*
go ye	to	the town	and	when	you enter	into	town the,

patahesc'ē	*dzez*	*ayr*	*mi*	*or*	*sap'or*	*džroy*	*y-us*
there will meet	you	man	a,	who	a vessel	of water	on (his) shoulder

unic'i,	*ert'ayk'*	*z-het*	*nora*
has,	go ye	after	him.

(Mark xiv, 13.)

The Old Armenian language as we find it in the fifth century is
much decayed and changed from its primitive state. Often it is
even more changed than the markedly decayed Albanian of the nineteenth century. For instance, *dy*, *tre*, the Albanian numerals for *two*,
three, are much more easily recognizable than the Armenian *erku*,
erekh. But, conversely, the primitive Indo-European inflectional
system has been preserved more clearly in Armenian than in Albanian, and thus Old Armenian must be regarded as closer to the original Indo-European than modern Albanian. Armenian *erekh* is more
useful than Albanian *tre* in determining the Indo-European inflection
of the numeral. But Old Armenian is in no respect a clear language
like Sanskrit, Lithuanian, and Gothic.

Moreover, the language is overrun with Persian loan-words, well
calculated to confuse earlier scholars, who had not yet attained that
insight into the regularity of the evolution of sounds which alone
makes it possible to differentiate accurately between loan-words and
native words. Hence for a long time Armenian passed as an Iranian

language. Even Rask for a time shared this delusion. There is no evidence of it in his prize essay, in which he describes Armenian as an Indo-European language (p. 51), and explains correctly one of the most remarkable Armenian sound-changes (*p-* to *h-*, as in Armenian *hayr*, "father," *hur*, "fire"; compare Greek *patēr*, "father," *pyr*, "fire"). Probably when Rask wrote his prize essay he had not yet acquired a very thorough knowledge of Iranian. But in a letter dat-

H. HÜBSCHMANN

ing from 1818,[1] the Iranian theory is definitely announced. Later, in his essay *On the Age and Authenticity of the Zend Language and of the Zendavesta* (1826), he places Armenian in the same relationship with Iranian as Indian, Greek, Slavonic, and Germanic.[2] The Iranian theory long remained the prevailing one, and it is definitely advocated by Schleicher in his work *Die Sprachen Europas* (1850.)

It was only during the linguistic awakening of the seventies, with its sharper eye for the laws of sounds, that the position of Armenian as a special branch of the Indo-European family was recognized clearly and fully. In a series of studies which appeared from 1875 to 1897, Heinrich Hübschmann undertook to differentiate between

[1] *Samlede Afhandlinger*, II, 281.　　　　[2] *Samlede Afhandlinger*, II, 374.

loan-words and genuine Armenian words, and pointed out the fundamental laws of the development of sounds. These works laid the foundation of Armenian linguistics, and on this foundation other scholars, such as the Frenchman Antoine Meillet, have worked further.

A. MEILLET
[After *Archiv. f. slav. Phil.*, xxv]

It would be unjust not to add that native scholars also, continuing the proud traditions of Armenian learning, have contributed substantially to the progress of the study during the nineteenth century. They have produced editions of the older literature, dictionaries of the ancient language, and so on; and they have not neglected the investigation of the modern language and of living dialects.

IV

THE CONTINUED STUDY OF THE CLASSICAL LANGUAGES

WITH the pouring in of this new material from unknown or insufficiently known sources, the study of Latin and Greek, which had been the starting-point for European linguistics, did not cease to be the great school for young scholars in all departments. Specialists in comparative linguistics turned back to them with delight.

But these far-travelled sons were not always heartily welcomed when they returned home. On the contrary, there was often a sharp antipathy between classical philologists and students of comparative linguistics. This antipathy arose not so much because the stay-at-homes were a little old-fashioned, or because the prodigal sons perhaps brought with them unnecessary foreign manners, superfluous Indian grammatical terms, and the like; it was due rather to a fear, perhaps not wholly unfounded, that the new tendencies might result in neglect of the older aims of investigation, or might impose upon classical philologists an obligation to acquire a mass of learning that bore only indirectly upon their own field. Such strained relations are now practically forgotten. The two disciplines are no longer confused with each other. They are no longer rivals, the death of one being the life of the other, but rather peaceful neighbors, each of whom has cause to rejoice in the thriving growth of the other's field; and experience has shown that workers can be found for one field without enticing them away from the other.

One contrast, however, will continue. For the philologist as a student of national culture Latin and Greek go naturally hand in hand, while for the student of comparative linguistics there is no particular connection between them. The Romans went to school to the Greeks so much that it is impossible to study Roman culture and literature without a knowledge of Greek; and even if Greek culture and literature are somewhat more independent, the Roman offshoot can often teach us something of the mother plant. The result has been that the philology of both tongues is studied as a unit — classical philology. It is true that students of comparative linguistics could not quickly disabuse themselves altogether of the inherited conception that Latin and Greek constitute a separate group (see pp. 3, f., p. 10).

Both Rask and Schleicher still accept some sort of special connection between them. But antiquity's crude conception of the relationship could not endure, and the better insight of the seventies into the laws of sounds removed the last vestiges of support for it. It became clear that when agreement occurs between the Latin and Greek vowel systems while Sanskrit or Lithuanian or Germanic differs, it is because Greek and Latin independently have sometimes preserved the old system which was once the common property of the whole Indo-European family, while the other languages have deviated from it. The agreement between Latin and Greek is not, however, a result of a Common Græco-Roman development. The Indian vowel system with its three vowels *a*, *i*, and *u*, over which Grimm (see above, p. 39) and Schleicher rejoiced, is actually more modern than the Greek and Latin system of five vowels, *e*, *o*, *a*, *i*, *u*. All of the Indo-European languages originally had *e*, *o*, and *a* distributed in the same way as in Greek and Latin:

	e	*o*	*a*
Latin	*ferō* I bear, carry	*orbus* orphan	*agō* I drive
Greek	*phérō*	*orphanós*	*ágō*

It is only by a secondary development that *e*, *o*, and *a* fell together in Indian and Iranian, and that *o* and *a* fell together in Germanic, Baltic, and Slavonic:

Sanskr.	*bhárati* he carries	*arbhaká-s* child	*ájati* he drives
O.N.	*bera* to carry	*arfr* heritage, what is left behind	*aka* to drive

Therefore it is no sign of a special kinship between the two classical languages when Latin *ferō* and Greek *phérō* resemble each other more than they resemble Sanskrit *bhárati*, or when Latin *orbus* and Greek *orphanós* resemble each other more than they resemble Sanskrit *arbhaká-s* or Old Norse *arfr* (and Gothic *arbja*, "heir"). This conception of the relationships of sounds was reached in the seventies, by examining the principal languages, especially Sanskrit. It is strengthened by the fact that two of the branches which were included somewhat late in the survey, Armenian and Celtic, have five short vowels, exactly like Latin and Greek:

Irish	*berid* he carries	*orpe* heritage	*agid* he drives
Armenian	*berem* I carry	*orb* orphan	*acem* I drive

There is no special agreement whatever between Latin and Greek beyond what can be found between any two neighboring branches of the Indo-European family. There is no more special kinship between Latin and Greek than there is, for instance, between Greek and Armenian; and Latin stands in a much closer relationship to Celtic than it does to Greek.

CLASSICAL PHILOLOGY

In the preceding chapters we have considered philology and linguistics under one head. But in the case of Greek and Latin we cannot avoid making a distinction. It is therefore not superfluous to say a word or two here about the relations between the discipline of philology and the science of linguistics as a whole. It is not superfluous because philology is Janus-faced and looks in two directions at once: toward the study of language and toward the study of history. One may define philology briefly as a study whose task is the interpretation of the literary monuments in which the spiritual life of a given period has found expression. This definition might seem to point in the direction of history, in so far as it is the understanding of spiritual life which is named as the ultimate aim of the work; and when the interpretation is not concerned with an individual monument, but seeks to derive all the information possible from an entire literature, then the philologist is on the way to encroaching upon the field of the historian. Yet it is clear that the process of interpretation requires first of all an insight into a linguistic system, and that it must proceed according to linguistic rules; it is therefore undoubtedly a linguistic task, even though it does differ from a purely linguistic study for the sake of the language alone. But, in turn, the philologist often crosses the boundaries of pure linguistics; for it has always been the philologists themselves who have written the grammars, dictionaries, prosodies, and so on, from which their activities as interpreters proceed. Philology, then, can be regarded as a sort of linguistic activity which concerns itself with the interpretation of the literary monuments of a given period; for this purpose it employs and itself produces aids of purely linguistic as well as historical kinds. From this, however, it must not be concluded that philology should have no use for aids made accessible by entirely different means: to name but one example of each kind, I shall merely mention that archæology as well as comparative linguistics may become an auxiliary science to philology. It is impossible to define philology as foreign to linguistics; despite all theoretical definitions to the contrary, philology and pure linguistics are inseparable. The general rule is that no philologist escapes labor in linguistic science, and no student of pure linguistics can dispense with philological studies.[1]

Classical philology is a continuation of the activity already begun by the Greeks during the Alexandrian period (the last three centuries before Christ), when their own ancient literature lay a considerable distance behind them. But, in spite of its two thousand years, it has

AUGUST BÖCKH
[After Max Hoffmann, *August Böckh*]

continued throughout the nineteenth century to show youthful energy and the ability to progress. Work on the sources has been systematized, and method in all its branches has become firmer than ever before. Among those who turned their attention most to the historical side (the investigation of national culture), we may name August Böckh, who rendered especially great services to "antiquities," the study of national and social life in ancient times, and who is likewise one of the founders of the science of inscriptions; Carl Ottfried Müller, who not only won renown as a brilliant historian, but

[1] The use of "philology" as a mere synonym of "linguistics" is to be avoided, as Leonard Bloomfield has urged in *Language, Journal of the Linguistic Society of America*, I (1925), 4. The term is not so used in this volume. — Translator's note.

has a claim on the gratitude of students of comparative linguistics for his study of two districts within the horizon of classical antiquity, Macedonia and Etruria; and among those now living, Ulrich von Wilamowitz-Moellendorff. In textual criticism and grammar, the Dutch scholar Carl Gabriel Cobet and the Dane Johan Nicolai Madvig (specialists in Greek and Latin respectively), not to mention others, have rendered great service.

CARL OTTFRIED MÜLLER
[After Otto and Else Kern, *Carl Ottfried Müller*]

The high significance of textual criticism in classical philology is the result of the long and often intricate process of handing down classical works. These have passed from hand to hand, and even our oldest manuscripts are separated by long centuries from the period of their original authors. In the process of continual recopying it was inevitable that errors should creep in; and one mistake might easily lead to another, when a subsequent copyist attempted a correction without penetrating deep enough into the text to discover the correct meaning. In the Middle Ages, when knowledge of classical culture and classical languages had sunk to a very low level, the tradition was particularly bad. When the editing of classical literature began, after the invention of printing, the process at first was quite without plan. Late manuscripts, full of errors, were accepted as the basis for editions, and efforts were made to eliminate the worst errors and to clear up unintelligible passages by means of conjectures made without any strict method. Not until the nineteenth century was a method devised, when it was recognized that it was necessary to draw up a family tree, so to speak, for the manuscripts of a given

C. G. COBET
[After Gudeman, *Imagines Philologorum*]

work. Errors common to two manuscripts, especially if they are numerous, or include especially curious mistakes, indicate some relationship between these manuscripts. One may be directly or indirectly copied from the other, in which case the later manuscript has no independent value, and an apparently plausible reading in the later manuscript does not indicate anything about the manuscript tradition, because it must be regarded merely as a conjecture; or the two manuscripts may be copies of a common original which no longer exists: in this case the problem is to discover by comparing them just what stood in that original. This last, and not the individual vagaries of the two copyists, is our concern. The relationship between the manuscripts may of course be more involved: one may be copied from one manuscript and corrected from another, and so on. But the thoroughgoing investigation of the families into which the existing manuscripts of a given work may be divided, and the determination of which of these families represents the best and most genuine tradition, make up the first step toward deciding how much reliance can be reposed on the various readings. Even with the most

J. N. MADVIG

thorough comparison of the manuscripts, however, it is usually impossible to work back to a faultless text. Here, then, there is still work for the philologist. By penetrating deeply into the content and train of thought of the work, and by an alert sense for even the most delicate shades of linguistic usage, he may discover and point out to us where the error lies. Next, he must know how copyists' errors are likely to arise. Thus he may possibly succeed in reproducing the original text. Where before there was only confusion, skilled philologists have sometimes restored clearness and continuity simply by changing a letter here and there.

A comprehensive treatment of the results of classical philology, including also Greek and Latin linguistics from the comparative Indo-

European point of view, is a work in many volumes edited by Iwan von Müller, the *Handbuch der klassischen Altertumswissenschaft*; there are other undertakings of a similar nature.

GREEK

The ancient Greek language was spoken in the southern part of the Balkan peninsula, on the islands in the Ægean Sea, including Crete, and in the numerous colonies which, besides hellenizing the entire western coast of Asia Minor, Cyprus, and the coasts of southern Italy and Sicily, extended westward to the farthest points of the Mediterranean Sea (Africa, Spain, Gaul), and eastward as far as the Black Sea and the Sea of Azov.

We have evidence of a pre-Hellenic population in inscriptions from some of the more remote Greek islands, not only from out-of-the-way Cyprus, but from Crete and Lemnos, in the extreme southern and northern parts of the Ægean Sea. On the mainland the neighbors of the Greeks on the north were the Illyrians and Macedonians. The Illyrians were certainly a foreign people,[1] but the little we know, through names and glosses, of the ancient language of the Macedonians seems to indicate that they were related to the Greeks. Their language was not a Greek dialect, but may have stood in the same relationship to Greek as Scandinavian does to High German in our own days. If this view is correct, we understand better how easily and how zealously they later appropriated the Greek spirit.

In the earliest period, the Greek language was subdivided into a number of dialects, which in some ways differed widely from one another. Some of the dialects came into literary use, but we get the best idea of dialectal differences from inscriptions. We may divide the ancient dialects into four groups, which we shall call respectively East, North, South, and West Greek. In historical times these groups have natural geographical boundaries to only a limited extent, and it is evident that the chief characteristics of the dialectal divisions go back to a period earlier than the wanderings and conquests of the West Grecian races, especially of the Dorians. The four groups were distributed thus:

1) East Greek (Ionian and Attic) in the extreme eastern portion of Greece proper (Attica and the Island of Eubœa); in most of the Cyclades (with the exception of the southernmost isles); on the cen-

[1] See above, p. 68.

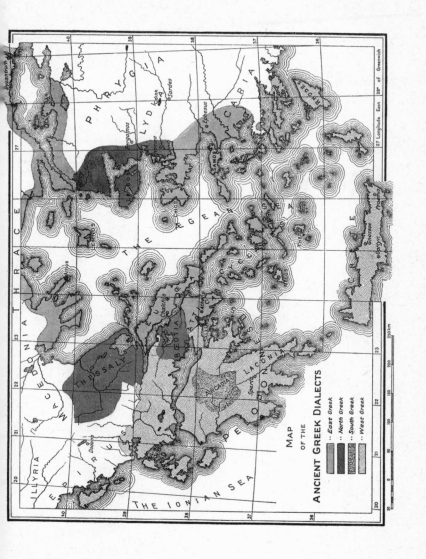

MAP
OF THE
ANCIENT GREEK DIALECTS

.. East Greek
.. North Greek
.. South Greek
.. West Greek

tral western coast of Asia Minor, together with the islands of Chios and Samos.

2) North Greek (Æolic) in the northern province of Thessaly; in the geographically disconnected central Greek province of Bœotia; and in the northern part of the western coast of Asia Minor, including the island of Lesbos.

3) South Greek, the speakers of which had suffered most from the advances of the Dorians, still maintained itself only in Arcadia (in the interior of the Peloponnesus); in Pamphylia (on the southern coast of Asia Minor); and on the island of Cyprus.

4) West Greek, with Doric, embraced Epirus, in so far as it was Greek; Central Greece, excepting Bœotia and Attica (thus it extended between the two North Greek dialects, Thessalian and Bœotian); the Peloponnesus, excepting Arcadia; and finally the southernmost islands in the Ægean Sea and the southernmost part of the western coast of Asia Minor.

To complete the picture it must be added that the Ionians had also settled along the northern coast of the Ægean Sea from the three-pointed peninsula projecting from Macedonia, to the peninsula of Gallipoli, and on the islands which lie within or inclose the bay between these two peninsulas. On the northern coast of the Sea of Marmora there were some Doric colonies, e.g. Byzantium. In southern Italy and Sicily there were many Ionian colonies, especially from the city of Chalcis in Eubœa, such as Naples; but there were also many Doric colonies, such as Tarentum and Syracuse.

With some reason, North and South Greek may be combined into one large group, which might be called Central Greek. This gives the triple division used by the Greeks themselves: East Greek, Central Greek, and West Greek correspond roughly to what the ancients called Ionian, Æolian, and Dorian.

In literature, South Greek plays no part. North Greek played its part for but a short time, and only in poetry (first the Æolic dialect in Asia Minor, and later Lesbian; still later, and to a very limited extent, Bœotian). Despite their political power, even the Dorians were unable to produce an enduring literary culture. The Dorian lyric, which begins about 600 B.C., was composed for public festivals of the Dorians; but it was created not by the Dorians, but by Ionians, Æolians, and so on. The most famous poet of all, Pindar, was a Bœotian. We find an attempt toward a Dorian literature, in both prose and poetry, in Sicily; and the famous mathematician Archimedes wrote in Dorian. But it was the Ionian-Attic group which brought about linguistic unity for Greece. And it was the Ionians of Asia Minor who began the movement. It is true that Athens early developed a literary language, but that, in its earliest period, was influenced by Ionian, and thus failed to retain the most conspicuous characteristics of Attic. After Athens had become the leading state of Greece, Ionian and Attic exchanged rôles: Ionian adapted itself to Attic, and not the reverse; and in the course of the fourth century before Christ Ionian became almost completely assimilated to Attic. The higher classes of Macedonia appropriated the common language thus developed, and Alexander's conquests made it a world language. At home, however, the non-Ionian dialects maintained themselves for a time. The dialect in Laconia, whose capital, Sparta, was a formidable rival of Athens, did not die out, but has continued its development down to the present day under the name of Tsaconian, though it survives only in a restricted area on the eastern coast.

With this single exception, all the ancient dialects succumbed before the Common Language based on the Attic dialect, which from the first century after Christ undoubtedly predominated. Yet it became a little altered in the course of its wide dissemination, and during the many centuries which have elapsed since then — in late classical times, in the medieval "Byzantine" period, and in modern times — it has not stood still. Modern Greek is at least as different from classical Greek as Italian is from Latin, if not more so. The language is still spoken widely. Yet of the world empire that Alexander the Great conquered for it in the East, only pitiful fragments remain: a few regions in the interior of eastern Asia Minor, in the province of Cappadocia. It has declined in the west also: there are some Greek-speaking districts in southern Italy, but there is no longer a "Greater Greece" there. In the homeland itself the old territory has been retained; i.e. Greece proper, and all the islands in the Ægean Sea including Crete, and Cyprus. On the northern coast of the Ægean Sea and the western coast of Asia Minor, Greek is spoken, as it was in classical times. On the southern coast of Asia Minor there is a Greek-speaking district near Adalia, in ancient Pamphylia. The coast of the Sea of Marmora and large portions of the western and southern coasts of the Black Sea are likewise Greek. Under these conditions it is not remarkable that the "common" language of the ancients has again divided into several dialects which often differ considerably from one another. But with the exception of Tsaconian they all descend from the Common Language based on the Attic dialect.

In one respect the comparison between modern Greek and Italian is not valid. While the Italian literary language has a tradition of many centuries to look back upon, the shadow of the classical language and the yoke of the Turks have combined to hinder the development of a modern literary language in Greece. Hence the modern Greek literary language was not established till the nineteenth century, and even now there is contention as to its correct form. In Greece, as elsewhere, the popular speech lacked the abstract words for which every modern language has such great need. The natural remedy was to take such words from the ancient language. But the use of the old words easily involves the use of the old inflectional forms, too. This archaizing tendency is pushed to an extreme by one party — the predominating one — so that a foreigner is likely to feel that the natural beauty of the language of the folk is being spoiled. At first sight one would think this artificial half-classical language would be quite incomprehensible to the people at large; but through the splendid Greek school system, acquaintance with it is being widely extended. There is an opposition which seeks to make the literary as much as possible like the living language. Its supporters are mostly poets, and it is almost powerless.[1] In spite of great changes in pronunciation, the spelling remains that of classical Greek, so that there is often a great discrepancy between the written and the spoken form of a word. Thus modern Greek orthography presents the greatest possible contrast to the regular spelling which is the pride of the Italians.

The oldest Greek inscriptions date from the eighth century before Christ. Literature may have begun even earlier. Homer's *Iliad* and *Odyssey*, treating of the war of the Greeks with Troy and of the crafty Ulysses' return home after the fall of the city, are invaluable sources for comparative linguistics; often they are the only sources which show clearly the connection between Greek and the oldest Indian usage. But the Homeric poems are not easy to date. The old naïve idea that these two epics — together making up almost twenty-eight thousand lines of verse, or a stately tome of seven hundred pages — are the work of a single individual (so that one could date the language if one were so fortunate as to determine the dates of

[1] An occurrence which illustrates the present attitude is the violent student demonstration in 1901 against the translation of the Bible into the language of the folk.

this poet), certainly cannot be entertained now. This notion was destroyed as early as 1795 by F. A. Wolf, and the nineteenth century struggled further with the problem. In 1846 Karl Lachmann attempted to throw light upon the subject by a comparison with the development of folk poetry among other nations, especially among the Germans, whose ancient literature he knew well. A. Kirchhoff in 1859, and later U. von Wilamowitz-Moellendorff in 1884, sought to discover the places where originally independent poems had been joined together. Whatever one's opinion may be about these attempts, it is certain that the Homeric epics have their roots in a time when there was not so much concern about an author's individuality as there has been since, a time when the poet stood in the shadow of his work. The poets' names were forgotten, but their poems lived and grew and became merged together. *The Iliad* and *The Odyssey* are the culmination of a folk poetry of long-lived tradition. It appears from linguistic evidence that this folk poetry must have had its first home among the Æolians, in Asia Minor. From them it passed over to their southern neighbors, the Ionians, and thus the Homeric poems come down to us in a form which is Ionian with Æolian reminiscences.[1] At first the poetry must have been transmitted orally; for though it may not be older than the Greek alphabet, it is certainly much older than the wide application of that alphabet to literary use. When the poems were finally written down, they appeared in an orthography unsuited to them, and have perhaps shifted it, since apparently they were first written in one of the older Greek alphabets which did not differentiate between different sorts of open and closed ĕ and ŏ, and later were transliterated into the usual Greek alphabet; a proceeding which, in the case of an already archaic language, must inevitably lead to mistakes. At least, a transposition from one alphabet to another was assumed in classical times; in modern times the theory has been controverted; it has been maintained by highly respected linguistic scholars, and it has been rejected by equally respected philologists.

Thus the history of the origin and transmission of the Homeric poems differs greatly from that of the other literary works with which classical philology has to do, and hence the study of this subject requires other methods than the usual ones. Historical knowledge of

[1] A well-known specialist in linguistics, A. Fick, in 1883–86 made the experiment of translating the poems back into Æolian; this experiment, however, was based on an overestimation of the powers of linguistics and philology. We do not know sufficient Æolian, and we are in no position to determine how much of the poems existed in that dialect.

the different dialects is required, a sort of "internal" Greek comparative linguistics, which can be undertaken with success only in the light of comparative Indo-European linguistics.

Greek dialect studies underwent a rejuvenation during the course of the nineteenth century, aided by Indo-European linguistics in general, and the more so because the number of available inscriptions in dialect was greatly increased. Nearly all of the more important dialect material was discovered during the nineteenth century. In spite of these discoveries, however, this material is still so incomplete that comparative Greek linguistics has nothing like the significance of comparative Germanic linguistics, founded by Grimm; and one can point to no Grimm among its exponents. Worthy of all honor is H. L. Ahrens's *De Graecae linguae dialectis*, 1839–43; but with the discovery of new inscriptions in the last half of the century, this work has become completely antiquated. Very useful is the *Sammlung der griechischen Dialektinschriften* which Hermann Collitz, with a large number of collaborators, edited during the years 1884– 1915, a work of over four thousand pages, with grammatical surveys and word-lists. This collection, with the manuals by Albert Thumb and the American Carl Darling Buck, both dated 1909,[1] is the century's most important comprehensive treatment of the steadily increasing material. The latest contribution is by F. Bechtel: *Die griechischen Dialekte* (1921–24).

The first scholar to make an effort to bring about a closer connection between comparative linguistics and Greek philology was Georg Curtius. This attempt did not run a wholly peaceful course. The Greek grammar for schools which he published in 1852, wherein he attempted to render some of the results of comparative linguistics accessible for practical instruction, evoked a series of violent attacks from the distinguished but contentious philologist K. W. Krüger (himself the author of a valuable Greek grammar), who denied Curtius all honor as a judge of Greek linguistic usage and accused him of plagiarism from his own grammar. Nevertheless, Curtius's grammar passed through sixteen editions before its author's death. But his most influential work is his *Grundzüge der griechischen Etymologie*, of which the first of five editions appeared in 1858. In form this book is a theory of etymology, its chief content being an exposition of the evolution of sounds. Curtius differentiates between regular sound

---

[1] Buck's excellent work (*Introduction to the Study of the Greek Dialects*) appeared in a new edition in 1928.

change and irregular or sporadic sound change; he has, indeed, an idea that rules operate in this field, but he still thinks that the validity of the rules has some limit. With the help of the index this book can be used also, to a certain extent, as an etymological dictionary. It is Curtius's great service that he thus made easily accessible the results of comparative etymological research, and held wild conjectures in check by his discriminating criticism. There is nothing

GEORG CURTIUS

very original in the works of Curtius, but they contributed greatly toward awakening interest in the problems and results of comparative linguistics in so far as these concern Greek. His personal influence seems to have been even more stimulating. This was shown, when in 1862, after having taught at Prague and Kiel, he accepted a call to Leipzig. He had been told that he might expect twenty to twenty-five auditors, as Leipzig was then attended by but few philologists; but in a short time he had double that number, and toward the end the average was nearly three hundred. Curtius had an extraordinary power of engrossing his hearers' attention. From his time Leipzig became the center for comparative linguistics which it has remained to our own day.

In recent years surveys of Greek linguistics have been undertaken repeatedly in the form of comparative grammars (the best is by Curtius's famous pupil, Karl Brugmann) and etymological dictionaries. But the material has increased greatly since the time of Curtius, and the well-rounded and readable form that Curtius was able to give his treatment has not been equalled by his successors.

It is the tendency of the newer linguistics to follow the evolution of the language down to the present. Byzantine language and literature have had an energetic worker in the German Karl Krumbacher; and the scientific study of modern Greek has been advanced particularly by the Greek Hatzidakis and the German Albert Thumb, among others.

LATIN

In classical times Italy was far from unified in language; linguistic relations, indeed, were still more complicated than in the Balkan peninsula.

We know that some of the peoples in Italy came there at a relatively late period. The Gauls in northern Italy are supposed to have crowded in about 400 B.C. The Greek colonization of southern Italy was some centuries older; and still earlier had come non-Indo-European Etruscans, who, after extending their power and influence over a large part of Italy, continued to maintain their nationality and culture in the province of Etruria, which to some extent corresponds to modern Tuscany and the region south toward the Tiber. They also maintained their nationality, if not their culture, in the Alps between Lakes Garda and Como, and far northward through the Tyrol, where they bore the name of Rhaetians (*Raeti*).

But even if we exclude these peoples, whom we know to have immigrated, the remaining languages did not constitute a single group. Certainly the largest area was occupied by a group of closely related languages which we are accustomed to call Italic. But on the eastern coast of Italy a number of inscriptions give evidence of languages which cannot be reckoned in the Italic branch, although they may have had something in common with it: Venetian, in the north, in the province of Venetia, which has given its name to Venice, and Messapian, in the heel of the boot. These two languages may have been interrelated and related to the Illyrian language on the other side of the Adriatic Sea, though unfortunately we know next to nothing of things linguistic in ancient Illyria.

There has also been some doubt about the northernmost and southernmost languages toward the west. The northernmost was Ligurian, which extended far into present-day France. Its old territory reached from the Cevennes into the plains of the Po, from the sources of the Rhine and the Rhone to the river Arno. Widely varying opinions have been expressed concerning this language. Place-names, and inscriptions found in the region extending from Lake Como to a point west of Lake Maggiore, indicate certainly, in my opinion, that Ligurian, though not strictly an Italic language, was closely related to the Italic branch, but must have separated from it so early that it had its own development; perhaps it stood in much the same relation to the Italic dialects proper as Macedonian did to Greek. The southernmost language to the west was Siculian, the language which the oldest non-Greek population of Sicily used. We know very little about it, but there seems to be no reason for not accepting it as an Italic dialect.

If we disregard Siculian, the Italic languages may be classified as follows:

A. Latin

B. Umbrian-Oscan
1) Umbrian
2) The central Italic dialects
3) Oscan

Of these languages Latin was originally the most restricted geographically. Its original home was Latium proper (the ancient Latium), a province of about twenty-five hundred square kilometers south of Etruria and the river Tiber, and in addition a small territory in southern Etruria surrounding the town of Falerii. There was some dialectal variation within this district, the Faliscan dialect in Falerii deviating most markedly, but the dialect of Rome prevailed. A much greater territory was occupied by Umbrian, in the province of Umbria east of Etruria. And Oscan had the greatest dissemination of all, covering as it did most of the southern part of Italy, and being spoken, among others, by the warlike Samnites, Rome's most dangerous rivals for the rule of Italy. A number of central Italic dialects between Umbrian and Oscan, south and east of the old Latin territory, were, in general, most closely related to Oscan. Volscians, Sabines, Æquians, Marsians, Vestinians, Marrucinians, Pælignians were the names of the tribes.

From a literary point of view, however, Latin seems to have had an advantage from the first over the other Italic languages. Latin literature begins in the third century before Christ, and there are Latin inscriptions as early as the sixth century before Christ. The oldest Oscan-Umbrian inscriptions are more than a century later, and we have no trustworthy evidence of a literature in these languages. It does not necessarily follow that none existed, but it cannot have been of much importance. With the growing power of the Romans, Latin spread more and more at the cost of the other Italic dialects. Just when these ceased to be spoken we cannot determine. The latest evidence comes from the excavations at Pompeii, where some of the Oscan inscriptions seem to date from the decades immediately before the town's destruction, A.D. 79.

Rome's world power converted Latin into an international language, spoken in the entire western part of the Roman empire and in some parts of the Balkan peninsula. It became the parent language of a group of widely disseminated languages now living, and it can be traced by loan-words all the way to Armenia and Arabia. As a learned language it dominated Western Europe throughout the Middle Ages and well into modern times. The Romance languages, which are descended from Latin, and whose independent existence can be reckoned as beginning with the eighth century after Christ, are as follows:

1) Portuguese
2) Spanish (Castilian)
3) Catalan (in eastern Spain)
4) Provençal (in the south- ern third of France)
5) French
6) Rhaetoromanic (in the Grisons, the Tyrol and Friuli)
7) Italian
8) Dalmatian (extinct, crowded out by Italian.) [1]
9) Rumanian (cf. p. 70, above)

Our knowledge of Oscan-Umbrian was all won in the nineteenth century. At the beginning of the century not even the boundaries between these languages and Etruscan had been made out. C. O. Müller first distinguished correctly between Umbrian and Etruscan in his book, *Die Etrusker* (1828); but the first steps toward a real understanding of the Oscan-Umbrian remains were made as late as the eighteen-thirties by the Sanskrit scholar Lassen, by Grotefend, who first deciphered the old Persian cuneiform inscriptions, and by the

[1] Anthony Udina, the last speaker of Dalmatian, an old man from the island of Veglia, was killed in a mine explosion in 1898.

future Egyptologist Lepsius. Since then important work has been done in this field by Mommsen, Kirchhoff, Bréal, and Bücheler, and in more recent years by von Planta, Conway, and Buck.

But there has been progress also in the study of Latin. The labor of collecting linguistic material has been prosecuted as never before. We may mention the Latin morphology (*Formenlehre*) published by Neue in 1866, which appeared later in new editions. But the great

MICHEL BRÉAL
Founder of comparative Indo-European linguistics
in France; specialist in the Italic languages

work of the century is an as yet uncompleted dictionary. Long the dream of philologists, it began to be realized toward the close of the century: a dictionary which within practicable limits should exhaust all the material valuable from a linguistic or philological point of view in all Latin literature, and in the whole mass of inscriptions from the beginnings to A.D. 600 (*Thesaurus linguae Latinae*). Five academies — those of Berlin, Göttingen, Leipzig, Munich, and Vienna — united for the accomplishment of this undertaking. The governments of some German states which did not participate in the plan have lent more or less support, and contributions from private sources have been considerable. As a preliminary, the editions of the texts had to be examined, and many had to be reëdited. Then the entire vocabulary had to be copied or clipped out, each word in its context; in this way some millions of cards were made available. On the basis of this material, single articles were written up by a permanent staff of scholars with headquarters in Munich, where the cards were sent. Each article gives a word's history through the whole of

FRIEDRICH DIEZ

the extensive period covered by the work, its forms, combinations, meanings, and usage in the changing periods and the different styles of literary and popular language. The etymology is also given, wherever it can be determined with some probability, this part of the work having been undertaken by Rudolf Thurneysen. It was estimated that five to seven years would be necessary for the preliminary step, and twelve to fifteen more for completion. Work began in 1894, and the first part was issued in 1901. According to the original estimate, the task should have been completed at about the beginning of the World War; but here the estimate broke down, for in 1915 only volumes V and VI (the latter containing the letter *F*) were in process of publication. The war crippled the enterprise, for it called the collaborators away, many of them never to return; but fortunately this great work is again being continued.

Latin philology has the greatest use for the new light from inscriptions and comparative linguistics in the study of Plautus, who lived from about 254 to 184 B.C. When Plautus wrote his comedies, Latin had in many respects a much older appearance than in the Golden Age, almost a century and a half later. But most of the manuscripts of his comedies have preserved the original forms of the text

GASTON PARIS
[After Bédier and Roques, *Bibliographie des Travaux de G. P.*]

badly. The possibility of restoring the original forms was increased by the unexpected discovery in 1815 of a palimpsest in the Ambrosian library at Milan. This manuscript had originally contained several of the comedies, copied in the fifth century after Christ; but the parchment had been used again in the eighth century: the old writing had been rubbed out, and over it, in a very coarse handwriting, had been written a Latin translation of the Old Testament. Difficult though the task was, scholars succeeded in reading much of the Plautine text. The most illustrious mind among those who struggled with the problems of Plautus was F. Ritschl (whose edition appeared in 1848–54), even though there may be much to criticize in his attempt to transcend what can be derived from the manuscripts themselves by strict philological methods.

Important contributions to Latin linguistics have been made also by Karl Lachmann and by the indefatigable interpreter of the oldest Latin inscriptions, Franz Bücheler. The results of comparative linguistics as applied to Latin are surveyed in several comparative grammars and etymological dictionaries.

KRISTOFFER NYROP

The historical study of the Romance languages was begun by the German F. Diez in his *Grammatik der romanischen Sprachen* (1836–44), and *Etymologisches Wörterbuch der romanischen Sprachen* (1853). The study was carried on later by many scholars of Romance or foreign nationality, such as the Frenchmen E. Littré, Gaston Paris, and Paul Meyer, the Italian Ascoli, the Germans Meyer-Lübke and Schuchardt, and the Dane Kristoffer Nyrop.

Within the Indo-European linguistic family the Romance languages are the best example of a widely spread branch the parent language of which is well known and need not be reconstructed like primitive Germanic or primitive Slavonic. Yet it must not be forgotten that the Romance languages do not descend from literary Latin, but from the ordinary speech of the common people. Hence the study of the Romance languages is very important for linguistic method. From them we can also learn many things about Latin which the literary remains do not teach us. Romance philology is now served by a number of periodicals, and is already surveyed in the *Grundriss der romanischen Philologie* (edited 1888– by Gustav Gröber).

V

THE STUDY OF NON–INDO–EUROPEAN FAMILIES OF LANGUAGES

OUR acquaintance with the languages not belonging to the Indo-European family has made great progress during the nineteenth century. The available material has grown extraordinarily, and our knowledge of the relations among these languages, and of their grouping in families, has gone far beyond that of the eighteenth century. In this connection, it would be unjust not to mention the great part played by Christian missionaries in broadening our knowledge of exotic languages.

However, very few of these families have been the subject of such thorough comparison as that undertaken within the Indo-European family. Hence there is often doubt even yet as to the extent of these families, and some of the current ideas about their grouping are in a way advanced on trust. Particularly questionable are the attempts to combine various families in larger units. No convincing method has been found for organizing this swarm of languages into a small number of groups.

In the course of the nineteenth century certain attempts were made to devise a short-cut by establishing a number of types under which all languages could be classified. Thus, some have been classified as isolating, others as agglutinative, inflectional, or incorporating. As an example of an isolating language, Chinese is cited: all words are monosyllabic and have no inflection of any kind. The relations which we express by means of inflection are indicated by independent words, wherever indications cannot be dispensed with entirely. This holds good even in cases in which inflection is indispensable with us (genitive, plural, tense of verbs). The classical example of an *agglutinative* ("glued together") language is Turkish. Here there is a mass of endings which express the relations of words, but the junction of word and ending is quite clear, so that there can be no doubt as to the boundary between the two; for example, *äv* "house," *äv-dä* "in the house," *äv-lär* "houses," *äv-lär-dä* "in the houses"; *säv* "love," *säv-di* "he loved," *säv-di-lär* "they loved." In the *inflectional* languages, on the other hand, it is difficult to determine the boundaries; word and ending are fused in an unresolvable unity, and internal changes in the word itself may be used to express changing relations (e.g. English *bear, bore, borne*). The most prominent of the inflectional types is primitive Indo-European. Thus *I, thou, he (she), we, you, they*, as subject were expressed not independently, but by means of changing inflectional endings in the verb:

Latin *ferō*	I bear	plural *ferimus*	we bear
fers	thou bearest	*fertis*	you bear
fert	he (she, it) bears	*ferunt*	they bear

There are languages where not only the subject, but also the object, the indirect object, etc., are expressed along with the verb form. These languages are called *incorporating*. The best example is the language of Greenland, where a whole sentence containing many details often has the form of a single word.[1] It is quite true, however, that these types of languages do not have much to do with linguistic relationship. It must be admitted that the characteristics of a language do not change quickly; languages very closely related will therefore rarely belong to entirely different types. But in the course of a considerable space of time, the type may become changed. We can find different types within one and the same family of languages. Thus some of the modern languages of the Indo-European family, such as English and modern Bulgarian, exhibit affinities with the isolating type; modern Armenian has a great similarity to the agglutinative type (*arev* "sun," genitive *arev-u* "of a sun," plural *arev-ner* "suns," genitive *arev-ner-u* "of suns"); and Old Irish has striking incorporating tendencies (cf. above, p. 61). Linguistic types are therefore not at all well adapted to indicate kinship between languages which are very distant from one another. Moreover, these types rarely appear pure; usually different principles are seen in use side by side in one and the same language.

The comprehensive surveys of the close of the eighteenth century had their successors in the nineteenth. There is Klaproth, *Asia polyglotta* (Paris, 1823); and later there are works on the languages of the Caucasus, of India, of America, which will be referred to below. But the only work of the nineteenth century which includes the entire field is Friedrich Müller's *Grundriss der Sprachwissenschaft* (Vienna, 1876–88). By comparing his treatment with Adelung's *Mithridates* one can best appreciate the tremendous progress ac-

---

[1] For instance, *qasuersarfigssarsíngitdluínarnarpoq*, "One certainly found no place to rest." The root is *qasu-* "tired, to be tired"; *qasu-er-sar-* "to cause to cease to be tired," and so on. *-nar-poq* is a personal ending.

complished. In the course of his general introduction Müller provides a genealogical survey of all languages, with references to the principal works in which they are treated; and then in several volumes he gives sketches of a great many typical languages. The sketches are short, but yet long enough to give an idea of the languages discussed. They are accompanied as a rule by specimens. Since the conclusion of Müller's work no little time has elapsed, and investigation has not ceased to advance. It was the aim of Franz Nikolaus Finck to give the latest results in *Die Sprachstämme des Erdkreises* (1909). But this book is very different from Müller's: it contains merely a catalogue-like enumeration of approximately two thousand languages, arranged according to their presumable relationships, but without grammatical information or specimens, and without references to sources. Some references to sources are found in a series of books by Trombetti. Nevertheless, a large work giving a treatment not less detailed than Müller's, and written from the vantage-ground of present knowledge, remained a desideratum until it was supplied in some measure by the French work *Les langues du monde, par un groupe de linguistes sous la direction de A. Meillet et Marcel Cohen* (Paris, 1924). This contains eighteen linguistic maps, but hardly any specimens. Finally, in 1926, the German scholar Father Wilhelm Schmidt attempted single-handed an exposition of the whole subject in *Die Sprachfamilien und Sprachenkreise der Erde* (with fourteen maps). In spite of many inaccuracies, this book may prove useful.

Müller and Finck arrange the languages according to the different races of man, Müller distinguishing the languages of woolly-haired, smooth-haired, and curly-haired races. Finck begins where Müller stops: he classifies Caucasian, Mongolian, American, and Ethiopian races. But it must not be inferred that there is any inherent connection between language and race. On the contrary, one of the first observations to be made when languages are examined is that races and languages do not have the same boundaries. In practice the classifications of Müller and Finck have no more value than a geographical arrangement with the necessary concessions to certain or probable linguistic relationship; and without much impropriety one might replace Finck's ethnographical classification by purely geographical names, such as the Mediterranean group (Europe, Northern Africa, the Near East), the Far East, America, and remoter Africa and Australia, with the reservation that languages which are known to have made their way into any of these regions from a neighboring one are treated as belonging to their original homes.

In the following survey of the most important languages and families of languages the arrangement is geographical; but special attention is given to families which have been most thoroughly investigated, and which have had the greatest influence upon Indo-European linguistic scholarship. Since in general these are the families which have been neighbors to our own from ancient times, it is convenient to discuss first the circle of foreign languages which surround Europe most closely; then the foreign families about India; and finally the more distant series of languages in the Far East, America, Africa, and Australia.

THE FOREIGN FAMILIES SURROUNDING EUROPE

1. *Finno-Ugrian and Samoyed (Uralian)*

From the point of view of scholarly investigation, the Finno-Ugrian family of languages has remained more closely in contact with Indo-European linguistic science than any other. This family, divided into seven branches, occupies three widely separated regions: the two which are in full reciprocal connection with European culture I shall name, somewhat arbitrarily, the western and southern sections; a third begins in Central Russia at the Volga and extends through the countries along two tributaries of the Volga, the Vyatka and Kama rivers, and the land north of these rivers as far as Siberia, on both sides of the river Ob. This eastern region is much split up in its southern part, so that it forms a number of islands, large and small, in the great sea of the Russian people; various Turkish tribes, also, project into it. Only the northernmost inhospitable land north of the Vyatka and Kama, and in the interior of Siberia, has been retained in peace by the Finno-Ugrian tribes.

Of the seven branches of the family, the following belong to the western geographical section:

1. *West Finnic* (Finnish in Finland, Esthonian, and some less significant dialects in the regions near the Baltic Sea).
2. *Lappish* (in the extreme north of Norway, Sweden, and Finland, and on the Kola peninsula in Russia).

To the eastern geographical section belong the four following branches of the family:

3. *Mordvinian*, farthest to the south, is spoken on both sides of the Volga in its course from north to south, and extends to about the fifty-second degree of latitude, or a little south of the town of Samara. The Mordvinians were once a great people, who had their home west of the Volga. Still rather numerous, — according to the census of 1897 about one million, or half the entire population of the eastern geographical section, — they are widely scattered among the Russians, and the language is steadily declining.
4. *Cheremissian*, north of Mordvinian, but separated from it by a Turkish tribe. Most of the Cheremissians live north of the course from west to east of the Volga.
5. *Permian*, two different languages between the Vyatka and the Kama, and north of these rivers all the way to the Arctic circle. The Permians were originally a numerous people with an early culture. The town of Perm takes its name from them.
6. *Ugrian* includes two hunting and fishing peoples, the Vogulians and the Ostiaks in the vicinity of the Irtysh and Ob rivers, north of the town of Tobolsk.

The southern geographical section, which is the result of immigration in historical times, consists of but one language:

7. *Hungarian* or *Magyar*. The Magyars reached their present homes in the ninth century.

With regard to the relationships between south, east, and west, it can be said that Magyar is closest to Vogulian, and West Finnic is closest to Mordvinian.

Like the Magyars, the West Finnic tribes are immigrants in the districts they now inhabit. There are clear indications that the whole Finno-Ugrian family originally dwelt together in some eastern region. There they received a number of loan-words from an Iranian or Indian language, or from the parent language which later separated into Iranian and Indian. These loan-words are to be found now in the branches of the family in forms which have undergone the laws of sounds peculiar to each branch. The most striking example is the numeral for 100:

Finnish *sata*   Hungarian *száz* (pronounced *sāz*)
Compare Sanskrit *śata-*,   Avesta *sata-*

We cannot say exactly when or where these loan-words were borrowed. But, just as it is certain that they must have been borrowed at a very early period, so it is clear that the borrowing must have taken place in some land far to the east of the historical home of the West Finnic tribes. The emigration from this eastern country to the vicinity of the Baltic Sea must have taken place very early. At the beginning of the Christian era the tribes we now call West Finnic must already have dwelt sufficiently near the Baltic Sea to have come under strong Baltic (Lithuanian) and, later, Gothic influence. The proof of this is the very large number of loan-words which the Finns took over in just the forms which we should expect in those ancient times for linguistic reasons; today these forms are modified only by the sound-changes which occurred in the various West Finnic dialects. These sound-changes have been so few, especially in Finnish, that the loan-words from Gothic, for instance, appear today in modern Finnish in forms which reflect a prehistoric stage with remarkable clearness. For example, Finnish *kuningas* "king," is certainly identical with the form which the Goths used about the time of the birth of Christ, and is older than any surviving Germanic form. From the country where the Finns underwent this Baltic (Lithuanian) and Gothic influence they later migrated to their present home. It is worthy of mention that the Lapps are very different culturally from the Finns, although the languages are closely related in vocabulary and inflectional forms (the developments in sounds are quite different). Hence it has been conjectured that the Lapps are a people of another race who have taken over the language of the Finns. If this conjecture is correct, the change must have taken place at a very early time, as Lappish sometimes preserves forms which, from a Finnish point of view, are prehistoric.

There are practically no ancient linguistic monuments in the Finno-Ugrian family. There is a Hungarian funeral sermon from the thirteenth century. In one of the Permian languages there are some texts from the fourteenth century, written in an alphabet invented by their apostle, Saint Stephen (†1396). In Finland and Esthonia, literature begins in the sixteenth century; and it is also only in the sixteenth century that sources become more numerous in Hungarian.

A special family, distinct from the Finno-Ugrian but having a distant relationship with it, is Samoyed. It includes a scanty population of about sixteen thousand, inhabiting the far-flung regions along the Arctic Ocean in Eastern Russia and Western Siberia, from approximately the mouth of the Petchora river to the mouth of the Khatanga. The tribe of the so-called Ostiak Samoyeds have their home between the Ob and the Yenisei rivers, south of the sixtieth degree of latitude. A Samoyed dialect used to be spoken also five degrees farther south, near the two eastern tributaries of the Yenisei, but it is now almost completely replaced by Turkish. Finno-Ugrian and Samoyed together are called Uralian.

With some reason, Finno-Ugrian linguistics can boast of being older than Indo-European linguistics. The resemblances between Magyar on the one hand, and Finnish and Lappish on the other, awakened attention early. But the Hungarians did not feel themselves quite flattered by kinship with the Lapps; it savored too

M. A. CASTRÉN
[After *Journal de la Société Finno-Ougrienne*, xxx]

strongly of fish oil. They would have much preferred kinship with the Turks, especially with the famous Huns, whose victorious plundering expeditions through Europe fourteen hundred years ago started the great folk migrations. As support for this claim they alleged the many points of agreement in vocabulary between Hungarian and Turkish, without perceiving that these were due to loan-words which the Magyars had taken over from the Turks at various times. Then, in 1799, appeared the work of Gyármathi referred to above (p. 11), in which proof was given for the relationship with Finnish. In this book the principle which became the lodestar of incipient Indo-European linguistics is clearly pronounced, i.e., the preponderant importance of the inflectional system for linguistic comparison. Agreement in vocabulary is placed last as evidence by Gyármathi, and he emphasizes the fact that Hungarian has taken over a great many loan-words from various foreign languages, such as Turkish and Slavonic. From this time the Turkish hypothesis has been echoed only in circles remote from systematic investigation.

In the nineteenth century, Rask, who valued Gyármathi's work highly, delved deeply into the study of Finnish and Lappish. He

K. B. WIKLUND

even contributed toward the awakening of interest in Finnish among the Finns themselves. He wrote a Lappish grammar and devised the Lappish system of spelling. And he was the first to make a substantially correct classification of the Finno-Ugrian family. The Germanic (Gothic) and Baltic (Lithuanian) loan-words in Finnish were studied by Vilhelm Thomsen in two admirable investigations (1869 and 1890), which have been the foundation of the study of loan-words in general.[1] The foremost specialists in Lappish

[1] Lately the question of the Germanic loan-words in Finnish has been much discussed, and different opinions have been proposed as to the age of these loan-words and as to the Germanic tribe from which they were borrowed. For a very short summary of the discussion see T. E. Karsten, *Die Germanen* (1928), pp. 169–94.

today are the Swedish scholar K. B. Wiklund and the Norwegian, Konrad Nielsen. But otherwise the centers of Finno-Ugrian linguistics during the nineteenth century have been Helsingfors and Budapest. In Finland it was M. A. Castrén who founded the study. He travelled very widely, and we owe to him grammatical works on several of the eastern Finno-Ugrian languages, on Samoyed, and also on certain northern Asiatic languages of other families, such as Yenisei and the three Altaic families. Among his successors may be

E. N. SETÄLÄ

named E. N. Setälä and H. Paasonen. In Hungary, Budenz was the leader. A German by birth, he became a professor at Budapest and wrote in Hungarian. Among his works is a comparative dictionary. After him, J. Szinnyei, in particular, has rendered great services to Finno-Ugrian linguistics.

2. *Yenisei*

In accordance with the geographical arrangement adopted, it is proper to name here the slowly expiring family, Yenisei, investigation of which is almost entirely the work of Castrén. The only extant representatives of this family are the dialects spoken by the so-called Yenisei-Ostiaks,[1] about eleven hundred people who live along the Yenisei River from the sixtieth to the seventieth degree of latitude, most of them south of the Arctic Circle. The advance of civilization has reduced them to extreme poverty. They are hunters and fishermen, with no domestic animals except dogs. Castrén found still another language of this family, Kottish, near Agul, approximately on the fifty-fifth degree of latitude; but it was spoken by only five persons, and is now extinct. Some tribes farther south had already given up their language in Castrén's time, and about them we know only what appears in Klaproth's *Asia polyglotta.*

It is only natural that this family, wedged in between Uralian and Altaic as it is, should give rise to various conjectures. Some ethnologists have made a fanciful attempt to find something in Scandinavian and Lappish which resembles this language of the Yenisei hunters and fishermen, who would thus be the most ancient pre-Germanic inhabitants of Scandinavia. This was the rôle attributed to the Finns in the eighteenth century; but they could no longer fill it after nineteenth-century linguistics had proved that their home was in a far eastern region, and that the points of similarity in the Finnish and Scandinavian vocabulary were due to loans made *to,* not *from,* Finnish. But the rôle will have to remain unfilled; the Yenisei family is not qualified to take it over. On the other hand, Finnish students of linguistics, from Castrén onwards, have maintained with growing conviction that there is a certain resemblance between the Yenisei languages and the great family to which Chinese belongs. Reasons can be advanced which point to the conclusion that the present Yenisei are the last remnants of a powerful folk who, with the Thibetan empire as their southern neighbor, ruled over a great part of Siberia, but were at length compelled to submit to the Turks. It is best at present to regard the Chinese theory as an hypothesis, however. The resemblances which have been adduced so far are not decisive.

3. *Turkish, Mongolian, Manchu (Altaic)*

The Turkish family covers a wide territory, the extreme limits of which are set by the Ottomans toward the southwest (Dobrudja, Constantinople and vicinity, Asia Minor); by Chinese Turkestan

---

[1] The designation *Ostiak* is meaningless from the linguistic point of view. It is borne also by one of the Ugrian tribes, and by the Samoyeds south of the sixtieth degree. Properly, then, it designates only the inhabitants of a particular territory, and is thus a purely geographical term.

on the southeast; and by the Yakoots on the north, on both sides of
the lower course of the Lena. The family belongs almost exclusively
to Asia; the only exceptions, save for the European branches of the
Ottomans, are some offshoots which extend into European Russia.
In addition to the Turkish population in the Crimea and in parts of
the Caucasus, we must name (1) the regions about the Caspian Sea,
where there is a division of the Kirghiz (who extend all the way
across to the Altai in Asia, and are the most numerous of the Turkish
peoples after the Ottomans), and (2) the northern offshoots, which
consist of the Bashkirs and the Kazan Tartars, wedged in among a
Finno-Ugrian population, together with the remarkable Chuvash
people, the southern neighbors of the Finno-Ugrian Cheremissians.

The numerical strength of the group does not correspond to its
wide dissemination, though its number is somewhat greater than
that of the Finno-Ugrian family. The population speaking Turkish
languages can be estimated at about thirty millions. Most of these
are so closely related that we need not distinguish languages and
dialects here. Only Yakoot and Chuvash diverge markedly from the
rest. Chuvash differs so greatly that many words which are pronounced approximately in the same way from the Arctic Ocean to
Constantinople are scarcely recognizable in Chuvash unless one is
acquainted with its sound-laws. For instance, we have Ottoman *taš*
"stone," Chuvash *čul* — admittedly an extreme example, as three
sound-laws have operated in the one word.

Since the end of classical times Europe has had much intercourse
with the Turks, and various names of Turkish tribes now extinct are
well known to the historian. The frightful Huns, who began the
great migrations, were of the Turkish race, as were the Avars, who
settled in Pannonia (Hungary), and were crushed by Charlemagne.
Of Turkish race also were the Bulgars, who bequeathed their name to
the Slavic people of the Balkans (see above, p. 44). It has been
confirmed by the investigations of the Finnish scholar Mikkola that
these Turkish Bulgars sprang from the same people who survive as
the Chuvash of our day. Thus the peculiar characteristic of the
Chuvash language is very old roots: it must have become separated
from the Common Turkish language at a very early period. The
most powerful of the Turkish peoples against whom the Russians
had to fight at the beginning of their history were the Kazarians,
whose capital lay near the Volga, not far from the present Astrakhan.
They ruled over a large part of modern Russia and had lively inter-

course with the Greeks. A Greek emperor of the eighth century married the daughter of a Kazarian prince. It is noteworthy that the Kazarians had adopted the Jewish religion. In the tenth century they were forced to submit to the Russians, and thereafter the chief rôle in Southern Russia was played by other Turkish tribes, such as the Cumanians, whom the Russians called Polovtsians. In the face

J. J. MIKKOLA

of the Mongolian onslaught at the beginning of the thirteenth century, they united with the Russians, and their ruler adopted Christianity. But the Mongolians conquered, and the Cumanian people broke up. Some of them passed to Hungary, where they maintained themselves for several centuries.

The Turkish languages have much older monuments than the Finno-Ugrian, which today stand so far in advance of them in culture. In Southern Siberia, along the upper course of the Yenisei river and in Northern Mongolia, long inscriptions from about A.D. 700 have been found, written in a special Turkish alphabet, the Old Turkish "runes"; and the most recent discoveries in Chinese Turkestan [1] have brought to light numerous Old Turkish manuscripts,

[1] See below, pp. 192 ff.

mostly fragmentary. A long didactic poem, *Kutadgu bilig* ("Auspicious Knowledge") in Uighurian, written in 1069 in the kingdom of Kašgar (redacted in an alphabet imported from northeastern Iran, the land of the Sogdians, and akin to the Syrian alphabet) has been known for a long time. A manuscript of 1303, written in the Latin alphabet, contains information about Cumanian as well as Cumanian texts of Christian import. At present all Turkish literary culture is under the influence of Mohammedanism.[1] Hence Turkish was until quite recently written in the Arabic alphabet, which is not at all suitable for the purpose. And not only was the language thus made almost illegible, but the lack of national feeling among the Mohammedans has allowed the language to be flooded with Arabic and Persian loan-words. The really fine literary style of the Ottomans is so overlaid with these borrowings that at times the genuine Turkish language is hardly visible.

Research in Turkish linguistics is entirely the work of foreigners; the Turks themselves have made no contribution. Our knowledge of the two most divergent Turkish languages, Yakoot and Chuvash, has been advanced considerably, and their significance for comparative Turkish linguistics has been clearly shown. In the case of Yakoot, the beginning was made in an excellent work by the famous Sanskrit scholar Otto Böhtlingk; and on Chuvash one of the most recent important works is a dictionary by the Finnish scholar H. Paasonen (1908). On the other hand, the general investigation of the whole family had to wait long for anything better than second-rate work. Neither the etymological dictionary by the Hungarian H. Vámbéry, nor the products of the German W. Radloff [2] (working in Russia) can be ranked higher than this. It was really Vilhelm Thomsen who laid the foundations of comparative Turkish phonology by his interpretation of the oldest Turkish inscriptions and his investigation of the language of the Uighurian didactic poem.

Widely different from the Turkish family are two others, Mongolian and Manchu, though they apparently bear a distant relationship to Turkish, and are usually included with the Turkish language under the common name *Altaic*. It is only on the assumption that

---

[1] The Yakoots, who are heathens, have no literary culture.

[2] Most important are his *Proben der Volkslitteratur der türkischen Stämme* and *Versuch eines Wörterbuches der Türk-Dialekte*.

this grouping is correct that these two families are named here: from a purely geographical point of view they do not belong to the nearest foreign families of languages surrounding Europe.

. The Mongolians, whose conquering expeditions in the thirteenth century brought them to the very doors of Europe — in 1241 they won the great battle near Liegnitz, in Silesia — and who continued their rule over Russia until 1480, live now in Dzungaria (West Mongolians), in Mongolia proper (East Mongolians), and on both sides of Lake Baïkal (North Mongolians). Linguistic variation among the three regions is so slight that it is better to speak of dialects than of different languages. A tribe of the West Mongolians, the Kalmuks, dwell in Russia west of the lower course of the Volga, near Astrakhan. In some districts of Afghanistan, also, east of Herat, there are scattered Mongolian tribes whose language belongs to the western group.

The Manchurian family of languages includes (1) the Manchus in Manchuria, who in the year 1644 placed their own royal house on the imperial throne of China, but had to pay for their domination over a people of ancient civilization by a steady decline in their own language; and (2) the Tunguses in Siberia, a widely distributed but numerically small people, whose home extends in a bow from the Taimir peninsula south of the Yakoots to the Sea of Okhotsk.

Both Mongolians and Manchus use the Uighurian (that is, ultimately the Syrian) alphabet, which they write in vertical lines, beginning with the line farthest to the left. The Mongols, however, experimented for a time with another script of Indo-Thibetan origin, the so-called square script, which was introduced by the Emperor Kubilai in 1259. It was the official script for a few centuries, but ultimately gave way to the older Uighurian script. In its original form the Uighurian system was ill suited to the phonological system of these languages, but it has been greatly improved in the hands of the Kalmuks and Manchus.

Considerable progress was made during the nineteenth century in knowledge of the Mongol and Manchu families. It is worthy of remark that Castrén wrote grammars of both North Mongolian and Tungusian. But the pivotal question of the relationship among Turkish, Mongolian and Manchu has not yet found a solution. We can merely record an opinion that a relationship exists, though it is an opinion in which all specialists in the languages have agreed,

KALMUK WRITING

arban dörbödügēr bödök.
ten- fourth chapter.
(fourteenth)

1. *tani (d) zürüken inu bičigei tükšitügei.*
your hearts — not be frightened.

ta burxan[1] du itege(d)ži nada čigi itegektün.
Ye God on believing me on also believe!

mini ecegein ger-tü-ni orošixu oron
My father's house in dwelling- place(s)

[*inu olon bui*].
— many are.

(John xiv, 1-2.)

MONGOLIAN WRITING

burxan Buddha

(The word is used in the Kalmuk New Testament for *God*.)

The first character is *bu*; the curve highest at the left and the curve to the right mean *b*; the lowest curve at the left means in Mongolian *u* or *o*; in Kalmuk *u* is different from *o* (and from *ö* and *ü*, which are written in Mongolian partly with the same characters as *o* and *u*). Of the three strokes below *r* the first two belong together and mean *x* (German *ch*), made plain in Kalmuk by the added dots. The third stroke means *a*, the final stroke *n*.

---

[1] *x* = German *ch*.

especially in so far as Turkish and Mongolian are concerned. But the evidence falls far short of proof. A careful distinction must be made between genuine native words and loan-words. Loan-words undoubtedly play a very great part in consequence of the considerable historical contact among the three peoples. It is not improbable that the Turks were usually the lenders. Then the sound-laws for the words supposedly common to and original in the three families must be investigated. Only in this way can it be definitely determined that there actually exists such a common vocabulary. The Finnish scholar Ramstedt and the Hungarian Gombocz have recently taken the first steps toward solving this last problem. But we can say already that if the conjecture of a relationship is confirmed, then Mongolian and Manchu are in a much earlier stage than Turkish; in comparison with them Turkish has been much changed in the course of phonetic development.

4. *Caucasian*

In the Caucasus Mountains are spoken, in addition to Turkish dialects and Indo-European languages like Armenian and Ossetic, about thirty different languages, which for the most part differ strikingly from one another. This multiplicity seems to be of ancient date; at any rate, the Greek geographer Strabo, who lived from 63 B.C. to A.D. 19, records it. Yet the Caucasian languages now existing may safely be included in two branches, North and South Caucasian.

The greatest complexity is found in North Caucasian; yet it is not so great that the relationships of these languages can escape close observation; and, in spite of the lack of thorough investigation, it is possible to get a glimmering of some sound-laws. The North Caucasian languages can be classified in two divisions, a western and an eastern. The western division consists of Abkhasian and Circassian. Large bands of these two peoples emigrated during the years 1864–66, when the Russians had subdued the country, and sought a new home in Turkish territory, especially in Asia Minor. A third small tribe of the same western division, the Ubykhians, emigrated *en masse*. The eastern division, which apparently preserves a considerably older stage than the western, consists of Chechentzian and several languages which are included under the name *Lesghian*. All of these languages are without literature. They are spoken by wild mountain tribes numbering on an average a few thousands of persons, the maximum number of any tribe being about two hundred thousand.

Thus linguistic investigation had to begin here on virgin soil. Texts, grammars and vocabularies for these various tongues, with their difficult phonological and morphological systems, had to be made accessible. By far the most important work in this field is that of the indefatigable A. Schiefner: from 1856 to 1873 he published detailed descriptions of eight different Caucasian languages. Later, the former lieutenant-general in the Russian army, R. von Erckert, printed a book with the title *Die Sprachen des kaukasischen Stammes* (Vienna, 1895). It is merely a catalogue-like survey of North and South Caucasian, with scanty information about each language, and with many serious errors. But the book is valuable because it includes many more languages than Schiefner described. Recently, rich material has come to light in other ways. Some has been published by workers in the interests of scholarship, and some has been made accessible primarily for the instruction of the natives. Much valuable material is to be found especially in the series published by L. Lopatinsky, in Tiflis: *A Collection of Materials for the Description of Places and Peoples in Caucasia* (in Russian). The Ubykhian emigrants, too, have been visited by students of linguistics in their home in Asia Minor, and their language will not pass undescribed into oblivion. Even outside Russia the languages of the Caucasus are being studied. From 1924 on, Adolf Dirr has been editing in Leipzig *Caucasia, Zeitschrift für die Erforschung der Sprachen und Kulturen der Völker des Kaukasus*; and in 1928 the same scholar published a comprehensive work on the Caucasian languages (North and South Caucasian): *Einführung in das Studium der kaukasischen Sprachen.* Thorough comparative investigation has not yet begun, however.

In contrast with the complexity of North Caucasian, South Caucasian consists, strictly speaking, of but one language, Georgian, with its dialects. This one South Caucasian people is more numerous than all the North Caucasians together: at the close of the nineteenth century the northern tribes totalled 1,000,000, the southern 1,350,000. The Georgians have an ancient literature. According to legend, one man, Mesrop, invented both the Armenian and the Georgian alphabets, in the fifth century after Christ.

South Caucasian is very different from North Caucasian. It is even doubtful if the two can be regarded as belonging to the same family. But at least it seems certain that the relationship between the two is as close as that between Samoyed and Finnish, or between

Mongolian and Turkish. The confirmation or refutation of the supposed relationship will be one of the chief tasks of Caucasian linguistic science in the future. In the distance beckons the hope that the study of Caucasian may cast some light on the Babel of tongues spoken in ancient times in Asia Minor and its vicinity, a linguistic world of which we have at present only very incomplete knowledge through ancient inscriptions. We might even discover something about the language of the Etruscans, who emigrated from Asia Minor to Italy. But all this is still no more than a hope, in spite of the sanguine statements of investigators who are unschooled in the methods of comparative linguistics.

5. Semitic and Hamitic

The Semitic family includes the following branches and languages:

A. East Semitic (Assyrian and Babylonian).[1]

B. West Semitic.
   1) Aramaic (between Assyria and Canaan).
   2) The languages of Canaan (Phœnician, Hebrew, Moabitic).

C. South Semitic.
   1) Arabic.
   2) Ethiopian (in Abyssinia).

The home of the race is undoubtedly to be sought in Asia, but many Semitic tribes have spread beyond Asia's borders. In very ancient times the Phœnicians had colonies along the coasts of the Mediterranean. Evidence of this activity is furnished partly by place-names (e.g. *Salamis*, name, of a town in Cyprus and of an island near Athens), and partly by inscriptions — some from Cyprus, but many more from Northern Africa, Carthage and its vicinity, where the language ("Punic") maintained itself much longer than in its native land, perhaps even as late as the fifth century after Christ. The Semites in Abyssinia certainly immigrated from southern Arabia, supposedly long before the birth of Christ. They adopted Christianity and have retained both it and their Ethiopian language to the present day. Finally Mohammedanism, which made the Arabians a conquering race, brought about the dissemination of the Arabic language throughout all northern Africa; and Mohammedan rule on

---

[1] *Accadian* has been used as the name in common for these two languages; but it was thought best to dispense with this name in the present work, and to adhere to the older though not unobjectionable use of Assyrian, both as a special and as a common name.

the other side of the Mediterranean is still evidenced by the Arabic dialect of the island of Malta. This dialect, however, is now completely separated from the rest of the Arabic world. The population is Christian, and the language is written in Latin characters.

Within Asia three Semitic languages in turn predominated: first Assyrian, then Aramaic, and finally Arabic. The Assyrians, who took over the culture and system of writing (cuneiform) of a foreign people, the Sumerians, were the first Semites to raise their language to world rank. In the fifteenth century before Christ Assyrian was still used as an international language in diplomatic intercourse throughout the Near East and between the Near East and Egypt. But from the eighth century before Christ, the Aramaic peoples began to crowd into Mesopotamia, and their language gradually superseded Assyrian. The change was complete about the time of Alexander the Great, although Assyrian was still written up to the first century before Christ. Aramaic also engulfed the languages of Canaan, and extended its influence to Arabia. In this way both Phœnician and Hebrew passed out of use. Some of the latest parts of the Old Testament were written in Aramaic, and Aramaic must have been the mother-tongue of Christ.

But Hebrew remained the sacred language of the Jews, even after they became scattered in foreign lands, where they spoke the language of their environment or sometimes of a previous environment (like the Jews in Russia, who speak Yiddish, a dialect of German). Since continuity with the past was never completely broken, Zionists have felt able to work for a revival of Hebrew, so that it may become the common language of the Jews in their mother country, Palestine. The future will show whether this extraordinary experiment can really succeed.

For some centuries Aramaic was the dominating language in the Near East. It had already become one of the chief languages in the old Persian empire, and its various dialects were still of considerable importance after the advent of Christianity. The Christian Syrians, whose center of culture was the city of Edessa, now Urfah, sent missionaries into many districts in the interior of Asia. Evidence of this missionary activity is found not only in the most recent excavations in Chinese Turkestan, but also in the remarkable Nestorian Stone, which was discovered in the year 1625 in Si-ngan-fu, China. It was set up in 781, and tells, in Chinese and Syrian inscriptions, of the vicissitudes of the Nestorian community in this region. But the mighty wave of Arabic which swept over the country of the Aramaic people with Mohammedanism, gradually submerged all the Aramaic dialects. There remained some remnants of Syrian in the country near Lake Urumia and in three remote villages in Antilibanus, near Damascus. These remains of Aramaic, the Ethiopian dialects, and Arabic are the only Semitic languages now living.

The Assyrians left behind them the oldest linguistic monuments of the Semitic peoples; their cuneiform inscriptions begin as early as 2500 B.C. The other Semitic peoples used different varieties and developments of one and the same alphabet, called by the Greeks the Phœnician. The oldest monuments in this alphabet come from the Phœnicians, about the tenth century before Christ, and from the Moabites, about 900 B.C. (cf. below, p. 177). The oldest Aramaic and Arabic inscriptions are two centuries later. The oldest Ethiopian inscription dates from the fourth century after Christ, and the oldest Ethiopian literature is a Biblical translation of about A.D. 500. But the primitiveness of the languages does not correspond to the period at which they first appear in history. Ancient Assyrian is much decayed phonologically; neither can the venerable language of the Bible, Hebrew, claim a high degree of primitiveness. Arabic plays the part of Sanskrit in this family of languages. The Semitic languages are very similar to one another — a fact which contributed not a little to the ease with which one language superseded another.

The nineteenth century inherited a good deal of knowledge of the Semitic languages from the preceding periods. The relationship among Aramaic, Hebrew, Arabic, and Ethiopian was clearly recognized; and Ludolf, as well as, later, Gyármathi [1] and students of comparative Indo-European linguistics, discerned the preponderant rôle of morphology in such investigation. The designation *Semitic* had been proposed first by Leibniz at the beginning of the eighteenth century, and by another scholar toward its close. Against this name, however, many objections can be made. [2] It is taken from the tenth chapter of Genesis, in which the author attempts to draw up a genealogical table for all the races of the earth, and to trace them back to Noah's three sons, Shem, Ham, and Japhet. It is odd that this name, used by the old Biblical writer as a link in a comprehensive classification which we cannot accept, should have been adopted

---

[1] See above, pp. 11, 106.

[2] It was no accident that Rask avoided it in his prize essay and adhered to the name *Oriental* which Ludolf used.

in usage as the name of a very restricted group of nations, whose individual languages are in much the same close mutual relationship as the Germanic dialects. But the name *Semitic* nations is in agreement with the old genealogical table, inasmuch as this table actually designates the Assyrian, Aramaic, Hebrew, and Arabian peoples as the descendants of Shem. The name has stuck; not only has it taken root in scientific language, but it has been used and particularly mis-

THEODOR NÖLDEKE
[After Bezold, *Orientalische Studien*]

used so much in daily speech that it has become hammered into the consciousness of everyone. Now it cannot be changed.

The nineteenth century broadened considerably the material of Semitic linguistics. The Assyrian-Babylonian language was rescued from oblivion and its monuments were interpreted. Nearly all of our ancient inscriptions in Western and Southern Semitic were discovered and interpreted during the nineteenth century. In addition to this, our knowledge of the living Semitic languages and dialects was much widened. Thus, almost all we know of the existing remains of the Aramaic (Syriac) language was learned during this period. Neither has there been any lack of summaries. The external history of the languages was sketched by E. Renan and T. Nöldeke; a comparative treatment of their grammar was first attempted by William Wright (Cambridge, 1890); the standard work is by C. Brockelmann (Berlin, 1908–13). But a great deal remains to be done; comparative Semitic linguistics is, as Brockelmann very properly says, not at its close but at its beginning.

Under the name *Hamitic* are included several languages which together have occupied the whole eastern and northern coasts of Africa from the equator in the east to the Senegal river in the west. They still have their homes there, but do not dominate the whole territory. As early as prehistoric times they had to give way in Abyssinia before the oncoming Semitic language, Ethiopian. But the advance of the Mohammedan Arabians proved much more portentous. The Hamitic family can be divided into three subdivisions:

1. South Hamitic, often termed Cushitic.
2. Egyptian.
3. The Berber languages.

The South Hamitic group comprises half a dozen languages south of Egypt. Two of them are best known as the Somali (in the entire eastern horn of Africa) and the Galla (a people of some millions, west of Somaliland).

The great cultural language of the Hamitic family is Egyptian, the oldest monuments of which go back to the fourth millennium before Christ, and which can be followed by means of texts written in hieroglyphics or in a development of hieroglyphics, until the beginning of the Christian era. Meanwhile ancient Egyptian civilization had outlived its day, and was overcome by the Greek culture which Alexander's conquest brought in. But Christianity created a new national life. The Greek alphabet was .adjusted to the Egyptian language, and from the close of the third century of our era a new Christian literature sprang up. In this period we usually call the language *Coptic*, the Arabic form of the name *Egyptian*. Coptic was replaced by Arabic as a spoken language during the sixteenth century, but it remained in use as a religious language.

The Berber branch, with about thirty different languages or dialects which are spoken by some seven millions of people altogether, has its home in Northern Africa west of Egypt. It is not entirely without ancient monuments. Over almost the entire northern coast brief inscriptions, the so-called Libyan inscriptions, are found, dating

from the time of the Romans. Some of them are written in Libyan
and Latin, or Libyan and Punic; a single one is in Libyan and Greek.
One of the oldest, and certainly the most curious of them all, is a
Libyan and Punic inscription from Dougga in Tunis, containing the
name of the famous king Massinissa. These inscriptions are written
in a special alphabet derived from the Semitic, and apparently identical with the alphabet used to this day by a tribe of Berbers, the
Tuaregs, in the Sahara. The inscriptions have been known since
1631,[1] but it was not until 1843 that they were made the subject of

TUAREG WRITING

꞉꞉Φ	·ⵥ+꞉+	IOⵄIΦ
whb	*(a)ytwt*	*nrznb*
(*abehaw* gray)	(*tawtiya* poor iron)	(*ibanzaren* gray)
	(Read from right to left.)	

a thorough study by the French scholar de Saulcy, who ascertained
the meaning of most of the Libyan characters. In spite of subsequent
work by other scholars, notably by J. Halévy, it must be said that the
study of these inscriptions is yet in its infancy. They are so short
that it is difficult to grasp their meaning.

Of the correctness of the grouping covered by the name Hamitic
there can be no doubt whatsoever; and it is equally undoubted that
the Hamitic languages are related to the Semitic. A very clear illustration of the kinship is provided by the prefixes which indicate the
different persons of certain forms of the verb:

Arabic		*Somali*	
'a-	I..	*ahai*	I am
ta-	thou..	*tahai*	thou art
ya-	he..	*yahai*	he is
ta-	she..	*tahai*	she is
na-	we..	*nahai*	we are
ta-	you..	*tahin*	you are
ya-	they..	*yahin*	they are

The prefixes in Berber have very similar forms. But the prefixes are
not always of assistance. Some of the languages have dropped them;
they are not found in Galla, for example, which otherwise is very

[1] The alphabet of the Tuaregs, however, only since 1822.

close to Somali; and they are not found in Egyptian. On the other hand, the numerals can be used to show the distance both between Semitic and Hamitic and between the various Hamitic languages. All of the Semitic languages from Assyria to Abyssinia agree throughout in the numerals from 3 to 10; but Egyptian agrees with Semitic only in 6, 7, and 8: no similarity can be perceived in 3, 4, 5, 9, and 10. And in the whole series from 2 to 10 the Berber languages show a clear resemblance to Egyptian only in 2 and 6, while the South Hamitic numerals are totally different from the Egyptian, and do not even agree with one another.[1] This indicates how distantly the various Hamitic languages are related, and how difficult their comparative treatment is. It is natural, then, that this treatment should not yet be complete, and so there is still some question how far the boundaries of Hamitic extend. One of the disputed languages is Nubian. As a rule it is placed outside the Hamitic group, but in 1911 Leo Reinisch, the distinguished specialist in South Hamitic languages, confidently asserted that it is Hamitic.

Nubian is interesting because of its ancient literary monuments. At the beginning of the twentieth century, Nubian texts a thousand years old on Christian subjects were found. There are also Nubian inscriptions dating from imperial Rome, in an alphabet based on Egyptian characters. But we still do not understand much of them. The Nubians are not negroes; but to the negro race belong the Haussa, whose language is also disputed. Haussa, spoken between the river Niger and Lake Tchad, is the most widely disseminated of all the negro languages of Africa, and is used as a commercial language in many parts of Central Africa. It was described by the Egyptologist Lepsius as Hamitic, and it cannot be denied that there is evidence pointing in that direction. But the relations of both Nubian and Haussa must be left an open question pending further inquiry.

Under these conditions it is impossible to prophesy how the Semitic-Hamitic problem will develop in the future: whether Semitic and Hamitic will continue to be regarded as two distinct families side by side, or whether all will be thrown together under one family and subdivided, not into two, but into several parallel branches: (1) Semitic, (2) Egyptian, (3) Berber, etc. What we can best discuss at present is the relationship between Semitic and Egyptian. The

[1] There are some fundamentally different systems of numerals within the South Hamitic group.

resemblances are very great in grammatical structure, but are far less in vocabulary. Yet new cognates are being discovered continually, and certain sound-laws are beginning to show up clearly. In comparison with Semitic, Egyptian gives the impression of having decayed considerably.

Unlike Semitic linguistics, modern Hamitic linguistics did not have much preparatory work from previous centuries upon which to build.

RENÉ BASSET

The eighteenth century's horizon included, besides Coptic, only an incomplete acquaintance with the living Hamitic languages. The nineteenth century can boast of having widened this knowledge greatly. Among the scholars who have worked in the South Hamitic field we find specialists in Semitic like H. Almkvist, J. Halévy and F. Prätorius, but Leo Reinisch deserves the greatest distinction. For the Berber languages, Hanoteau and René Basset may be named. In his Nubian grammar, published in 1880, R. Lepsius gave a general introduction to the languages of Africa, including a survey of the Hamitic group, in which he included Haussa but not Nubian. One of the greatest accomplishments of the nineteenth century in this field was the interpretation of the Egyptian hieroglyphics, of which an account will be given in another chapter. The problem of the relationship between Semitic and Egyptian was the subject of a thorough investigation by the German scholar Theodor Benfey in 1844. He relied upon Coptic. Recently Adolf Erman, especially, has contributed trustworthy evidence. Several etymological comparisons have been made by Harri Holma and A. Ember. An elaborate work on the subject was nearly ready for the press when in 1926 a fire destroyed Ember's home in Baltimore. Ember himself lost his life, and the manuscript was burned.

6. *Basque*

Basque is now spoken by only half a million people on the innermost corner of the Bay of Biscay on both sides of the Pyrenees, partly in French, partly in Spanish territory. The oldest linguistic material dates from the fifteenth and sixteenth centuries.

The Basques are the descendants of a people who were much more widely spread at an earlier period, the Iberians in Spain and the Aquitanians north of the Pyrenees. This fact was determined as early as 1821 by W. von Humboldt on the evidence of place-names. Thus *Iliberri* is known from antiquity as the name of a town in southern Spain (now *Elvira*, near Granada) and of a town near the Golfe du Lion, in the Mediterranean, just north of the Pyrenees (now *Elne*). Both the towns are far outside the present territory of the Basques, but the derivation from Basque *iri* "city," *berri* "new" is just as certain as the derivation of English place-names like Newstead or Newton. The connection between Iberian and Basque can be shown in still another way. The Iberians left inscriptions and coins in a special alphabet; and though this material [1] is so scanty that even determining the meaning of the characters has cost much trouble, and though we still understand but little of the inscriptions, Hugo Schuchardt [2] established several of the Iberian inflectional endings, particularly from the evidence of coins. And they agree so well with Basque that they serve as grammatical proof of the kinship of the two languages.

In its present form Basque is very peculiar, especially in the involved verbal system. What we express in English by the three forms *have*, *has*, and *had* requires one hundred and fifty different

---

[1] Collected by Hübner, *Monumenta linguae Ibericae* (Berlin, 1893).

[2] *Die iberische Deklination* (1907).

forms of the verb in Basque; the forms vary not only as in English
with present and past time, and not only as in Latin and the other
ancient Indo-European languages with the different subjects (*we*

HUGO SCHUCHARDT

have, you have, etc.), but also according to the various direct and
indirect objects. "I have given the woman the apple" reads

eman	*diot*	*emaztekiari*	*sagarra*
given	I have	to the woman	the apple

But in the sentence "I have given you (plural) the apples," *I have*
reads

dauzkitzuet

Some of the forms for *he has*, in sentences like "He has seen it, me,
us, you (plural)," respectively, are

du, nau, gaitu, zaituzte.

The Basque dialects vary sharply. The material for our knowledge
of them has been rendered accessible especially by Prince L.-L.
Bonaparte. Comparative treatment was begun by the Dutchman
van Eys in a *Grammaire comparée des dialectes basques* (Paris, 1879),
and continued later by his countryman C. C. Uhlenbeck in *Beiträge*

zu einer vergleichenden Lautlehre der Baskischen Dialekte (Amsterdam, 1903).

The next enterprise of research must be to discover whether a relationship can be postulated between Basque and any other language known to us. In this matter scholars have held two differing opinions. Some, as for instance Trombetti, have conjectured a relationship between Basque and Caucasian. But it is a long way

C. C. UHLENBECK

from the Caucasus to the Pyrenees, and we have absolutely no proof that there ever existed a linguistically homogeneous population between these two points. Even if the Etruscans in classical Italy were an offshoot of the Caucasian family, they prove nothing, because they had immigrated from Asia at a relatively late period, about 1000 B.C. Very convincing proofs have not yet been furnished, although it cannot be denied that there is a striking similarity between one of the inflectional endings of nouns in Basque and in South Caucasian. Others have supposed that Basque might be related to the Hamitic languages. This would be much easier to understand from a geographical point of view. One can conceive that the Iberians at some distant prehistoric time followed the same path the Arabs followed in the Middle Ages when they reached Spain. But from the linguistic side this supposition also hangs by a very slender thread. Earlier attempts to prove the relationship failed, and Hugo Schuchardt's material in the *Revue internationale des études basques* (1912, 1913) is merely a collection which does not carry conviction, though it does contain points well calculated to awaken attention. Thus it cannot be denied that there is a similarity in the numerals 6 and 7:

Coptic *sou* six	*sašəf* seven
Basque *sei*	*zazpi*

It is a little awkward that the resemblance is greater to Coptic than it is to Old Egyptian, comparison with which shows that the two last consonants in Coptic *sašəf* originally occurred in reverse order; so that if the relation is to be maintained, we must also accept an inversion of the consonants in the Basque *-zp-*.

THE NON–INDO–EUROPEAN FAMILIES SURROUNDING INDIA

One of the great works of recent linguistics is the *Linguistic Survey of India* directed by Dr. G. A. Grierson, a survey of the several Indo-European and foreign languages in the Indian Empire. The plan of the work was set forth by Grierson at the Orientalist Congress in Vienna in 1886; the Congress recommended the matter to the Indian government, and work began in 1894. Almost all the government officials participated. Printed questionnaires were sent to the most remote parts, and in 1898 Grierson was able to commence determining the number of languages, dialects and sub-dialects, and the boundaries between them. In 1903 detailed treatments of them began to appear. The gigantic work was finished in 1927. Of its nineteen heavy folio volumes, five, mostly written by the Norwegian scholar Sten Konow, treat of the non-Indo-European families of languages. Three distinct foreign families are represented in or near British India: the Dravidian, the Austro-Asiatic, and the Indo-Chinese.

7. Dravidian

The Dravidian family includes a group of nations, numbering a population of more than sixty millions, in India south of the twentieth degree of latitude, and in Ceylon. The race is not without culture; within its territory are no less than three civilized languages with literatures which go back to the tenth, and even to the fifth, century after Christ. The principal language is Tamil. Outside India the Brahui language in Baluchistan seems to be related to the Dravidian family. Some scholars have fancied that the family once

STEN KONOW
[After *Norges universitet,* 1911]

reached even farther to the north and west, and that the language contained in the cuneiform inscriptions of Elam, north of the Persian Gulf, might belong here. Others prefer to assume relationship between Elamitic and Caucasian; but nothing whatever is proved.

The whole family is treated by R. Caldwell in *A Comparative Grammar of the Dravidian or South Indian Family of Languages* (London, 1856).

8. *Austro-Asiatic and Austronesian*

In the eastern part of India, north of the Dravidian districts, we find a family of languages, spoken by not more than three million people, which is quite different from the Dravidian. Various names have been employed to designate it: the term *Munda* now in vogue is a misnomer; that formerly used, *Kherwarian,* is a little better. The best-known language of this family is Santhali. An investigation by E. Kuhn in 1889 has shown that the Kherwarian languages must be related to what one may briefly call the border languages of Farther India, Mon in Pegu, Khmer in Cambodia, etc., some dialects in the peninsula of Malacca, and also some scattered linguistic districts in the interior along the rivers and in Assam, and finally the language of the Nicobars. All these languages together make up a family which scholars have recently designated as the Austro-Asiatic

ERNST KUHN
[After *Festskriftet for Ernst Kuhn*, 1916]

("Southern Asiatic"). The various branches of this family — Kherwarian and the Farther Indian branches — are, however, only very remotely interrelated.

Parallel with the name Austro-Asiatic the term *Austronesian* has been used recently of that family which was earlier called Malay-Polynesian. In spite of its enormous dissemination from Formosa and Hawaii to New Zealand, from Madagascar to Easter Island, this family everywhere betrays very clearly its original unity. It may be divided into various branches: Indonesian, Melanesian, Polynesian. The Indonesian branch includes, in addition to the Indian islands, Madagascar and the Malay language in parts of Malacca. Some of the languages in the Indonesian branch have their own script, which is usually derived from the Indian; among the Malays of Malacca, however, the Arabic script is the basis. Malay, which has spread throughout almost all Indonesia as a commercial language, boasts a literature some centuries old; the literature of Java is even older, dating from about A.D. 900.

Wilhelm von Humboldt treated the ancient language of Java in his famous work *Über die Kawi-Sprache auf der Insel Java* (Berlin,

WILHELM VON HUMBOLDT
[After *W. V. H., Eine Biographie,* Cassel, 1853]

1836–39), in which the kinship between Indonesian and Polynesian is clearly proved. The relationship of the Melanesian languages to Indonesian and Polynesian was determined by H. C. von der Gabelentz in 1861–73. Many Dutch scholars have inscribed their names in the history of Austronesian (and especially Indonesian) studies, the most illustrious being Johan Hendrik Caspar Kern, likewise renowned as a Sanskritist. It may be mentioned also that the chief language of the Philippines was first phonetically described and scientifically analyzed by the American, Leonard Bloomfield.

Lately a very distant relationship has been accepted, largely on the work by W. Schmidt, between Austro-Asiatic and Austronesian, and both groups have been combined under the name *Austric*.[1] The designation may be usable, but one must remember that Australia, which bears the name by an older claim, does not belong to the Austric double family. *Austric* thus becomes almost an opposite to *Australian*, which includes the languages of Australia, Tasmania, the greater part of New Guinea, and the dialects of the Andaman Islands.

9. *Indo-Chinese*

The Indo-Chinese family includes Thibet and Burmah, Siam and China. A number of dialects in the mountains of the northern boundary of India belong to it. Farther India is divided between Indo-Chinese and Austric in such a way that the Austric languages are largely confined to the border regions. It may be remarked that the Austric languages in Farther India resemble the Indo-Chinese languages to some extent in their structure; like these, they are monosyllabic, and it was not until the nineteenth century that the correct distinction between these two groups was made; even today the kinship of the Annamite language is a point of controversy, although the best authorities include it in the Austric, not in the Indo-Chinese family.

Of the four principal languages of the Indo-Chinese family, three (Siamese, with Thibetan and Burmese) are written in alphabets developed from the Indian. Thibet possesses a Buddhistic literature from the seventh century of our era. The spelling is historical, and has maintained itself unchanged during alterations in pronunciation, so that now many of the characters are mute; thus in *brgyad*, "eight," both *b* and *r* are silent. The literature of China begins about 2000 B.C., and is written in the most markedly ideographic script we know, a script which completely conceals the profound dialectal differences within the huge territory where Chinese is spoken. Naturally, this system conceals also the changes in pronunciation during the centuries, and it is therefore an extremely difficult task to determine anything about the pronunciation of the language in past times; yet rhyme, the transcription of foreign words and names, old loan-words in Chinese and other factors, combined with the testimony of living dialects and the related languages, all give us some hints of an older

---

[1] As a matter of fact the three newly-invented names *Austro-Asiatic*, *Austronesian*, and *Austric* are for obvious reasons not very convenient in English. For the same reasons they are not convenient in Italian, as Trombetti has remarked. But they are not impossible, and they have the great advantage of brevity.

pronunciation of the characters than that now prevailing. But in spite of these glimpses of the history of sounds, it is not ancient Chinese, but the far younger language of Thibet which teaches us most about the oldest linguistic forms of this family. A good example is the numeral *eight*:

Thibetan *brgyad*
Chinese *pat* or *pă*

The Thibetan form cannot be explained from the Chinese, not even from the older form, where -*t* has not yet become mute; but from the old Thibetan form as preserved in the orthography, both the Chinese and all the varying forms in the different Indo-Chinese languages and dialects can be explained, although the word begins in the Indo-Chinese dialects with very different sounds: *bhr-*, *pr-*, *rhy*, *ry*, *r*, *y*, *č*, *ts*, *š*, etc.; all these forms point to the *brgy-* of the Thibetan.

Chinese is thus not a primitive language, but one which has passed through a long process of development. It is an excellent example of how far phonological decay can go without making a language incomprehensible. Not only does Chinese consist of mere uninflected monosyllabic words, not only do words and syllables thus become one and the same, but in addition the syllables in Chinese are very simply constructed. Our rendering of Chinese proper names will provide some idea of what types of syllable occur: *Pe-king* (North City), *Nan-king* (South City), Hoang-ho, Yang-tse-kiang. There is no real consonant group at the beginning of the syllables (*ts-* as in *Yang-tse-kiang* being felt as one "affricate," not as two consonants), and the possibilities for the ending of the syllables are even more limited; scarcely more than vowels, including diphthongs, and nasals, need be considered; the *k*, *t*, or *p* in which some words originally ended has become mute in the principal dialect; *eight* is no longer pronounced *pat*, but *pă*. With such a limited range of sounds, it is obvious that there cannot be any very great variety in the forms of the words. The musical accent adds some variety. Five — in the Cantonese dialect eight — different pitches are distinguished which are as invariable in the make-up of a word as vowels or consonants: *mai* pronounced in one pitch means "buy," in another "sell." But even the variation produced by pitch is insufficient. Chinese is rich in words pronounced alike but having different meanings (cf. English *meat*, *meet*, *mete*). Such words must be differentiated by means of the context; but this possibility is not unlimited; therefore it may be that, so far as phonetic decay is concerned, Chinese has reached the uttermost limit; development in this direction certainly cannot continue much farther without calling forth a reaction which will again give the words more scope. One may perhaps guess at the method by which this can be done by observing the great part that compounds play in modern Chinese: *girl-child* = *girl*; often two synonyms are compounded, like our *part and parcel*, but without the use of *and*.

Among the scholars who have applied themselves to the history of Chinese may be named August Conrady, who showed in 1896 that the difference in pitch sometimes occurs in connection with the dropping of a syllable; also, very recently, the Swedish scholar Bernhard Karlgren.

The question of some ultimate relationship between Indo-Chinese and Yenisei has been discussed above, p. 108.

THE MORE DISTANT NON–INDO–EUROPEAN LANGUAGE FAMILIES

We have now concluded the survey of all the foreign linguistic families which were neighbors of our own family in ancient times. There remains the treatment of the more distant families: the languages in farthest Asia (in so far as they have not been included in some greater family extending toward the west), the languages in America, in South and Central Africa, and in Australia. If we begin our journey in Asia, we shall meet some civilized languages at first; but our subsequent wanderings will bring us only to barbarous tongues. The investigation of these languages still leaves much to be desired.

10. *Japanese and Korean*

Japanese, with its ancient literature beginning in the eighth century after Christ, is clearly related to the dialects of the Lu-chu (Riu-Kiu) Islands, which extend south of Japan to Formosa. There seems to be a more distant relationship between Japanese and another ancient language, Korean, whose literature goes back to the fourth century after Christ. The theory of such a relationship is advocated, not without ability, by a Japanese scholar, S. Kanazawa, in a little volume *The Common Origin of the Japanese and Korean Languages* (Tokio, 1910). These languages have nothing to do with Chinese; but it is well known that both Japan and Korea have been dominated by Chinese influence. This influence is so great that both the Japanese and the Koreans have taken over intact the Chinese system of numerals, without, however, entirely giving up their own. Thus, in both Japanese and Korean there is a double series of numerals. *Eight* in Japanese-Chinese is *hači*, with a Japanese change of *p* to *h* and a Japanese ending, while in Korean-Chinese it is *phal*, with a Korean change of *t* to *l*.

JOHN BATCHELOR AND AN AINU PRINCE
[After Batchelor, *The Ainu and Their Folklore*]

Both Japan and Korea have freed themselves partially from the Chinese ideographic script, Japan by means of a syllabic system of fifty characters, Korea by means of an alphabet.

11. *Ainu and Gilyak*

In the southern part of Sakhalin, on Yezo and in the Kuriles, excepting the northernmost island, dwell the Ainus. Their anthropological characteristics have been often discussed, some authors exaggerating their hairiness, while others emphasize their similarity to the white race. Our knowledge of their language is due for the most part to the missionary John Batchelor, who lived among them

AN ESKIMO OF ANGMAGSALIK COUNTING SIX
[Photograph by William Thalbitzer, 1906]

for many years. In the northern part of Sakhalin and on the lower course of the Amur the Gilyaks have their home. Their language is very different from that of the Ainus; if there is any relationship at all, it must be very distant.

12. *The Kamchatka Languages*

These languages are spoken in Kamchatka, including the northern-most island of the Kuriles, and in the country north of Kamchatka all the way to the Arctic Sea. Three different languages are spoken which are very clearly related: Kamchadale, Koryak, and Chukchee.

13. *Yukaghir*

The Yukaghirs dwell along the Arctic Ocean between the Yakoot and Kamchatka peoples. Their language, which we know chiefly through the work of A. Schiefner, is giving way to Yakoot, and is now spoken by not more than one thousand persons.

14. *Aleut and Eskimo*

Rask had seen [1] that there is a relationship between the language of the Aleutian Islands, which connect Kamchatka with Alaska — Asia with America — and the Eskimo languages, which, spoken by a scanty population, extend along the entire northern coast of America past Baffin's Land and Labrador to Greenland, the eastern coast of which is the other extreme of their territory.

Eskimo is remarkable for its extremely involved structure, which in a way surpasses that of Basque (we find a similar complication in many of the American languages). Of extraordinary interest is the fact that the difference between the Eskimo language of Greenland and that of the other side of Davis Strait is not so great but that mutual understanding is perfectly possible after a little experience; and yet the two tribes have been separated for at least six hundred years, and possibly for a thousand or more. Even between the extreme points, Alaska and Greenland, the similarity in language is very clear; the difference is perhaps not greater than that between English and German.

15. *The American Languages*

The term *American Languages* should not be understood as a linguistic grouping; it is simply a geographical designation.

America shows striking linguistic contradictions: a linguistic unity which the Old World never had, and a differentiation to which it is

---

[1] Witness a manuscript written as early as 1818, printed a hundred years later in *Oversigt over det danske Videnskabernes Selskabs Forhandlinger* (1916), pp. 211–49. Cf. *International Journal of American Linguistics*, I, 40 ff.

difficult to find a parallel. The unity is due to the wide dissemination achieved by a few immigrating languages. While the traveller through Europe comes upon a score of civilized languages, a knowledge of English, Spanish and Portuguese suffices for the whole of the much larger American continent. But the ancient American languages, which this survey has in view, offer a more complicated picture.

It is still uncertain into what large groups the American world of languages should be divided — a world which includes such different stages of culture as that of the North American Indians, of the ancient civilized peoples in Mexico and Central America, who had developed a system of hieroglyphic writing, and of the almost totally uncultured Fuegians. Much has been accomplished in the study of these languages, especially by Americans, among them Franz Boas and Edward Sapir,[1] but even yet we have not got beyond a picture of dizzying complexity: more than one hundred and twenty different *families* of languages are computed. It is incredible that there should be no kinship at all among some of these; but a peculiar course of linguistic development may make it difficult to discover what the original relationships were. Yet in time scholars will no doubt be enabled to simplify the picture somewhat.

An important survey is the work edited by F. Boas, in collaboration with many others, *A Handbook of American Indian Languages* (Washington, 1911, 1922).

16. *The South and Central African Languages*

If we commence our journey in Africa from the south, we meet, at the outset, distinctly divided linguistic territories.

First we come to the Bushmen and the Hottentots. Hottentot we know quite well, but the Bushmen's language very incompletely; and we have practically no information on the speech of the pigmy races which are spread throughout the forests of Central Africa. It is generally assumed that there is some kinship between the language of the Bushmen and that of the Hottentots; but if it exists at all, the kinship is very distant. One peculiarity which they have in common is the remarkable "clicks," which resemble the inspiratory sound we make with the front of the tongue as an expression of regretful sympathy, or the smacking sound ("chirrup") used in driving horses, or the sound of a kiss. But these occur in Hottentot

[1] European scholars have also had a share: the Dutchman C. C. Uhlenbeck is an example.

and Bush language as regular, well-differentiated elements of speech. However, since similar sounds are found outside this territory, they do not allow us to infer relationship.

If we exclude Bushman and Hottentot, the greater part of Africa south of the Equator belongs to one family, the Bantu, which has attracted much attention because of its peculiar structure and clear relationship, and has repeatedly been the subject of comparative treatment — by W. H. I. Bleek (1862–69), J. Torrend (1891), and C. Meinhof (1899, 1910). One of its most discussed characteristics is the prefixes with which all nouns are supplied, according to the class to which they belong: names of persons, plants, round shiny things, animals, long things, inanimate things, diminutives, etc. We find, for instance, in Herero, spoken on the western coast, between the twenty-first and twenty-second degrees of latitude:

Singular		Plural
omu-ndu	human being	ova-ndu
e-yuva	sun	oma-yuva
o-ngombe	head of cattle	ozo-ngombe
otyi-na	thing	ovi-na
oru-veze	time	otu-veze
oka-natye	child	ou-natye

These prefixes occur in varying though easily recognizable forms in all the Bantu languages; thus, "human being" in Kaffir (on the East Coast) is aba-ntu, — whence the name Bantu, — while in some of the other languages it is oa-ntu, wa-ntu, ba-tu, etc. In the versions given by Europeans of the names of these languages, the prefixes cause a good deal of confusion, since they are sometimes included, sometimes excluded: one author speaks of the Ovaherero, another of the Herero, or the same author omits the prefix in the name of the Herero but retains it in the name Be-chuana. The names of the languages have the thing-prefix, which is also sometimes retained in the European version: Otyi-herero, Ki-suaheli, Se-chuana. But it is not sufficient that all the nouns should appear with one or another prefix, a sort of article which serves no other purpose than to indicate the class of the noun: every class of nouns requires also its special adaptation of adjectives, pronouns, etc., and its special prefix for subject and object with the verb; and the prefixes of adjectives, pronouns and verbs do not always recall clearly the form of the noun itself. The similarity is easily seen in the following Herero constructions:

ova-ndu v-andye	my people
ozo-ngombe z-andye	my heads (of cattle)
otyi-na ty-andye	my thing
oka-natye k-andye	my child

But the similarity has disappeared completely in:

e-yuva r-andye	my sun

The verbs are supplied with prefixes, as if one were to say, "The boy he-it-shot the hare" (for "the boy shot the hare"): the first prefix echoes the prefix of the subject noun, the second echoes the prefix of the noun which functions as object; but the similarity in sounds is even here not always evident. Although systems of congruence between nouns, adjectives, and verbs are well known in languages other than Bantu, and although there is scarcely a single element of the Bantu system of congruence for which an analogy cannot be found in entirely different groups, the system as a whole is nevertheless very characteristic of the Bantu languages.

North of the clear and well-defined Bantu group there extends from the Equator to the Sahara, and from the West Coast to the Nile, a broad belt which can be combined under the geographical name of Sudan languages. To find any order in the interrelationships in this extremely varied belt is a difficult task which has not yet been accomplished. On page 122 above I have pointed out that the boundaries between the Sudan languages proper and the Hamitic family cannot be drawn with certainty, and I have mentioned Nubian, along the Nile, and Haussa, between the Niger and Lake Tchad, as two of the languages in dispute. The remaining languages, after we have rendered unto the Hamites what is the Hamites', may be mutually related and may be more remotely related to the Bantu group; but these relationships cannot be more than hypothetical until we have further information. On the other hand, it is certain that the multiplicity of languages in the Sudan is very ancient. The scanty information afforded by Arabian geographers of the Middle Ages (from the eleventh to the fourteenth century) seems to point to a state of things very similar to that now prevailing and to prove that the pronunciation has not changed very much during the last five hundred years.

17. *The Australian Languages*

The linguistic world of Australia includes Australia and Tasmania, the greater part of New Guinea, and the dialects of the Andaman

Islands. It is surrounded on the east and north, and, in a manner of speaking, on the west (Madagascar) by the Austronesian group of languages, in such a way that the boundaries between races and languages do not fall together; the Andaman dialects lie wedged into Austro-Asiatic territory. But the Australian languages have the unenviable distinction of being almost the least thoroughly investigated in the world, so that we cannot pronounce with certainty on their relationships. That they constitute a genealogical unity may be regarded as credible.

VI

INSCRIPTIONS AND ARCHÆOLOGICAL DISCOVERIES.
THE STUDY OF THE HISTORY OF WRITING

A CONSPICUOUS feature in nineteenth-century investigation is
the discovery and interpretation of a great number of linguistic
monuments descending to us directly from past times; monuments
which did not pass from copyist to copyist through a long chain of
tradition: inscriptions on rocks, in buildings and ruins, but most of
all upon "portable" objects, found largely in the earth, ranging from
heavy stones to things as small and easily moved as seals or rings.
The material upon which they are written varies: stone, metal, clay
tablets, wood. The method of writing varies also: the characters
may be raised in relief, carved with a chisel, scratched with a knife,
impressed in the soft clay, and so on. In the same class with inscriptions may be considered, from the linguistic point of view, a series of
manuscripts (on papyrus, etc.), which were found under similar conditions, and, in much the same way, bring us direct messages from
times long past and often forgotten.

All that had been found of such monuments in previous centuries
is but little in comparison with what was discovered during the nineteenth century. And, indeed, most of the material which had been
found previously to the nineteenth century had to wait until then
for interpretation, if it was written in languages not known through
tradition.

For many reasons it is expedient to combine in one chapter the
accounts of these inscriptions and archæological discoveries. Here
another kind of work had to be undertaken and another kind of investigator was needed than in ordinary linguistic research. The division of labor has been quite different also. It is a conspicuous characteristic of ordinary linguistic research that the activity of the individual is limited to a single group of related languages, or that, if his
activity includes several groups, it is at least delimited by linguistic
relationships, because most of the information which throws light
upon a given language is to be found within the circle of relationship.
But in this field the divisions are quite different, at any rate in the
beginning. Egyptologists, Iranologists, Assyriologists laid the first

foundations for the study of the Oscan and Umbrian inscriptions of Italy, and of the Greek inscriptions from Cyprus; and the ancient Persian inscriptions served as keys for Assyrian and Elamitic, although there is no linguistic relationship. This is of course only the first step. In Oscan, Umbrian, and Cyprian the leadership quickly passed over to classical philologists; and it was only in the deciphering, not in later developments, that research in the Assyrian and Elamitic tongues got its light from Persian inscriptions. But this first step has great interest in an historical treatment of the subject.

One of the reasons why entirely different linguistic territories could be of assistance to one another in this way is that most of the difficulties to be overcome resided not in the language itself, but in the writing. Therefore the study of inscriptions and archæological discoveries has elicited important information on the history of writing and its development, as well as on linguistics in the narrowest sense. Nearly all of our material for the earlier history of writing is due to discoveries and decipherings made in the nineteenth century.

The systems of writing which have come to light in this way may be classified in four groups:

Pre-alphabetical systems.

  1) Word- and syllable-script.
  2) Syllable-script.

Alphabetical systems.

  1) The Semitic alphabet (a syllable-script, which to us may seem to be a consonant-script).
  2) The Greek alphabet (vowel- and consonant-script).

Of the relationship among the various pre-alphabetical systems we can speak with only partial security. It follows that we cannot make out how many independent beginnings of a script should be assumed. The oldest systems — the most important are the Egyptian hieroglyphics, the Assyrian cuneiform inscriptions, and the Chinese script still in use — are geographically not so remote from one another as to preclude some historical relation. But ancient systems of writing occur elsewhere also, as in America; [1] and thus, taking everything into consideration, we must proceed on the assumption that the invention was made in several places and by different races independently; otherwise we should have to indulge in fantastic hypotheses.

[1] See above, p. 138.

It is almost certain that writing developed from the narrative drawings which savage races such as the North American Indians have in abundance. Naturally these drawings are much less completely carried out than the narrative drawings for children in our comic strips, and custom plays such a great part in them that many must be called symbols rather than pictures; for example, seven horizontal lines on a North American Indian's gravestone mean the seven campaigns of the dead chief, and three perpendicular lines indicate the three wounds he received in battle. But no matter how much of this type of simplification occurs, the drawings remain drawings, and they can be read with a varying choice of words: they become genuine writing only when they are brought into connection with the sounds of the languages. This connection undoubtedly occurred by means of the rebus method. The step from narrative drawings to writing took place, then, by the same sort of process which we apply when we allow a picture of the sun to stand for the first syllable in the word *sundry,* or let the picture of an eye stand for the pronoun *I*. But even after men had hit upon the use of pictures in this way for characters representing sounds, they went on using them as actual pictures for a long time. Hence all the most ancient systems of writing are mixtures of word symbols (or ideographic symbols) and syllable symbols.

One should not allow oneself to be confused by the Chinese script. There cannot be any contrast between word- and syllable-characters in Chinese, since all Chinese words are monosyllabic. So far the script is purely a word-character. But this script did not come into existence without the use of the rebus method. It is this method that the Chinese apply in their rendering of foreign names (place-names and personal names); here they use their characters as mere syllabic characters. But also in the characters for the ordinary Chinese vocabulary one can easily trace the rebus method. Thus, when the characters for *hung* [2] "a big-bellied person," *k'ung* [1] "impatient," *k'ang* [2] "carry on the shoulders," *kang* [4] "sedan chair," *kiang* [1] "river," *hung* [2] "red," *hung* [4] "quarrel," *hung* [3] "quicksilver" * contain one and the same common element compounded in various ways (most Chinese characters are compounded of two elements), and when this common element is identical with the character for *kung* [1] "work," it is quite clear that these coincidences do not indicate any common relationship in meaning, but solely a certain similarity in the sound. Such an element is usually called a *phonetic element.* On the other hand, the other element in all these characters is clearly enough an ideational element; this other element (the

---

* The numbers added to the Chinese words indicate the pitch in which the word is pronounced.

"key") is a hint as to the method by which the rebus is to be solved (compare the illustrations); thus in the fifth character the phonetic element in combination with the key says "Think of something that sounds somewhat like *kung*¹ and has something to do with water!" and the solution of the rebus is *kiang*¹ "river": but if the elements are arranged otherwise, as for example in the eighth character, the solution is *hung*³ "quicksilver"; the

EXAMPLES OF THE COMPOSITION OF CHINESE CHARACTERS

工 *kung*¹ 'work'

Keys:

1. 仜 *hung*² 'big belly'

1. 人 'human being'

2. 忪 *k'ung*¹ 'impatience'

2. 心 'heart'

3. 扛 *k'ang*² 'carry on the shoulders'

3. 手 'hand'

4. 杠 *kang*⁴ 'sedan chair'

4. 木 'wood'

5. 江 *kiang*¹ 'river'

5. 水 'water'

6. 紅 *hung*² 'red'

6. 糸 'silk'

7. 訌 *hung*⁴ 'quarrel'

7. 言 'word'

8. 汞 *hung*³ 'quicksilver'

8. 水 'water'

sixth character says "Think of something that sounds about like *kung* [1] and can be said of silk!" Answer: *hung* [2] "red." Other Chinese characters are compounded according to other principles, but that is another story.

It must also be noted that Chinese writing is not a writing based on ideas, but one based upon words; the characters are not signs for abstract conceptions, but for the Chinese words themselves, as they sounded in past times or sound now in the various Chinese dialects. These characters can indeed be transferred to other languages, and they have been so transferred in Japan, Korea, Annam; but transference cannot be effected without adapting them.

Even though the Chinese script is not an exception to the above statement that the oldest systems of writing are a mixture of word-characters (ideographic characters) and syllable-characters, it is not well calculated to give us any clear conceptions of the origin of writing. For it is not a primitive script, but one which has passed through a long process of development, though this development has taken place in the opposite direction, so to speak, from that in which writing developed among other peoples. Any genuine conception of primitive writing can be gained only through the systems with which the discoveries of the nineteenth century have made us familiar — Assyrian and Egyptian.

The normal development of the combined word- and syllable-character type of writing is that the word-characters are used less and less, until we have a pure syllabic script. Then comes a struggle to lower the number of syllable-characters; this lowering is brought about by the help of various artifices, — by more or less arbitrary resolutions of the more complex syllables, or by the use of the same character for syllables which resemble one another but are not exactly identical. An individual method of reducing the number of syllable-characters was developed by the Egyptians and taken over from them by a West Semitic people. The principle is that the reader is given the responsibility of guessing the vowels in the syllables. The syllable-characters may indicate one of many vowels, but are definite with regard to consonants, and therefore it appears to us, who have learned to analyze a syllable into consonants and vowels, as if the characters were consonant-characters. The Semitic alphabet thus originated has made a victorious and unparalleled progress throughout the world. In most places it was used as a syllabic system of writing — which it actually was. It could be improved (the Indians in particular improved it drastically, without, however, causing it to lose the traits of a syllabic writing), but it was also liable to a relapse in the direction of the older types of syllabic writing. The Greeks alone converted the Semitic alphabet, when they took it over, into both a consonant and vowel script, and thus undertook the analysis of syllables into individual sounds, an accomplishment which any six-year-old child can carry out now, but which at first was a tremendous achievement, one which completed the evolution of writing and made it into a supple instrument for rendering human speech.

In the course of this long evolution the ingenuity of individual men must certainly have played a part. There is no reason to doubt that. But what is most striking is that language itself worked in behalf of the speaking man. The various types of language have all made their own contributions to the development of writing. A language with many simply constructed monosyllabic words, and also with some words of more than one syllable, was the best foundation for the formation of the first mixed word- and syllable-script: such a language was spoken by the Sumerians, the masters of the Assyrians in learning. The transfer to a language richer in syllables, especially one with simple syllables, necessarily furthered the transformation of the script in such a way that word-characters became rarer, and syllable-characters increased: Assyrian was just such a language. A language with many complex syllables, like Old Persian and the other ancient Indo-European languages, must necessarily provide an incentive for breaking up syllables artificially. In this way the number of syllable-characters was materially reduced. And the particular method of leaving the syllable-characters indefinite as to vowels could be discovered most easily in languages like Egyptian and Semitic, where the vowels continually changed under inflection and derivation. Thus, different forms of the verb *to kill* in Arabic run as follows:

katala	he killed
kutila	he was killed
katalta	thou didst kill
ya-ktulu	he will kill
katlun	killing, murder

Here we observe the alternation of *ta* with *ti*, *tu*, and *t*. Hence it was no accident that the alphabet originated with the Egyptians and Semites. When it was transferred from them to a language with fixed vowels and many complex syllables, like Greek, the last step — that of resolving syllables into vowels and consonants — lay very near, and the Greeks were assisted in this solution by a combination of auspicious circumstances.

Thus long was the way, and there is no doubt that most of the stages we can point out were virtually necessary steps in the development. We must not allow ourselves to be confused by later systems of writing which seem to have skipped one stage or another, but which have done so only in appearance, and actually have developed through insight previously attained. It was perhaps not wholly without external help that the Japanese developed a very simple syllabic script of only fifty characters from the involved Chinese script with its thousands and tens of thousands of characters. Their language invited just such a script by its whole structure; but

ワ wa	ラ ra	ヤ ya	マ ma	ハ ha	ナ na	タ ta	サ sa	カ ka	ア a
ヰ wi	リ ri	イ yi	ミ mi	ヒ hi	ニ ni	チ chi	シ si	キ ki	イ i
ウ wu	ル ru	ユ yu	ム mu	フ hu	ヌ nu	ツ tsu	ス su	ク ku	ウ u
ヱ we	レ re	エ ye	メ me	ヘ he	ネ ne	テ te	セ se	ケ ke	エ e
ヲ wo	ロ ro	ヨ yo	モ mo	ホ ho	ノ no	ト to	ソ so	コ ko	オ o

THE FIFTY JAPANESE SYLLABIC CHARACTERS IN THE ARRANGEMENT
USED BY JAPANESE PHONETICIANS.[1]

[After Kanazawa, *Ueber den Einfluss des Sanskrit auf das japanische Schriftsystem*, Tokio, 1907.]

it is not certain that the Japanese would have been able to create it if both they and the Chinese had not learned phonetics from the scholars of India. Certainly the Korean alphabetical writing (vowel- and consonant-script), which we know from the fifteenth century, can lay no claim to being an independent invention. Of its origin nothing has been proved; Indian influence does not seem to explain anything, but there were other ways in which the results of the evolution of the alphabet might reach the borders of Korea. — We have several examples of syllabic systems of writing invented in the nineteenth century or on the verge of the twentieth through the ingenuity of Indians or negroes. The one most discussed is a syllabic system of over two hundred characters which was found in use during the fifties among a heathen tribe of negroes, the Vei, on the extreme northern coast of Liberia. It was invented by a negro, Doalu, and was encouraged by the chief of the tribe. Schools were established for boys and girls and men and women. They wrote with a reed and plant juices on slabs of wood or on paper got from Europeans. The more clever among them wrote books of miscellaneous content. But two wars, in which the Vei were defeated by neighbor tribes and their capital was twice destroyed, put an end to the literary development. Certainly this Doalu was a gifted man. But his syllabic system was not an independent invention. As a child he had re-

[1] In the transcription *y* and *ch* denote the corresponding sounds in English *yoke* and *chat*. There is another but unsystematic arrangement of the characters: *i ro ha*, etc. In this arrangement the syllables together make up Japanese words which constitute a verse with fairly clear meaning.

ceived instruction for three months from a missionary, and, however little he may have retained, he may very well have remembered the idea that a word of several syllables can be split up into unit syllables, and that sound units can be represented by arbitrary symbols. Given the idea, the sources of the individual symbols have relatively little interest. Doalu seems to have followed the principle implied in "Je prends mon bien où je le trouve." Some of the characters are obviously European letters and numerals whose meaning he did not know, but which he used as seemed best to him. $P = be$, $B = gba$, $N = po$, $H = re$, $E = to$, $8 = so$, $5 = fa$, $K = mbe$, etc. Most of the characters are arbitrary figures: squares, circles, crosses, etc., with non-functioning "diacritics"; many characters begin with a superfluous $\sim\sim\sim$ (in imitation of European handwriting).

Comprehensive treatments and investigations on the history of writing have not been lacking. We owe such works to Klaproth, Steinthal, Taylor (*The Alphabet*, London, 1883), P. Berger (*Histoire de l'écriture dans l'antiquité*, Paris, 1891) and Hans Jensen (*Geschichte der Schrift*, Hanover, 1925).

A survey of the contributions which the discoveries of the nineteenth century have made to the science of language can be divided into the following five sections: (1) the languages of cuneiform inscriptions, (2) languages written in hieroglyphics, (3) the Semitic alphabet (in its easily recognizable forms), (4) more remote and greatly changed offshoots of the Semitic alphabet, (5) the Greek alphabet and its successors. In our brief treatment there will be no opportunity to go into the inscriptions which belong to the field dominated by the Chinese system of writing and its various derivatives; and with regard to the American systems of picture-writing learning has as yet no great achievements to boast of. In each of the five fields to be considered we shall find very different linguistic families represented.

THE LANGUAGES OF THE CUNEIFORM INSCRIPTIONS

By the name *cuneiform inscriptions* we designate a number of old systems of writing whose external characteristic is that all the characters are compounded of — or, more correctly, resolved into — wedges. This peculiarity is of course not primitive, but was evolved as a result of the prevailing writing material: men wrote on soft clay with a sort of wooden stylus shaped like a narrow ruler, which was pressed down into the clay. If this instrument were held slantwise, as we hold a pen, the lower part would go deepest into the clay, and the stylus would leave a cuneiform line, and this cuneiform or wedge-like appearance was further developed by changing the shape of the stylus. In the home of cuneiform writing, the land of the Tigris and the Euphrates — where it was first practised by the Sumerians and later by the invading Semitic conquerors, the Assyrians — we can point out to a certain extent how the cuneiform characters arose from older characters more like pictures (hieroglyphs).

Outside the land of the Tigris and Euphrates, the proper home of cuneiform writing, we know four centers of culture where it was used. Two lie to the west and north: (1) the region about Lake Van; this district is now the home of the Armenians, but the inscriptions originate with an entirely different people who dwelt here before the Armenians did. The country is called *Ararat* in the Bible. Noah landed upon its highest peak; the Assyrians used the name *Urartu*, and the Greeks called the people *Alarodians*; (2) the capital city of the Hittites in the ancient province of Asia Minor, Cappadocia, where the village of Boghaz-köi now is. The other two are to the south and east: (3) Elam, the southern portion of the province of Susiana with the capital city Susa, at the northern point of the Persian Gulf; (4) Persia. Persia proper lies to the southeast of Susiana, but Old Persian inscriptions are found in other regions of the great Persian Empire also, especially in ancient Media, north of Susiana.

But we have not exhausted the list of languages about which cuneiform inscriptions teach us something. In the Hittite empire in Asia Minor there seem to have been spoken, in addition to the prevailing language, various others which are likewise represented in the discoveries from Boghaz-köi. Through another discovery we know the Mitanni language, which belonged to the eastern boundary of Asia Minor on both sides of the Euphrates. And the Cossæans (in Assyrian *Kassi*), who dwelt in northern Susiana and ruled Babylon between 1600 and 1200 B.C., are not wholly unknown to us linguistically, since the Assyrians have left us various bits of information about their speech. In geographical order from west to east and from north to south we can name, then, the following languages which used the cuneiform system:

1) The principal language of the Hittite empire in Asia Minor.
2) Other languages of Asia Minor within the Hittite empire.

Fifteenth to thirteenth centuries before Christ.

3) The language of Van.   Ninth to seventh centuries before Christ.
4) The language of Mitanni. About 1400 B.C.
5) Assyrian-Babylonian. From about 2500 B.C.
6) Sumerian. From about 4000 B.C.
7) Cossæan. A great power from 1600 to 1200 B.C.
8) Elamitic. From about 2000 B.C.
9) Old Persian. Sixth to fourth centuries before Christ.

Of these cuneiform languages, two belong clearly to well-known families: Assyrian-Babylonian is Semitic, and Old Persian is Indo-European of the Iranian branch. The other languages are disputed. Some investigators are so liberal as to turn them all over to the Caucasian family; but justification for this generosity has not yet been advanced. Pending further investigation it is best to divide them into four groups. The principal Hittite language shows such close resemblances to Indo-European that it very probably belongs to that family in spite of its foreign appearance. But other languages of the Hittite empire, of which we as yet know very little, may have to be classified with the Caucasian, along with Van and Mitanni, although proofs are scanty. But it should be noted that Van and Mitanni agree with Indo-European in individual features: in nouns the nominative ends in -š in both, and in Mitanni the accusative ends in -n. Thus we may cite forms of Mitanni and Van proper names which agree very well with the forms of the Greek name *Homēros* or the Hittite word *antuḫša-š* "man":

Nom.	Mitanni *Gilia-š*	Van *Menua-š*	Hitt. *antuḫša-š*	Gr. *Homēro-s*
Acc.	*Gilia-n*		*antuḫsa-n*	*Homēro-n*

Such similarities might also prompt the conjecture that the non-Indo-European languages of Asia Minor, along with Van and Mitanni, belonged to a family which had approximately the same relationship to Indo-European as Hamitic has to Semitic. If they do actually belong to the Caucasian family, then the latter must have been relatively close to the Indo-European family, a relationship which is no longer apparent in the modern languages. Elamitic, to which it is not impossible that Cossæan was akin, is very different from Van and Mitanni, and Sumerian in turn is entirely different from these and from all the other cuneiform languages.

Assyrian script consists of sound-characters and word-characters. The sound-characters are altogether syllabic. There are characters for more complicated syllables like *gal*, *kus*, *kur*, etc., for simpler

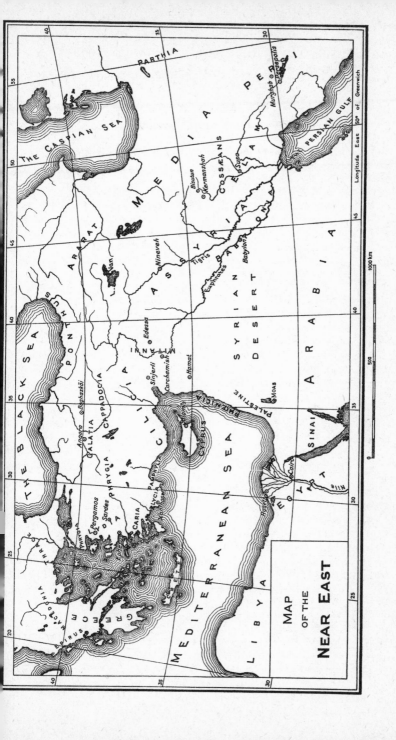

MAP
OF THE
NEAR EAST

syllables like *ba, bi, be, bu, ab, ib, ub,* etc., and for syllables which consist simply of a vowel: *a, i, e, u.* The complex syllables can also be expressed by the combination of two simpler syllabic characters; for instance, *dur* by means of *du* + *ur,* ḫil by ḫi + il. A remarkable peculiarity, which is due to the rebus origin of the sound-characters, is that very often one and the same character has more than one value. Thus, the four entirely different syllable-values *tar, kud, šil, ḫaṣ* can all be expressed by means of the same character.

The word-characters occur partly as independent, partly as auxiliary characters. The independent word-characters may be followed by a sound-character which indicates more exactly the pronunciation of the final syllable, just as in an expression like *the 30th.* As auxiliary characters — "determinatives" — the word-characters may come both before words which are written with syllabic characters, and before words written with word-characters; they give the approximate meaning of the succeeding word — that is, they designate the category of meanings to which the word belongs. Thus the word-character for *god* is placed before the name of a divinity, the character meaning *mountain* or *country* is placed before names of mountains and countries, before names of cities the character *city*, before river-names *river*, before names of trees or articles made of wood *tree*, before certain personal names *man*, before masculine proper names a vertical wedge, before feminine proper names *woman*. These determinatives must not be read separately. Thus, "god" + *a* + *šur* must be read simply *Ašur* (name of one

SPECIMENS OF ASSYRIAN
WRITING

tar, kud, šil, ḫaṣ

'god'

a

šur

Ašur

gal, 'large'

ē, 'house'

'palace'

'horse'

('donkey'   *kur*   *ra*)

of the principal gods of the Assyrians). These determinatives may be compared to the "keys" in Chinese writing, but they are not so widely used. They may be compared also to the use of capitals in the spelling of names in modern European orthography; but the information which determinatives give about the content of the following words is much more detailed than that afforded by our capitals.

Obviously, the same character can be used both as a word-character and as a syllable-character. But the complete lack of agreement often observed between syllable-values and word-values of the same character is striking: the pronunciation of the word very often has no similarity at all to the syllabic value. The syllable-character *gal* means "large," and "large" in Assyrian is *rabū*; the syllable-character *ē* means "house," and a house was called in Assyrian *bītu*. Here there seems to be no bridge between word-meaning and syllable-value. But this is due to the fact that the Assyrians took over both word-meanings and syllable-values from their predecessors in the rule of Babylon. In Sumerian "large" is *gal* and "house" is *ē*. The lack of connection between syllable-value and word-meaning in Assyrian was really a step forward, in comparison with the situation in Sumerian, and must necessarily have contributed much toward giving the method of sound-writing the advantage over the method of word-writing; consciousness of the difference between the two principles necessarily became much clearer. Another fact which contributed here is that monosyllabic words were exceptional in Assyrian, while they were much more numerous in Sumerian. But the mechanical adoption of the Sumerian "spelling" sometimes had also the effect of making the writing stranger and more involved. It was perhaps not so perceptible in the word for *palace*. The Sumerians wrote *ē* + *gal* and read *ēgal*, "large house." They would have been quite indifferent to the question whether the characters were to be understood as syllable-characters or as word-characters. On the other hand, the Assyrians wrote the same two characters and read *ēkallu*, because they had borrowed the Sumerian word, which has wandered still farther to Hebrew, where it appears as *hēkāl*. But where they used their own words with Sumerian groups of characters, the result was likely to be very strange. Thus when they wrote "donkey" + *kur* + *ra* meaning "horse," the first character might lead the thought in the right direction; but the syllables *kur-ra*, which had a clear meaning in Sumerian, meant absolutely nothing in Assyrian, where "horse" is *sisū*.

In general, it cannot be said that the Assyrians promoted in any special degree the tendency toward simplification which lay inherent in the cuneiform character. Until their fall as a nation they conservatively continued the use of their entire complicated system of some hundreds of characters, although they might well have been satisfied with their hundred characters for simple syllables. They stuck to it long after the simple Semitic alphabet had spread over a great part of Asia. Yet they were not wholly without excuse for holding to their ancient system of writing. We can well imagine with what scorn the learned Assyrians looked down upon the Semitic alphabet, which had acquired its ease of writing at the cost of great inexactness in its phonetic system. It must have affected them in much the same way that the impressionistic spelling of a washwoman affects a modern educated person. We can put ourselves to some extent in their place: if we find a text in an unknown language written in the Assyrian script, the word-characters furnish us with an excellent guide for understanding what the subject matter is, the determinatives show us, among other things, where we are to expect proper names, and unless we mistake completely the syllabic characters — say, by reading *kud* or *šil* or *ḫaṣ* instead of *tar* — we get, at least in a language with a relatively simple structure, a fairly exact reflection of the pronunciation; and we are at any rate partly protected even against misreading the polyphone characters by certain niceties in the rules of spelling. It is quite another matter with the Semitic alphabet. If one does not know in advance how a word is to be pronounced, one cannot learn much from the spelling, because the alphabet is quite mute as to vowels; and the content of a given text in an unknown language is impenetrable unless some other language can be used as a key.

But outside Assyria, cuneiform writing was simplified somewhat. People were less learned, and waived unnecessary complications. Elamitic was written in the period of the Persian kings with a considerably smaller number of characters than Assyrian, although the system of writing is in principle the same. Among the Persians cuneiform writing underwent an astonishing change. An indication where the Persians learned to write lies in the Old Persian word for inscription, *dipi-*, surely no other than Assyrian *duppu* "table," which must have reached Old Persian through Elam, since the change from *u* to *i* is Elamitic. But the Persians improved cuneiform writing in a very radical way. With but few exceptions they rejected the word-characters, and of the syllabic characters they retained only the simplest, such as *da, di, du, a, i, u,* etc. — thirty-six in all. They introduced such rules of spelling that the system of writing is just on the verge of becoming a consonant- and vowel-system: instead of writing *di, du* they usually wrote two syllabic characters, *di-i, du-u*; the missing character for *ti* is replaced by *ta-i,* and so on, so that the syllabic characters *di, du, ta* are on the verge of becoming the letters *d, t,* etc. The form of the characters is simplified to complete un-recognizability. This conversion of cuneiform writing is so astonishing that some investigators have supposed that the Persians did not accomplish it independently, but worked under the influence of the Semitic alphabet. This is incredible, however, as the internal principle of Persian writing, involving a careful designation of the vowels, is entirely different from the plan of the Semitic alphabet. But we must certainly assume that the Persian cuneiform writing which is known to us only from the sixth century before Christ on is the result of a lengthy process of development, of which the older documents are lost. The system of writing certainly was not invented by King Darius, then, although the Greeks seem to have thought so. He had hardly any more influence on the Persian system of writing than Peter the Great had on the Russian.

The first cuneiform writing to be deciphered was the Old Persian. The Persian inscriptions are mostly on stone and buildings; many were found in the ruins of the royal palaces of the ancient Persian capital, Persepolis. Earlier travellers had already reported these inscriptions, but the first exact and trustworthy copies were brought back by the famous German scholar, Carsten Niebuhr, from the journey he made at the expense of the Danish king Frederick V to Arabia and neighboring lands. The inscriptions were published in his travel book in 1778, and they gave the first basis for deciphering. The other Persian inscriptions were not published until after the work of deciphering had begun. The Englishman Rawlinson and the Dane Westergaard may be named among those who have done the greatest service in adding to the material. We now have inscriptions not only from Persepolis and other places in ancient Persia, but also from Susiana, Media, Armenia, and Egypt (Isthmus of Suez). The most remarkable of them all, larger than all the others put together, is the great rock inscription from Bisutun, in the neighborhood of the town of Kermanshāh, in ancient Median territory, which was first copied by Rawlinson in the years 1836–47. It is inscribed beneath a piece of sculpture: nine persons with their hands bound behind their backs approach a majestic figure which treads upon a fallen foe with the right foot, raising one hand aloft as in prayer. Behind him stand several of his retinue, and above them all hovers a divinity, Ahuramazdā, Ormuzd. The inscription cost a tremendous amount of labor. It is cut into a steep rock several hundred feet high.

G. F. GROTEFEND (1805)

The whole surface was polished, holes being filled so carefully that it is almost impossible to distinguish the inlaid material from the surrounding stone; and the entire inscription, which when transcribed in Latin letters fills half a hundred printed octavo pages, was cut in with the greatest care, so that it is unique in its beauty and exactness. Like most of the royal inscriptions of Persia, it is set down in all three of the principal languages of the empire; but unfortunately the Assyrian (Babylonian) text was badly damaged when a brook made its course across it.

This great inscription, which we may well call the most remarkable in the world, originated with King Darius (522–485 B.C.). From him and his son Xerxes (485–465 B.C.), come most of the Persian inscriptions. A single very brief inscription from Murghāb, a little north of Persepolis, bears the name of Cyrus. It is much debated whether this Cyrus is the ancient king celebrated in story, the conqueror of Babylon — from whom we have two inscriptions in Assyrian alone, written on the same material as that used by the Assyrians, a clay cylinder and a tile, — or the prince named Cyrus who fell in the year 401 B.C. in a rebellion against his brother the king. The latest royal inscription from Persia is from Artaxerxes Okhos (358–338 B.C.).

The learned bishop of Sealand, Frederik Münter, can be said to have laid the first foundation, however slender, for deciphering the Persian inscriptions. From the varying number of characters in the three parallel texts, he concluded in 1802 that the first kind of cuneiform writing, that in the first column, was a system in letters, the second a syllabic system, and the third a word-system. We know now that these inferences were not quite correct: the first kind, Persian, is not a genuine letter-system, but merely a much simplified syllabic system; the second, Elamitic, and the third, Assyrian, belong principally to the same type, although the word-characters play a much less important part in the Elamitic than in the Assyrian column. But Münter was nevertheless on the right track. He made still other observations which broke ground for the deciphering: he discovered that the words were separated by an oblique wedge, and found the group of characters which could be accepted as meaning "king." But the actual deciphering is the work of a German scholar, Grotefend. He began with the correct assumption that the inscriptions originated with the ancient Persian kings whom we know from the Greek historians; and he rightly inferred also that the first kind of cuneiform writing must represent the language of the ruling nation, Persian, simply because it was invariably placed first; on this basis he succeeded in ascertaining, by the aid of two small inscriptions from Persepolis, the names Hystaspes, Darius, and Xerxes, and through them in determining in an approximate way the meaning of many of the characters. The deciphering was laid before the Academy of Sciences of Göttingen in 1802.

The two inscriptions used are subjoined here, partly in the cuneiform character, partly in a transcription according to pronunciation. Those who have sufficient patience to study the cuneiform characters without using the transcription will thus be enabled to experience something of what the first decipherers underwent. But this can be experienced even with the help of the transcription, since presumably the Old Persian words will seem sufficiently incomprehensible to most readers to function as unknown quantities.

1.

𒋾 𒈨 𒌋 𒆠 𒂊 𒋡 𒍑 𒀸 𒑲 𒍑 𒈨 𒆠 𒁹 𒐊 𒆠 𒀸

𒂊 𒐊 𒌋 𒌋 𒁹 𒀸 𒑲 𒍑 𒈨 𒆠 𒁹 𒐊 𒆠 𒀸 𒑲 𒍑 𒈨

𒆠 𒁹 𒐊 𒆠 𒈨 𒈪 𒈨 𒐈 𒀸 𒑲 𒍑 𒈨 𒆠 𒁹 𒐊 𒆠 𒀸

𒋾 𒈪 𒆠 𒋡 𒈪 𒈨 𒐈 𒀸 𒌷 𒐊 𒍑 𒐈 𒈨 𒌋 𒑲 𒈪 𒆠

𒈨 𒀸 𒑲 𒋡 𒑲 𒀸 𒈪 𒑲 𒍑 𒈨 𒐈 𒈪 𒐊 𒍑 𒐊 𒆠 𒀸 𒈪

𒆠 𒀸 𒐊 𒐈 𒐈 𒀸 𒐈 𒋡 𒌋 𒐈 𒀸 𒈨 𒐊 𒋡 𒈪 𒑲 𒍑

2.

𒑲 𒍑 𒆠 𒈨 𒌋 𒍑 𒈨 𒀸 𒑲 𒍑 𒈨 𒆠 𒁹 𒐊 𒆠 𒀸 𒂊 𒐊 𒌋 𒐊 𒌋

𒂊 𒀸 𒑲 𒍑 𒈨 𒆠 𒁹 𒐊 𒆠 𒀸 𒑲 𒍑 𒈨 𒆠 𒁹 𒐊 𒆠 𒈨

𒈪 𒐈 𒀸 𒋾 𒈨 𒌋 𒆠 𒂊 𒐊 𒋡 𒈪 𒍑 𒀸 𒑲 𒍑 𒈨 𒆠 𒁹

𒋾 𒆠 𒐊 𒆠 𒈨 𒀸 𒑲 𒋡 𒑲 𒀸 𒐊 𒑲 𒍑 𒈨 𒐈 𒈪 𒐊 𒍑 𒐊 𒆠 𒀸

In transcription the inscriptions read thus (I add an interlinear translation):

1.

Dārayavahuš Darius	*xšāyaþiya* king	*vazarka* great,	*xšāyaþiya* king	*xšāyaþiyānām* of kings,
xšāyaþiya king	*dahyunām* of countries,	*Vištāspahya* Hystaspes's	*puþ'a* son,	*Haxāmanišiya* the Achæmenid,
hya who	*imam* this	*tačaram* palace	*akunauš.* made.	

2.

Xšayāršā Xerxes	*xšāyaþiya* king	*vazarka* great,	*xšāyaþiya* king	*xšāyaþiyānām* of kings,
Dārayavahauš Darius's	*xšāyaþiyahyā* the king's	*puþ'a* son,	*Haxāmanišiya* [1] the Achæmenid.	

Grotefend perceived that the man who was named as king in the last inscription was designated as the son of the king in the first.

[1] *x* is pronounced like German *ch.*

On the other hand, the king of the first inscription was not indicated as the son of a king. The first king could not be Cyrus, because that name was too short for the seven characters in the first inscription. In the entire succession of Persian kings there were no names other than Darius and Xerxes that would fit. In the determination of the meaning of the individual characters, however, Grotefend necessarily made some errors, both because he incorrectly regarded the writing

G. F. GROTEFEND (1848)

as a system of letters, and because his point of departure — partly the Greek or Hebrew rendering of the foreign names, partly later Persian forms — was inadequate. For the word *king* he had nothing more to depend upon than the Modern Persian *šāh*, and he could not know, as we do now, that the *h* in this word arose from an older *th(þ)*. The relation between the correct reading and Grotefend's is as follows:

Actual spelling: *da-a-ra-ya-va-hu-ša* = *Darayavahúš*
Grotefend   : *d-a-r-h-e-u-š*

Actual spelling: *xa-ša-ya-a-ra-ša-a*   = *Xšayāršā*
Grotefend   : *x-š-h-a-r-š-a*

Actual spelling: *vi-i-ša-ta-a-sa-pa*   = *Vištāspa*
Grotefend   : *g-o-š-t-a-s-p*   (later Gustasp)

Actual spelling: *xa-ša-a-ya-þa-i-ya* = *xšāyaþiya* king
Grotefend   : *x-š-a-h-i-o-h*   (Mod. Persian *šāh*, shah).

It can be easily seen that Grotefend hit fairly close to the truth in these four words, in spite of his errors. But much else he read and interpreted quite erroneously. His name-keys contained too few characters, his linguistic keys were too rusty; what could be learned about the *Avesta* from Anquetil du Perron (see above, pp. 24 f.) was too doubtful, and Grotefend could not suspect anything whatever of the thorough-going Modern Persian development of sounds.

H. C. RAWLINSON
[After George Rawlinson, *H. C. Rawlinson, A Memoir*, London, 1898]

Other scholars were needed with keys finely polished by a good knowledge of the *Avesta* and of Sanskrit. And they were at hand. In 1826 Rask determined the meaning of the $n(a)$- and $m(a)$- characters, which occur several times in the inscriptions cited above; and with their determination the family name of the royal house of Persia, Achæmenid, was discovered. In 1836 Christian Lassen published a distinguished work which contains the beginnings of the correct interpretation of the character of this script as a syllabic character (he saw that a series of characters read by Grotefend as d, r, and so on, imply the vowel a and are to be read da, ra, and so on). In 1846–47 the work was completed by Hincks, Rawlinson, and

Oppert. From this time, Old Persian, and especially the Bisutun inscription with its ninety names, was an invaluable key to the other languages in the inscriptions of the Achæmenides, and to the deciphering of the inscriptions discovered in the native countries of these two languages.

In Assyria excavations were undertaken in 1842–45 by the Frenchman Émile Botta, who perceived that the inscriptions found here were written in the same script as that of the third column on the monuments of the Achæmenides. Then followed a great many other excavations, such as those of the Englishman Henry Layard in Nineveh in 1845–47 and 1849–51. They continued throughout the nineteenth century. Hand in hand with the excavating went the deciphering. In 1849 the Irishman Hincks determined the syllabic nature of the Assyrian characters. In 1851 Rawlinson discovered the polyphony of the syllabic characters — i.e., that one character could denote quite different syllables — and began to interpret the language as Semitic. The deciphering was brought to a preliminary conclusion by Oppert, *Expédition scientifique en Mésopotamie* (II, Paris, 1859). Among the many gifted scholars of Assyrian since that time it must suffice here to name Friedrich Delitzsch, author, among other works, of an Assyrian grammar (1889; second edition, 1906) and of an Assyrian dictionary.

The result of the work of which we have just sketched the outlines has been the revelation and interpretation of an immense literature: Hammurabi's laws (about 2000 B.C.), the kings' accounts of their deeds — among them we find names as well known in the Bible as King Sennacherib — religious, astrological, astronomical, mathematical texts, letters and all sorts of documents. These texts are written on various kinds of material, but mostly on clay tablets of one size or another, which may be compared to the manuscripts of a later period. Grammatical texts are found, also; for instance, the so-called syllabaries, in which many characters are explained with reference to their sound-values and word-values. Thus, that a given character has the syllabic value *lah* and the word-value "minister," Assyrian *sukkallu*, is shown by explaining it first as *la-ah*, then as *suk-kal-lu*.

Hincks, Rawlinson, and Oppert already recognized that, in addition to the Semitic language, in its slightly varying forms Assyrian and Babylonian, there was an entirely different language, Sumerian, in the Mesopotamian discoveries. This belonged to the predecessors of the Semites in these regions, the Sumerians, whose power the Semites destroyed, but whose culture they took over, and whose language they respected as a sort of holy tongue. Therefore a series of aids for learning Sumerian was devised for use in the schools for Assyrian priests: glossaries, tables of paradigms and the like, which, in connection with texts in both languages, have given us an insight into Sumerian. This insight enables us to interpret in some degree the extraordinarily numerous exclusively Sumerian texts. Great difficulties, however, are involved in the study of this language. The Assyrian "school-book" literature, of which we have fragments, is naturally not to be compared with modern linguistic literature with its precise terms and phonetic niceties; it is much more like a school-boy's notebook glossary, and gives no direct indications as to what was merely graphic and what was spoken. That the word "palace" in Sumerian is $\bar{e}gal$ naturally cannot be doubted, because the word went over as a loan into Assyrian as $\bar{e}kallu$ and into Hebrew as $h\bar{e}k\bar{a}l$; but, after all, the pronunciation $\bar{e}gal$ cannot be inferred from the method of writing $\bar{e}$-gal, for we could not tell beforehand whether the two characters should be spelled together according to their sound-value or whether they constituted together a new ideographic character whose pronunciation we could no more guess than we can guess the pronunciation of the Chinese character for "housewife," fu, from the fact that it is compounded of "woman" and "broom." Moreover, we have no key-language for Sumerian to help us as the other Semitic languages help us in Assyrian. Sumerian is neither Indo-European nor Semitic, neither Uralian nor Altaic, and it certainly is not Indo-Chinese. The conjecture that it might be a Caucasian language is worthless, for there are no resemblances which can be of any use to us.

The manifold doubts which come to mind in the study of Sumerian have given occasion to a most remarkable view which was advocated especially by J. Halévy, a Jew born in Adrianople who lived in France. From 1874 on he insisted with great energy but little clearness that the difference between the Assyrian and "so-called" Sumerian linguistic monuments is a difference not in language but merely in writing. According to his opinion, the Sumerian monuments were composed not in a language different from Assyrian, but merely in another writing, a sort of artificial cryptography. This whole hypothesis is refuted by its inherent impossibility. Strangely enough, Friedrich Delitzsch was at one time an adherent of Halévy, and in the first edition of his Assyrian grammar he gave a complete discussion of the reasons tending to prove that the Sumerian theory was incorrect. He soon abandoned this idea, and in 1914 published an extensive collection of material for learning Sumerian, including a Sumerian grammar in two forms — one exhaustive, the other brief.

Also to Delitzsch we owe the principal work on the language of the Cossæans, written on the basis of Assyrian information: this

FRIEDRICH DELITZSCH
[After *Illustrierte Zeitung*, Jan. 11, 1923]

basis is so slender, however, that we have no trustworthy idea of the language.

For Elamitic the inscriptions of the Achæmenides were a no less excellent key than for Assyrian. The first attempt to translate the Elamitic (second) column in these inscriptions is the work of the Dane N. L. Westergaard, printed in 1844 and 1854. He was followed by the Englishman Edwin Norris, and the most recent treatment is by the German F. H. Weissbach, who published in 1911 a collected edition of the inscriptions of the Achæmenides in all three languages, with German translation. At first, scholars were greatly perplexed as to the language to which the second column belonged. We now know that it is in the language of Elam, where French excavations in particular brought to light a wealth of material published by

V. Scheil in a series of volumes from 1900 on. These texts enable us to survey a cultural development of thousands of years. They are written partly on stone, partly on clay tablets. The investigation of this material is as yet only in its first stages. In 1926 Friedrich Wilhelm König began to publish a *Corpus inscriptionum Elamicarum*.

Inscriptions in the neighborhood of Van, mostly on buildings and cliffs, were discovered in 1828 by F. E. Schulz, who travelled through

A. H. SAYCE

the country under the auspices of the French government. The forty-two inscriptions found by him were published in 1840, and others have been added since. Some of them are Assyrian; one is written in both the language of the country and in Assyrian, but most of them are in only the language of the country. The most important contribution to their interpretation was made by Sayce in 1882. A German expedition investigated the inscriptions in 1898–99 with the purpose of bringing forth a collected edition, which began to appear in 1928 under the title *Corpus inscriptionum Chaldicarum*, edited by Carl F. Lehmann-Haupt. It will include the results of other expeditions (especially of a Russian expedition in 1916, the results of which were published in 1922).

The Mitanni language is known so far through but one text, a letter belonging to the great collection of several hundred clay tablets discovered in 1887 near Tell-el-Amarna in Egypt. The contents of the collection are letters dating from about 1400 B.C., written by or to various princes in the Near East — correspondence with the Egyptian kings Amenophis III and Amenophis IV. Some of the letters are from rulers in Palestine. With three exceptions, all are in Assyrian, which at that time was the international language of diplomatic intercourse in Western Asia and Egypt. The three letters not in Assyrian are also written in Assyrian cuneiform. And we have good reason to rejoice that this system of writing was used. If the letters had been a few centuries later, and had been written in the much more highly simplified system which was at that time in process of dissemination, the Semitic alphabet, the contents — and the pronunciation of the words — would have remained a secret. But the Assyrian script, with its many word-characters and determinatives, gave a preliminary glimpse of the content, and the stereotyped nature of the Assyrian style of letter-writing, such as fixed introductory formulas and the like, gave a key to the language, so that scholars were in a position to understand a considerable portion of the content and to determine not a few facts about the nature of the language. The one letter which proved to be written in the Mitanni language has been the subject of a number of investigations by Sayce, P. Jensen, L. Messerschmidt, and Ferdinand Bork.

The other two letters concern the king of Arzawa, a country which was sought by scholars somewhere in southeastern Asia Minor. They were published separately in 1902 by the Norwegian J. A. Knudtzon, with a translation and an attempt to determine the relationship of the language. He reached the conclusion that it was Indo-European, an opinion which soon gained both adherents and opponents. Meanwhile our knowledge of the language of the Arzawa letters was to be widened in an entirely unexpected way. In an expedition conducted by Ernest Chantre in 1893, the results of which were published in Paris in 1898, there were found near Boghaz-köi, some one hundred and fifty kilometers east of Angora in Asia Minor, fourteen damaged tablets of cuneiform inscriptions in an unknown language. The far-sighted English scholar Sayce explained that this language was the same as that in the Arzawa letters. Subsequently, in 1905, the Berlin professor, Hugo Winckler, undertook an expedition to the same region, and found more tablets in the language of the Arzawa letters. The investigations were continued in 1906–07; tablets in the unknown language were found by thousands; tablets in Assyrian were also found, a fact which showed that the ruined city below was the one which the Assyrians called *Hatti*, the capital of a

J. A. KNUDTZON
[After *Norges universitet*, 1911]

people which extended its power over Syria and had much intercourse with Egypt. The name *Hatti* is the same as that known from the Bible as *Hittites*. Among other things was found an agreement between King Hattušil and Rameses II of Egypt, about 1300 B.C. The unknown language thus showed itself to have been the principal language of the Hittite empire, and it is therefore permissible to call it simply Hittite. The publication of the enormous abundance of Hittite material has already made considerable progress; and there is no doubt that an ancient and almost forgotten people with a civilization of its own will live again for us when all of the material is interpreted. The interpretation will certainly succeed completely, as there are many points of attack. It is worthy of remark here that several tablets have been found which have word-lists in Sumerian, Assyrian, and Hittite; these have been discussed by Delitzsch and Harri Holma. The most thorough investigation of the language is by the Czech scholar F. Hrozný, who, like Knudtzon, maintains that it is Indo-European. At any rate, so much is certain: the inflectional system has a decidedly Indo-European appearance; the foreign impression that the language makes is due in large degree to the vocabulary.

The question is of great significance, for it concerns actually much more than the province of Cappadocia. P. Kretschmer (*Einleitung in die Geschichte der griechischen Sprache*, 1896) is certainly right when he insists, on the basis of place-names and proper names, that mutually closely-related languages were spoken throughout the whole central and southern parts of Asia Minor. If the Hittite language of Cappadocia is Indo-European, it must be agreed that this whole region spoke Indo-European languages.

A closer examination of the Boghaz-köi discoveries has shown that, in addition to Hittite, certain other languages occur. But it is impossible as yet to say much about them: at present there exist merely a few preliminary investigations by F. Hrozný and E. Forrer.

THE LANDS OF THE HIEROGLYPHS

By the name *hieroglyphs* we designate several systems of primitive writing which, in contrast with cuneiform writing, have preserved picture-like characters. The principal systems of hieroglyphs that we know are the Hittite, the Cretan, and the Egyptian. The first two have not yet been deciphered; but a syllabic system of writing which was used in the island of Cyprus, and no doubt was derived either from the Cretan or the Hittite hieroglyphs, was deciphered long ago.

The Hittite Hieroglyphs

Scattered about in Syria and parts of Asia Minor, especially in Cilicia (the southeastern province bordering upon Syria) are many monuments, mostly stone and cliff inscriptions, in hieroglyphic writing, some of them in relief. They were not discovered until late. After some previous vague reports and futile attempts by other scholars, William Wright succeeded in 1872 in procuring accurate casts of the inscriptions in Hamat (Hamah). By-and-by more inscriptions were discovered. The latest considerable addition to the material is the result of English excavations in Djerabis (Carkhemish), of which an account was published by D. G. Hogarth in 1914 and 1921. The inscriptions seem to belong to the period between 1000 and 550 B.C.; but see below. Wright designated them as Hittite, but it is not probable that they originated with the same people as the Hittite cuneiform tablets. The regions in which the two sorts of inscriptions were found coincide only to a very small degree.

The first scholar to attempt their interpretation was Sayce. His point of departure was a double inscription in cuneiform characters and hieroglyphs engraved on a seal bought in Smyrna by a merchant from Constantinople. It was offered to the British Museum about 1860, but was rejected because it was mistakenly regarded as a forgery. The original seems to have been lost in a great fire in Pera, but copies exist. Scholars have thought the cuneiform inscription read: "Tarkudimme, King in Metan." Whether this should be considered as Hittite or Assyrian it is difficult to say, since the inscription

FRAGMENTS OF A HITTITE INSCRIPTION
[After Wright, *The Empire of the Hittites*]

consists only of names and word-characters.[1] But the key in the double inscription was quite insufficient,[2] and Sayce was not sufficiently on his guard against the temptation to allow his imagination to supply what his acuteness could not. Later P. Jensen studied the inscriptions thoroughly, and very cleverly treated a number of preliminary problems. His general analysis, and his determining which are word-characters and which are sound-characters, what is the method of connecting word-characters and sound-characters in writing, which signs belong together in one group, and what approximate meaning certain groups seem to have, are extraordinarily penetrating and valuable. But according to his analysis the contents seem to be very meager. The royal inscriptions apparently contain not much more than the kingly name and title. Jensen has not succeeded in fixing the sound-values of the characters. The keys he used are far too uncertain and insufficient, and in his further efforts he has gone altogether astray. The most recent noteworthy attempt was made by C. Frank in 1923.[3] The future alone can show whether the Boghaz-köi discoveries can be of assistance.

The Syllabic Writing of Cyprus

In classical times the Greeks in the island of Cyprus used a remarkable syllabic system of writing which we know from inscriptions and coins dating from the seventh century before Christ to about 300 B.C.

This Cyprian system was richer in characters than the Old Persian system. We know nearly sixty characters, and we can say with approximate certainty that there must have been still more which accidentally fail to occur. Of these, some express more complex syllables, such as *ksa*, *kse*, and, perhaps — depending upon the reading and interpretation of a solitary inscription — *ros*, *nos*, but most of them are expressions for syllables of the simplest structure: *ka, ke, ki, ko, ku; la, le, li, lo, lu; a, e, i, o, u*. A language like Greek, which contains many very complex syllables, can be written in a system of this sort only by means of artificial tricks. The familiar

---

[1] There has been found in Boghaz-köi a document in cuneiform, with a seal in cuneiform and hieroglyphs. Unfortunately the hieroglyphs are much worn and are almost illegible; but the document is important for the chronology of the hieroglyphs: it was presented by King Arnuandash I in the fourteenth century before Christ.

[2] Compare the reproduction on p. 339.

[3] Cf. now Piero Meriggi, *Die hethitische Hieroglyphenschrift, Zeitschrift für Assyriologie* xxxix (1929).

✳ *a*	✳ *e*	✳ *i*	◡̆ *o*	⋎ *u*
◯ *ya*	⸲̌ *ye*		W *yo*	
)⟨ ✕ *va*	⊥ *ve*	)⟨ *vi*	⌒̂ *vo*	
▽ *ra*	⋀ *re*	⇁ *ri*	Ƣ *ro*	)⟨ *ru*
⌣ *la*	8 *le*	∟ *li*	+ *lo*	⌒ *lu*
)⟨ ✕ *ma*	✕ *me*	⋎ *mi*	◍ *mo*	✕ *mu*
⊤ *na*	ʻ�runeʼ *ne*	�⤸ *ni*	�𝖨Γ *no*	)ː *nu*
‡ *pa, ba, pha*	⟩ *pe, be, phe*	⋁̆ *pi, bi, phi*	⸑ *po, bo, pho*	⊍ *pu, bu, phu*
⊦ *ta, da, tha*	⤓ *te, de, the*	↑ *ti, di, thi*	Ƒ *to, do, tho*	Ƒ̄ₗₗ *tu, du, thu*
⬆ *ka, ga, kha*	⤨ *ke, ge, khe*	⊤̄ *ki, gi, khi*	⋀ *ko, go, kho*	✳)⟨ *ku, gu, khu*
⋁ Y *sa*	⊢⊣ *se*	⌂̲ *si*	⋁̆⋮ *so*	)⊹ *su*
)⟨ *za*			)) *zo*	
)⟨ *ksa*	Ꮳ *kse*			
	)⊹ *ros*	)⟨ *nos*		

THE SYLLABIC WRITING OF CYPRUS

Greek *anthrōpos* with its three heavy syllables is written thus, with five characters: *a-to-ro-po-se*. The Duc de Luynes first drew attention to the inscriptions of Cyprus; he collected them, including those on coins, in a book entitled *Numismatique et inscriptions cypriotes* (1852). But they long remained undeciphered, and no one thought that the remarkable writing concealed Greek.

A change came in 1871. In that year the English consul, R. Hamilton Lang, read at a meeting of the Society of Biblical Archæology in London an article on an inscription found by himself in an ancient temple at Idalion, which contained a dedication in both Phœnician and Cyprian. The Assyriologist George Smith then began an energetic effort to decipher the writing. With the assistance of the proper names, he attempted to determine the meaning of a number of the characters, and he succeeded to a considerable extent. With these keys he attacked the proper names in the pure Cyprian inscriptions. When some of the characters in a proper name can be read, the rest can often be guessed, if the ground is familiar. George Smith was actually successful in reading some names correctly, but naturally he did not escape errors. He perceived that the writing was a syllabic system; he read the word for *king* and found that it was the same as in Greek. He found some other similarities with Greek also, but did not yet draw the conclusion that the language was simply Greek, a conclusion which nevertheless became unavoidable. The deciphering was carried further by the Egyptologist Samuel Birch, by the Assyriologist Johannes Brandis, whose work appeared posthumously in 1873 (Curtius saw it through the press), and by the classical philologists Moriz Schmidt, W. Deecke, and Richard Meister.

Quite recently some inscriptions in the same syllabic system of writing have been brought to light, written in an unknown tongue. They all seem to originate from the city of Amathus. Attention was first drawn to them in 1911 and 1913 by Richard Meister and J. Vendryes. In 1924 they were fully and acutely discussed by Ernst Sittig, but so far we understand next to nothing of them. Yet some day they may reveal what sort of language was spoken in the island of Cyprus before the Greeks and Phœnicians came.

It is a natural consequence that the Cyprian syllabic system of writing must be much older than the oldest documents preserved. In the seventh century before Christ, no Cyprian would have been able to devise such a syllabic system of writing, which, with its threescore characters, was decidedly inferior to the Greek alphabet with a third as many characters, and could not approximately express the sounds of the language with the same accuracy as the alphabet.[1] On the other hand, conservatism in spelling might have held fast to a syllabic system already in existence, both in the seventh century and much later, the more so since it was undeniably quicker to write than the Greek alphabet. Naturally, the Cyprian syllabic system is no independent invention. It must have been developed from an older word- and syllable-system. And that older system can have been neither the Assyrian nor the Egyptian; internal evidence determines that. It is easier to guess in the direction of the writing used on the closest stretch of mainland to the north and east: the Hittite hieroglyphs. Certain similarities in the shape of the characters, however, have caused investigators recently to turn their attention westward to

The Cretan Systems of Writing

In Crete Arthur J. Evans has undertaken excavations which have revealed inscriptions partly in hieroglyphs and partly in a later script which has dropped the picture-like form and acquired simpler lines. Accounts were published by Evans in 1895 and 1909. The most recent work on the subject is by the Finn, J. Sundwall. The simpler system occurs in two varieties: one, which has about ninety-two characters, is disseminated throughout Central and Eastern Crete, and dates from the seventeenth century before Christ; the other, with about seventy characters, belongs to the city of Gnossos, during the period from 1550–1400 B.C. Because of the small number of characters we must suppose that these simpler modes of writing are approximately pure syllabic systems.

Thus far, the deciphering of the Cretan systems has hardly begun. It is agreed, however, that they do not belong to the Greek immigrants, but to the pre-Greek population of Crete, who, according to the historian Herodotus, were related to the Lycians in the southwestern part of Asia Minor. That this ancient population had at least partly preserved its language long after Greek culture had conquered the island is shown by three inscriptions from the city

---

[1] As Hans Jensen remarks, the syllabic characters *a-to-ro-po-se* might be read not only as *ánthrōpos*, but also as *átropos*, *átrophos*, or *ádorpos* (and in several other ways not yielding real Greek words). One may add that the syllabic system could not differentiate the accusative *anthrōpon* "man" from the vocative *androphóne* "man-slaying" (both *a-to-ro-po-ne*).

of Praisos, which are written in a non-Greek language absolutely incomprehensible to us.

The Egyptian Hieroglyphs

The best known of the hieroglyphic systems is the Egyptian. It seems to compete in age with the Sumerian script: the oldest monuments go back to about 3500 B.C. As for the internal system, the Egyptian, like the Assyrian, is a mixture of word- and sound-characters, and the two kinds supplement each other in a similar, though not in quite the same way as in Assyrian. The sound-characters denote partly more complex syllables consisting of a consonant plus a vowel unknown to us, plus another consonant (*wr*, *mn*, etc.), partly simpler syllables consisting of a consonant plus vowel. The peculiar thing, however, is that the quality of the vowel is not indicated. One and the same syllabic character thus has the meanings *ta*, *te*, *to*, etc., and such a syllabic character may also indicate a consonant alone when no vowel followed. On the other hand, there was no character for a vowel plus a consonant, and there was none for syllables consisting of a vowel alone, simply because there were no such syllables in Egyptian.

All this is related to the peculiar syllabic structure of the Egyptian language, which was originally very similar to Semitic. In Egyptian as well as in Semitic, every syllable originally consisted of a consonant plus a vowel. But the vowels varied under inflection and derivation, and could also be dropped entirely. Thus *ta*, *te*, *to*, etc., and *t* interchanged with one another in forms of the same root, and could therefore be written with the same character. A syllable never began with a vowel; where there was no other consonant at the beginning of a syllable it began with a glottal stop, a sort of coughing sound like that in German *mein 'Eid* as distinguished from *mein Neid*. It is produced by suddenly opening the closed glottis to a stream of air. By a little practice one can learn to produce this sound alone. The Semites and Egyptians pronounced it very energetically. For them it functioned as well as a consonant as *k* or *t* or *p* does for us. Syllables and fragments of syllables like *'a*, *'e*, *'o* and *'* were quite the same to them as, for instance, *ta*, *te*, *to*, *t* (the Egyptian character for such syllables was the picture of an eagle).

Thus Egyptian writing leaves us in complete ignorance of the vowels. It is only through Coptic (see p. 120) that we learn anything about them (and we can also infer a little from a foreign nation's rendering of Egyptian names). When we copy Egyptian with Latin letters, we can therefore give only the consonants: *fdw* "four," *sfḫ* "seven," *nfr* "good."

Hence it is often said of the simple Egyptian syllabic characters that they are consonant-characters. But this is an unhistorical conception. The Egyptians did not analyze the syllables into vowels and consonants, and then make the remarkable resolve to represent only the less sonorous sounds, the consonants, and to leave the more sonorous sounds, the vowels, unrepresented. On the contrary, their system of writing, like all other ancient syllabic systems, is founded upon a stage of development at which a clear analysis of the syllables had not yet been attained. It was syllabic characters which the inventor of the script created. The device of representing *ta*, *ti*, *tu*, etc., by a single character was a purely practical means of simplification, a means which the language itself offered, and which has more to do with the principle of word-writing than with that of our own consonant- and vowel-system. Just as a word-character gives only the idea, and lets the reader guess the required inflectional form, so the syllabic characters that did not indicate the quality of the vowels gave an unmistakable indication of the idea, on the basis of the special structure of the language, but left the reader to guess the precise inflectional form to be read.

	ꜣ		ḫ
	i̓		
	c		
	w		s
	b		š
	p		ḳ
	f		k
	m		g
	n		t
	r		ṯ
	h		d
	ḥ		ḏ

THE EGYPTIAN ALPHABET[1]

As a means of simplification, the Egyptian method with characters not indicating vowel-quality had enormous consequences. While the Assyrians used a hundred simple syllabic characters, the Egyptians were content with twenty-four. These alone would have been sufficient; but the Egyptians did not give up the compounded syllabic characters and word-characters any more than the Assyrians did. The total number of characters in the Egyptian system is therefore very large. It reaches thousands, and at least six hundred were in common use.

The deciphering of the Egyptian hieroglyphics is connected with Bonaparte's expedition to Egypt in 1798. While the French troops were working (in August, 1799) on fortifications at the westernmost mouth of the Nile near Rosetta, they unexpectedly came upon a stone with inscriptions in three different kinds of writing. The first was in Old Egyptian hieroglyphics. The second was in a script about which scholars were not at once clear: it was the cursive form of the

[1] The first and third characters stand for differing gutturals; the second character originally meant j; numbers 13–14 and 15–16 are two different kinds of *ḫ* and s sounds.

Egyptian script from the last pre-Christian centuries ("Demotic").
The third was in Greek. The stone was taken to Cairo and studied
by members of the Egyptian Institute which Napoleon had founded
there, and copies were sent to France. They were included in that
imposing work in many folio volumes, the *Description de l'Égypte*,
which began to appear in 1809. Meanwhile, in 1801, the stone itself
had been seized at the general's house by the victorious English,
despite the attempt of the French to save it by representing it as
his private property. The sarcastic remarks of the French officers
and men were of no avail. In 1802 it was taken to England and given
a place in the British Museum, where it still stands, with the legend
"Conquered by the British Armies." Yet, it was not an Englishman, but a French scholar who was to conquer the stone in
earnest.

The Rosetta inscription is an adulatory decree, quite uninteresting
in itself, passed by the Egyptian priests on the coronation of the
child king Ptolemy V in 196 B.C. It served for Egypt much as the
trilingual inscriptions of Darius and Xerxes served for Babylon: as
a key to the ancient tradition which, after maintaining itself for four
thousand years, had been forgotten, when, at the threshold of the
Christian era, the last sparks of ancient culture died out and were
succeeded by a new foreign culture which only gradually grew strong
enough in the course of two thousand years to take up other tasks
than those inherited from its own past.

The Greek text contains some well-known proper names: *Ptole-
maios, Berenike, Alexandros.* Scholars attempted to find these repeated in the Egyptian texts, first of all in the Demotic. The Swede
Åkerblad may be named as the first to work intensively on the
Demotic text. He perceived that the names must be spelled in some
form of alphabet, and determined the meaning of a great many characters. The alphabetical system was not particularly surprising in
the Demotic script, which in its external appearance resembles
closely various purely alphabetical systems of writing. But that the
picture-characters of the hieroglyphics contained an alphabet was a
much less obvious idea, which did not accord with opinions previously held. Yet comparison with the Greek text turned scholars'
thoughts in that direction, and in 1822 and 1824 François Champollion succeeded in deciphering the hieroglyphics and in pointing out
the relationship of the language with Coptic. The hieroglyphics now
led the way to an understanding of the Demotic system of writing,

which was definitively deciphered in 1848 by the German Heinrich Brugsch.

A great many Egyptian texts have revealed their contents to us in the course of the nineteenth century: royal edicts and reports of victory, religious documents, medical books, household remedies for everything imaginable — against fleas and flies, mice and snakes — didactic poems, epics, prose tales. A multitude of scholars have

FRANÇOIS CHAMPOLLION
[After H. Hartleben, *Champollion*]

labored with this material and recognized more and more clearly the true form of the language. It must suffice here to name the Frenchmen Emmanuel de Rougé and G. Maspero, and the Germans Richard Lepsius and Adolf Erman.

Ancient Egyptian writing did not disappear without leaving some influence behind it. When the Christian Egyptians began to write with Greek letters they used a number of Demotic characters to supplement the Greek alphabet, which lacked signs for some of the Coptic sounds. And in Nubia, near ancient Meroe, we find monuments from the Roman period inscribed in a system almost completely alphabetical (with characters for vowels and consonants) based upon Egyptian characters. This system has been deciphered by F. Ll. Griffith, but the language is still obscure. If the script and the language belong to the ancestors of the present Nubians, that people has not kept faith with its invention, for its ancient Christian

RICHARD LEPSIUS
[After Georg Ebers, *Richard Lepsius*]

literature (see above, p. 122) employs an alphabet which is based on the Coptic system.

THE SEMITIC ALPHABET

Of course the Semitic alphabet *per se* did not require discovery in the nineteenth century. It lives, indeed, to this day in various forms, and the whole world, so to speak, knows two of them: the Hebrew alphabet is that of the Old Testament and the Arabic alphabet is one of the most widely used today as the script of all Mohammedans. But the oldest forms of the Semitic alphabet were not known before the nineteenth century.

That century brought to light the most ancient documents written in the Semitic alphabet, and in so doing shed unexpected light upon the relations between this alphabet and various other alphabets, so that it may now be regarded as proved that all known alphabets descend from the Semitic.

The oldest monuments in the Semitic alphabet come from people inhabiting regions adjoining Canaan: the Phœnicians toward the north along the sea, the Moabites toward the south, east of the Dead Sea.

The most ancient documents originate with the Phœnicians. A very brief inscription on a bronze bowl broken into eight pieces was discovered in 1877 in an antique shop at Cyprus. The author designates himself as the "servant of King Hiram of Sidon." If this is Solomon's contemporary, King Hiram of Tyre, the inscription must be dated in the tenth century before Christ. But some scholars prefer Hiram II (eighth century before Christ). A chronological uncertainty of another kind attaches to a large inscription discovered in a tomb at Byblus in 1923, published in 1924: the epitaph of Ahiram, king of Byblus. Since the tomb contained also some canopic fragments with the name Rameses II, scholars have ascribed the inscription to the thirteenth century before Christ. But the tomb was not intact: it had been opened and plundered in remote antiquity, and we therefore must consider the possibility that the fragments were taken there by the plunderers. If such was the case, there is no direct criterion for determining the exact date of the inscription.[1] It is very old, at any rate. From Moab we have a very remarkable triumphal inscription of King Mesha, dating from about 900 B.C. It was large — thirty-four lines long — sufficient to give us the whole alphabet, and important in that its date could be determined with certainty, since King Mesha is mentioned in the Bible, and the inscription treats precisely of the wars of the Moabites with the Israelites and their king Omri and his son. It was found in 1868, and both French and German scholars attempted to gain possession of it. The Berlin professor Petermann represented the Germans in the bargaining with the Bedouins; but when Clermont-Ganneau, representing French interests, entered the field, the Bedouins advanced the price far beyond the sum that Petermann was authorized to pay. He then made the mistake of trying to obtain the stone by the help of the Turkish authorities. The Bedouins, whose feelings of independence were out-

---

[1] But cf. now on the Byblus inscriptions *Comptes rendus de l'Académie des Inscriptions et Belles-Lettres*, 1929, p. 251.

raged, resolved to prevent Turkish intermeddling, and smashed the stone by heating it and throwing cold water upon it. Fortunately Clermont-Ganneau had a copy, which is now preserved in the Louvre, along with some fragments of the original.

The ancient form of the alphabet which we know through these inscriptions is especially important in that it makes possible the proof that both the Greek and Indian alphabets descend from the Semitic. This relationship becomes obvious the moment one places the oldest forms of the Greek and Indian alphabets side by side with the Semitic, as in the accompanying table.

The Greeks called the alphabet Phœnician, because they themselves had learned it from the Phœnicians. But we have no reason to believe that the Phœnicians had any proprietary rights in it above the other peoples of Canaan. We cannot even call it the Palestine alphabet if that term implies that it originated in Palestine; for the alphabet appears very early also in an entirely different region, Southern Arabia. Here we find inscriptions which go back, if not to so ancient a period as those in Palestine, at least as far as the eighth century before Christ; and these portray the alphabet in a shape which cannot be explained by the Palestine forms, but which points back to an original common to both.

Niebuhr (see p. 154) drew attention in his travel book to the fact that old inscriptions exist in Southern Arabia. In the nineteenth century a great number of travellers, enduring unspeakable hardships and dangers which cost the life of many an intrepid scholar, achieved a knowledge of about two thousand of these inscriptions. Joseph Halévy in particular distinguished himself; disguised as a poor Jew from Jerusalem, he travelled in 1870 through the most difficult and inaccessible parts of Southern Arabia, proceeding from one Jewish community to another, and sharing the security the Jews enjoyed — according to the chivalrous ideas of the Bedouins, it was a disgrace to kill an unarmed Jew — as well as the contempt with which they were regarded. Nothing worse than a sound beating happened to him, and he returned with about seven hundred inscriptions. Later the Austrian Edward Glaser visited Southern Arabia repeatedly (in 1882–84, 1885, 1887–88, and 1892), likewise under most adventurous circumstances. On his last journey he met with such unsettled conditions that he had to give up travelling in the country; but he instructed some Bedouins in the art of making paper copies, and paid them in cash for each copy they brought him.

THE OLD SEMITIC ALPHABET COMPARED WITH THE GREEK AND THE INDIAN ALPHABETS.

OLD SEMITIC			OLDEST GREEK ALPHABET			OLDEST INDIAN FORMS	
Character	Name in Hebrew	Indicates syllables beginning with	Character	Name (later and older pronunciation)	Designates	Character	Designates
𐤀	'alef	'	𐤀	alpha	a	𐤀	a
𐤁	bēth	b	𐤁	bēta (bäta)	b	𐤁	ba
𐤂	gimel	g	𐤂	gamma	g	𐤂	ga
𐤃	dāleth	d	𐤃	delta	d	𐤃	dha
𐤄	hē	h	𐤄	epsilon (ē)	e	𐤄	ha
𐤅	wāw	w	𐤅	digamma (vau)	w, v	𐤅	va
𐤆	zayin	z	𐤆	zēta (dzäta)	dz	𐤆	dža
𐤇	ḫēth	ḫ	𐤇	ēta (hāta)	{ h, later ā	𐤇	gha
𐤈	ṭēth	ṭ	𐤈	thēta (thäta)	th	𐤈	tha
𐤉	yōd	y	𐤉	iōta (iäta)	i	𐤉	ya
𐤊	kaf	k	𐤊	kappa	k	𐤊	ka
𐤋	lāmed	l	𐤋	lambda	l	𐤋	la
𐤌	mēm	m	𐤌	mȳ (mū)	m	𐤌	ma
𐤍	nūn	n	𐤍	nȳ (nū)	n	𐤍	na
𐤎	sāmech	s	𐤎	ksī (ksē)	khs	𐤎	sa
𐤏	'ayin	'(1)	𐤏	omicron (ō)	o	𐤏	ē
𐤐	pē	p	𐤐	pī (pē)	p	𐤐	pa
𐤑	ṣādē	ṣ	𐤑	(sampī)	s	𐤑	ča
𐤒	ḳof	ḳ	𐤒	koppa	k	𐤒	kha
𐤓	rēś	r	𐤓	rhō (rhä́)	r	𐤓	ra
𐤔	šīn	ś and š	𐤔	sigma	s	𐤔	śa
𐤕	tāw	t	𐤕	tau	t	𐤕	ta

(1) A peculiar h-like guttural.

This method gave surprisingly good results. The Bedouins were zealous, and succeeded in reaching places where no European had yet set foot. The greater part of the results of Glaser's journey has not yet been published, for he hoarded many hundreds of inscriptions until his death, and the study of this material will require considerable time.

The Ethiopian alphabet is a descendant of the Southern Arabian form. From the Palestinian form all the other Semitic alphabets are derived, including North Arabic, which through the power of Islam became not only the Common Arabic, but, so to speak, the Common Mohammedan alphabet.

The Semitic alphabet is a syllabic script of quite the same sort as the twenty-four simple characters of Egyptian. The characters are neutral as to vowels. A given sign designates all the syllables which consist of a given consonant and any vowel, and can also designate the consonant alone when it is not followed by a vowel: *'alef* means *'a, 'i, 'u, '*, etc., *bēth* means *ba, bi, bu, b*, etc. All this was just as natural in Semitic as in Egyptian, because the syllabic structure was the same (cf. above, p. 146; in Assyrian alone some of the original characteristics of the Semitic syllabic structure had worn off). The method of procedure in leaving the vowel undetermined and thus saving a great number of syllabic characters was quite tolerable from the Semitic and Egyptian point of view. In spite of this vagueness, the syllabic characters quickly led the reader's thoughts to the proper sphere of meaning, and the exact reading would appear from the context. In Semitic, instances could not occur where a false vowel would conduct one into a wholly different sphere of meaning, as in the cases of English *kill call, den done, hat hate hit hot hut*.

The only effort toward a more exact determination of the vowels which can be pointed out in Semitic from ancient times is the use of *y, w*, and *'* to indicate that the preceding character is to be pronounced with a long *ī*, long *ū*, or long *ā*. In some cases this method of writing was etymological (*ī* arose from *iy*, etc.), and it was imitated in other cases where there was no etymological justification. These *y-, w-*, and *'alef* characters were called *matres lectionis*, "mothers of reading" (reading aids).

On the other hand, it was not until quite late that the device was hit upon of indicating the short vowels by the addition of lines, curls, dots, and so on, over and under the old syllabic characters. In Arabic a line is put over the syllabic character if it is to be pronounced with *a*, under it if it is pronounced with *i*, a comma-like curl above it if it is with *u*, a not completely closed circle over one pronounced without a vowel (قَتَلَ *ḳatala*, قُتِلَ

kutila, يَقْتُلُ *yaktulu*). But these so-called vowel-marks are not letters, not the expressions of an analysis by which the syllables are divided into two parts, but merely distinguishing (diacritical) marks like our accents and signs of length, or like the dots, curls, and hooks over *ö*, *â*, *š*, etc. In this connection, it is characteristic that the absence of a vowel also has its special diacritical mark, and that all of this embellishment is not in daily use, but is employed only when one wishes to be particularly clear. The fundamental syllabic character of the system is not abandoned because of this late device. In one Semitic alphabet, the Ethiopian, the vowel-marks are not written over or under the basic characters, but are united with them (i.e. not like our *ö*, *š*, but like *φ*, *ð*, etc.). This is in a way a retrograde movement in the direction of the pre-alphabetic systems. The situation is almost the same as in Cyprian, where there are special characters for *ka*, *ke*, *ki*, *ko*, *ku*, although it is not so refractory, as the characters for syllables which begin with the same consonant at least resemble one another and are derived from one and the same original character according to a definite rule.

As a result of the neutrality of the characters as to vowels, the Semitic alphabet informs us only of the consonants. We see, for instance, in the oldest Phœnician inscriptions, that the word for *king* contains the consonants *mlk*. Here we readily recognize Hebrew *melech*, Arabic *maliku(n)*, Assyrian *malku*, but how the word was pronounced in Phœnician we cannot know. Yet it does not follow that the characters are consonant-characters: they are syllabic.

The question of the origin of the Semitic alphabet has set many pens going in the course of the century. Unfortunately it must be said that a great deal that has been written on the subject has been a waste of paper. It may be taken for granted that one or another foreign system of writing must underlie it. Such a simple system does not come into existence without a long historical development. But in its home it apparently has no very long pre-history. Perhaps we dare not infer too much from the fact that the princes of Palestine about 1400 B.C. still failed to use this script in their correspondence with Egypt (evidenced by the Amarna discovery; see above, p. 164). This fact is no positive reason for believing that it was not yet in existence. Indeed, there is no reason for denying that it may be considerably older than the period at which it suddenly appears within our ken. But, on the other hand, we cannot regard it as accidental that there is neither in Palestine nor in Southern Arabia any trace of the older stages of development which are prerequisite for such a system. If these older stages were not completed in the native land, they must have been completed elsewhere; and in general it seems to be the rule that the great simplifications in methods of writing occur in the course of their transference from one people to another.

If we glance over the systems of writing current in the ancient world, we quickly perceive that it is possible to seek in but one direction. It is quite impossible to consider deriving the Semitic system from the Assyrian, as some scholars have wished. The Semitic system cannot derive from one so uniform as the Assyrian, but only from a picture-system, a system of hieroglyphics; for the characters are obviously pictures: *'alef* means "ox," and the character is a conventionally-drawn ox-head; *dāleth* means "door," and the character may very well represent a three-cornered tent-door; *'ayin* is "eye," *šīn* "tooth," and the characters correspond well enough. Quite certainly the Babylonian system was originally a picture-system (see above, p. 149), but it had ceased to be such two thousand years before the Semitic system appears. And even if one were willing to reckon with a two-thousand-year hiatus, and to disregard the difference in direction — Assyrian being written from left to right, Semitic from right to left — the Assyrian hypothesis will nevertheless founder upon another rock. A system of writing which had arisen through the simplification of the Assyrian would *not* be neutral with regard to vowels; like the Old Persian, it would have different characters for syllables with different vowels. For similar reasons it is hardly possible to consider the Hittite hieroglyphs or the Cretan system. Thus, we can consider only the Egyptian hieroglyphs, to which Champollion and de Rougé had already referred, and which geographical and historical reasons would naturally suggest as a probable source.

Here is precisely the internal agreement which above all else is a requisite for accepting relationship. In comparison with this fact, it is of little significance that there are many difficulties involved in pointing out similarities between Semitic and Egyptian in the form of the characters. In particular, no one has succeeded in indicating any thorough and evident similarity between the Semitic alphabet and the twenty-four simple characters of Egyptian.

Quite recently it has been thought that the connecting link between the Egyptian and Semitic systems of writing had been found on the Sinai Peninsula. Here, in 1905, an expedition sent by the Egypt Exploration Fund under the conduct of Flinders Petrie discovered, in copper and malachite mines used by the Egyptians and in the ruins of a temple dedicated to the goddess Hathor (the divinity of malachite), a number of roughly made objects in the Egyptian style, but obviously not of Egyptian workmanship — a kneeling human figure, a bust, a sphinx, eight inscribed stones — with inscriptions which gave the impression of Egyptian hieroglyphics in meaningless order mixed with unknown characters.[1] The sphinx has such inscriptions on its right and left sides, but on its shoulders are genuine Egyptian inscriptions. Thus this sphinx may serve in some degree as one of the bilingual monuments so extraordinarily important in deciphering. These Sinai inscriptions seem to belong to a period between 1850 and 1500 B.C. Scholars have therefore thought of bringing them into connection with the Hyksos people, a Semitic pastoral tribe who broke in upon Egypt from the desert toward the east about 1700 B.C., and ruled there for over a century, until they were driven out into Palestine about 1500 B.C.

Petrie had insisted that the Sinai inscriptions were not meaningless combinations of characters, but an actual system of writing, and an alphabetical system at that. In 1916 Alan H. Gardiner attempted to decipher the script, starting with the assumption that the language was Semitic. Almost all the characters exhibit clear resemblances with Egyptian hieroglyphics; but by employing, instead of the Egyptian sound-values, the Semitic names for the things represented or the names of the characters in the Semitic alphabet which resembled the hieroglyphics most closely, and then spelling the initial consonants of these names together, Gardiner extracted a plausible meaning from a group of four characters which was repeated in several of the inscriptions. It might very well be the Semitic name for the goddess Hathor.

If Gardiner's deciphering is right, we must conceive of the Semitic alphabet as having been formed in a way somewhat different from that which we might perhaps have supposed *a priori*. Naturally, the Semites learned the principles of spelling from the Egyptians; but they did not compound their alphabet from characters which in Egyptian already possessed either partially or altogether the sound-values required in Semitic. On the contrary, they chose their characters quite freely, without regard to their application in Egyptian, and used them with a value suggested by the Semitic names of the

[1] In 1927 an American expedition (Kirsopp Lake, Robert P. Blake, Arthur W. Johnson) discovered more Sinai inscriptions.

hieroglyphic pictures. For instance, they took over the Egyptian hieroglyph for "eye," but did not concern themselves in the least with the Egyptian pronunciation of that hieroglyph. In Semitic "eye" was 'ayin, and they applied the hieroglyph in the alphabet to agree with this. Thus they did not take over the Egyptian alphabet of twenty-four characters, although it could easily have been brought into conformity with Semitic, but constructed an entirely new alphabet. To the modern, in whose mind letters are connected only with

According to Gardiner's deciphering this probably reads:

m ' h b ' l (t)
y w d l b ' l t

This has been interpreted:
From him by the goddess beloved.
A memorial to the goddess.

THE SINAI SPHINX AND THE INSCRIPTIONS ON ITS SIDES
[After Eisler, *Die kenitischen Weihinschriften*, and Sethe, *Nachrichten der Gesellschaft der Wissenschaften*, Göttingen 1917.]

completely abstract conceptions of sounds, this may seem a remarkably roundabout method, but for the naïve ideas of that time, when it was impossible to forget that letters were pictures, such procedure must have appeared quite natural.

Meanwhile, however, Gardiner's deciphering cannot be accepted as fully proved, since thus far there has been no complete interpretation of the inscriptions. The latest attempt was made by H. Grimme in 1923.

The alphabet spread north of Palestine very early. Since 1890 we have known of a number of old inscriptions from the region near Zendžirli, in the extreme north of Syria on the boundaries of Asia Minor. They go back to the eighth century before Christ, perhaps to an even earlier period. One of the oldest, perhaps the oldest, which was first thoroughly investigated by Lidzbarski in 1909–10, is composed in a language incomprehensible to us. It is obviously the language spoken here at the zenith of the Hittites' power, but it contains a few names of Semitic divinities, and, apparently, other scraps of Semitic. The remaining inscriptions are Semitic (Aramaic), though some of them contain traces of the ancient language of the country. The Aramaic inscriptions of Nineveh and Babylon begin a little later.

From the Arameans the alphabet made its way to Iran, where, under the name of the Pehlevi ("Parthian") alphabet, it has acquired a sorrowful renown. The strength of the Aramaic alphabet here became its weakness. It was easy and quick to write, but rapidity brought about hasty cursive forms by which many originally different characters (for instance, *wāw* and *nūn*) fell together so that they could not be distinguished. The same sort of thing happened in Middle English manuscripts, where *n* and *u* coincided so closely that the scribes resorted to the arbitrary change of the vowel to *o* to distinguish the two; or we may compare the similar indistinctness in German handwriting, where confusion is avoided by putting a curl over the *u*. But in the Pehlevi alphabet no remedy was attempted for these coincidences. On the contrary, the difficulty of reading was increased by writing whole words in Aramaic, although undoubtedly they were read in the language of the country itself; an instance is *malkā* "king," read *šāh*. We know something of this method from our own usage: we write the Latin abbreviation & = *et*, but read *and*; *viz.* = *videlicet*, but read *namely*, and so on. In Pehlevi this sort of thing occurs wholesale.

The Pehlevi alphabet undoubtedly developed among the Parthians, who were the rulers of Iran under the dynasty of the Arsacides, from the time of Alexander the Great to the third century of our era. But it passed from the Parthians to the Persians, who continued to use it until the advance of the Mohammedans; and to the close of the nineteenth century it was known almost exclusively from Persian inscriptions and coins and from Middle Persian literature.

SPECIMEN OF THE
AVESTA ALPHABET

ō r t š u þ a r a z
Read from right to left:
Zarapuštro (nominative of the name of the founder of the religion)

The great discoveries in Chinese Turkestan (see p. 192) first revealed the existence of a Middle Parthian literary language written in the Pehlevi alphabet. However refractory the Pehlevi alphabet was, it was yet susceptible of reform, and the Persians improved it materially when they employed it in recording their sacred book, the *Avesta* (see above, p. 25). Every character was given its own easily recognizable form, and vowel characters were introduced. But however much we may admire the men who constructed the Avestan system, they cannot be regarded as the independent inventors of a method of writing vowels and consonants. It must be remembered that they worked in the fourth century after Christ in a country which had passed through a Greek period.

From the center of culture of the Syrians (Edessa, now Urfah) a new form of the alphabet was disseminated in the post-Christian period even more widely than the Aramaic alphabet in the pre-

F. C. ANDREAS

Christian period. The recent discoveries in Chinese Turkestan have shown us that an alphabet very close to the Syrian had reached the territory of the Sogdians, in the northeastern extreme of Iran.[1] From here the alphabet made its way to the Northern peoples of the Altaic family — the Uighurians, the Mongols, and the Manchus,[2] where the Semitic *matres lectionis* were applied so widely that the script was almost converted into a vowel- and consonant-system. But this is simply a discovery of America after Columbus, and in these North-

[1] It was the German F. C. Andreas who fixed one of the newly found Iranian languages as Sogdian; the French scholar Gauthiot has written a Sogdian grammar.

[2] See above, pp. 111, 112.

ern alphabets there are still many traces of the Semitic origin and the original syllabic character of the script.

Of the third thrust of the Semitic alphabet we do not need to seek information in inscriptions. It went forth from Arabia with Mohammedanism. But this thrust did not give rise to a number of national alphabets, as in the earlier instances. The Arabian (North Arabian) alphabet maintained itself everywhere. At the most, it has been ex-

ROBERT GAUTHIOT

tended here and there with more of the diacritical marks, distinguishing dots, which it had already largely adopted to designate shades of sound or to distinguish between letters which had coincided in the course of the development of the cursive style (to the Arabians' ؟ *b*, ؟ *t*, ؟ *p*, ؟ *n*, and ؟ *y*, the Persians and Turks added a character ؟ to designate *p*). For some of the Mohammedan peoples — the Persians, for instance — the Arabic system was passably sufficient, whereas for others, like the Turks, it was a misfortune. The wealth of vowels in Turkish simply cannot be expressed by means of the Arabic alphabet; Turkish written in Arabic letters is virtually illegible. Yet few Turks raised their voices in the wilderness to recommend the adoption of another alphabet; the great majority shuddered at any attack upon the sacred alphabet of the *Koran*, and, indeed, the Turks even attempted, not long ago, to force this alphabet upon another race, the Albanians. Only quite recently a change has taken place. First the Soviet republic of Azerbaijan adopted the Latin alphabet. Then in 1926 a Turkish congress held in Baku passed resolutions in favor of adopting it; and finally in November, 1928, the government in Angora sanctioned a law that the Latin alphabet should be the only one allowed in the whole Osmanli republic. The change of alphabet has been carried through with admirable energy; but certainly all the difficulties have not yet been overcome.

THE MORE DISTANT OFFSHOOTS OF THE SEMITIC ALPHABET

As more distant offshoots of the Semitic alphabet we may mention the Berber alphabet, the Indian alphabets, and the Old Turkish alphabet — the Turkish "runes." The Berber alphabet, which is discussed above on p. 121, is easily recognizable as Semitic; only the Indian alphabets and the Turkish runes require further discussion.

The Indian Alphabets

India had to be discovered twice by nineteenth-century linguistics. The first discovery came about through acquaintance with the uninterrupted literary tradition which from time immemorial — perhaps from 1500 B.C. — has passed from generation to generation in India. This is discussed above, pp. 18 ff. But later there followed a new discovery of the country, in that we came to stand face to face with antiquity — came to read, not what had been copied by one hand after another through long centuries, but the very writing which an Indian king had caused to be hewn into rock more than two thousand years ago. This now had to be laboriously deciphered, for no tradition had preserved recollection how it should be read.

The most ancient Indian inscriptions date from the Buddhist king Aśoka (263–222 B.C.). This king, ruler of the greatest empire which ever existed in India, was in the beginning of his reign a worldly-minded, cruel, and revengeful prince, who among other atrocities is said to have slain his nine brothers. Through a miracle he was visited by pangs of conscience for his terrible deeds against the Buddhists, was converted to Buddhism, and became the powerful protector of his new faith. In various parts of his mighty empire, from the extreme west to the extreme east, from Nepal in the north to Mysore in the south, he had inscriptions hewn on cliffs and pillars propagating the teachings of Buddhism and disclosing one fact or another about himself. He names also the contemporary kings in the various Greek empires, and his inscriptions have become the fixed point for Indian chronology, of which the literature teaches us almost nothing.

Aśoka employed two different alphabets. Toward the northwest on the borders of Afghanistan an alphabet is used which is written from right to left. In the rest of the empire another and more advanced alphabet is used, which reads from left to right. We now know that the first (the local) alphabet is that designated in Indian literature by the name *Kharōṣṭhī*, while the other (the Common Indian) bears the name of the *Brāhmī* alphabet.

Some of Aśoka's inscriptions were known as early as 1784 and were published in 1801. But they resisted all attempts at deciphering until, in 1837, the Englishman James Prinsep succeeded in extracting their secret. Prinsep first worked on the northwestern characters, for which assistance could be found in the bilingual coins from the Greek empires bordering on India; but his really great accomplishment was the interpretation of Aśoka's inscriptions in the Common Indian character. Without outside help these inscriptions could hardly have been deciphered, but in 1837 Prinsep obtained a key: a number of brief inscriptions from a temple near Bhopal, in Central India. He saw that these must have been inscribed on gifts made to the temple by private individuals, and that the obvious content must be "so-and-so's gift." Then it was easy to find the characters which must mean " ——'s gift," and not particularly difficult to ascertain how these must be pronounced in an Indian language (Prakrit). The few characters thus ascertained by Prinsep, and his acquaintance with the forms of Indian names, enabled him to read the proper names. Then he attacked the ancient royal monuments, and succeeded in translating one of Aśoka's inscriptions, cut upon a pillar which a Mohammedan prince of the fourteenth century had taken to Delhi and used to ornament a fort. The next year Prinsep turned to two of Aśoka's great cliff inscriptions. But over-exertion and the unhealthy climate put an end to his activity in 1840. Since that time investigation has been carried further by the Frenchman E. Senart and the German Georg Bühler.

To Bühler we owe the most recent study of the origin of the Indian alphabets. With regard to the Northwestern (the Kharōṣṭhī) there could not be much doubt, as the similarities with the Aramaic alphabet are striking. It must have come from Iran. It is natural to turn to Iran when the introduction of writing in India is under discussion. The word for "writing" in Indian is *dipi-*, which we know from Old Persian.[1] From the form of the characters it may be supposed that the Kharōṣṭhī alphabet originated in the fifth century before Christ. But it is much more difficult to reach an opinion on Brāhmī writing, which shows much older forms. Its origin has been sought by some scholars in Southern Arabia, but in all probability Bühler is right in his belief that it also is of Aramaic origin. Several characters which may well be considered the original nucleus of the Indian alphabet agree, some of them very strikingly, with the oldest North Semitic alphabets (compare the table opposite p. 168). The transformations can be explained in part by certain definite principles. The Indians did not write the characters upon the line, as we do, but underneath (i.e. hanging down from an upper line). In connection with this usage, some characters were inverted, so that the "heaviest" part pointed down. Moreover, there is nothing at all improbable in Bühler's conception of the meaning that the twenty-two Semitic characters might have acquired in Indian. The twenty-two Indian sound-values agree very naturally with the Semitic, and together constitute a system by which Indian could have been written, though very roughly. But undeniably the Indians needed several more characters, and these they added, doubtless very quickly. If we follow Bühler in his juxtaposition of Semitic and Indian characters, then we must necessarily follow him in his chronological conclusions and push back the beginnings of the Brāhmī alphabet to a very ancient period, conjecturally 800 B.C. Much more difficult is the question of its provenience. Bühler guesses that it came overseas from Mesopotamia, by an entirely different route from that followed by the Kharōṣṭhī. The points of agreement in the internal systems of both alphabets would then be explained as due to the fact that the Kharōṣṭhī had been influenced by the Brāhmī.

It lies outside the limits of the present condensed treatment to examine more closely the development of the Indian characters which has given them the form that we know from the Sanskrit alphabet

---

[1] See above, p. 154. The word occurs exactly in this form in Aśoka's Kharōṣṭhī inscriptions; the Common Sanskrit form, however, is *lipi-*.

(Dēvanāgarī) now in use. These changes in shape have little interest
for us, and the internal system of the script has not changed, for to
this day it is what it was from the first, a syllabic system brought to
its greatest perfection, so that it expresses the sounds of the language
with complete phonetic exactness, and yet comprises but a small
number of characters. The greatest part is played by the thirty-
three characters for syllables consisting of a consonant plus *a* —
ka, kha, ga, gha, ta, na, ya, ra, etc. By additions to these, above and
below the line, or before and after the basic character, syllables with
other vowels are expressed — *tā, tē, ti, tu*, etc. If the syllabic character is written together with the following character, it is to be read
without a vowel. This method of expressing a consonant without
a following vowel is applied without regard to the beginning or ending of words; the writing runs consecutively, without separation of
words. At the close of a sentence, however, another method is
employed: a special mark is added to the syllabic character to indicate that it is to be read without a vowel. This system of expressing

SPECIMEN OF DĒVANĀGARĪ

sa mā di śa tpi tā pu traṁ li kha lē kham ma mā ǰña yā

na tē na   li khi tō lē khaḥ pi tu rā ǰñā na kha ndi tā

To be read:

samādi´at pitā putraṁ likha lekham mamāǰñayā
natēna likhitō lēkhaḥ pitur ājñā na khānditā

"The father commanded the son: write a letter after my command! Bowing wrote he the letter; the father's command was not broken." But in
the last line the reader will almost unavoidably read *na tēna*, etc., "He wrote
not the letter; the father's command was not broken." This may be compared with the sort of pun possible in English (only orally) with such words
as *an ice-man, a nice man*.

vowels or their absence can be followed in principle back to the oldest inscriptions. It can easily be seen that it has a strong similarity
to the method which the Semites themselves hit upon much later,
but used as a rule only under extraordinary circumstances (see
above, p. 180). But the Brāhmī script has also had from the very
earliest times to the present day a series of characters which consist

of a vowel alone — $a, i, u, \bar{e}$, etc. This must be considered the greatest deviation from the principles of the Semitic alphabet.

But otherwise the Semitic foundation, the originally vowel-neutral syllabic character, appears so clearly that this characteristic alone would be sufficient proof of Semitic origin. And in spite of the great independence with which the Indians developed the alphabet, they did not get so far away from its origin but that a return to it is still possible. Even in recent times business men in India have shown a tendency to omit the distinguishing vowel marks, but this has been combated strongly by the English government and by the native rulers. The courts refuse to recognize as legal evidence accountbooks which do not have the vowel-marks, and the schools teach the children to write correctly. Naturally the omission of the vowelmarks in a non-Semitic language produces uncertainty, and anecdotes are current evidence of the confusion attendant upon their omission. Thus, once upon a time a merchant is supposed to have sent his relatives a letter which immediately called forth tears and wailing. They read (in Modern Indian): "Uncle died to-day, and Aunt beats her breast." A sympathetic neighbor asked to see the letter, and found the correct meaning: "Uncle has gone to Ajmīr, and Aunt is in Kot."

From the Indian alphabet a whole series of other alphabets are descended, which extend throughout the large territory in Southern Asia, from Thibet to Java.

Discoveries in Chinese Turkestan. Tokharian

Very recently discoveries of the highest importance have been made in the desert regions of Eastern Turkestan, which in late antiquity and during the early Middle Ages seem to have been meetingplaces for Chinese, Indian, Iranian, and (through Iran) Semitic cultures, while at the same time the proximity to the Turks had its influence also. These discoveries are of significance for many different fields of languages and systems of writing, and not least for the languages using the Indian system.

At the beginning of the last decade of the nineteenth century attention was directed to certain fragmentary manuscripts which had reached Calcutta, St. Petersburg, and London from Eastern Turkestan, and several expeditions (Finnish, Russian, Anglo-Indian, German, French, and Japanese) were soon sent out with the object of systematically investigating the ruined towns of Central Asia

(Turfan, Khotan, etc.). The results were astonishing. The extraordinarily dry climate and the shifting sand which covered places previously inhabited had preserved a great many manuscripts, wooden tablets, and so on, as well as paintings and other treasures. For example, the leader of the second Anglo-Indian expedition in 1906–08, the Hungarian Marc Aurel Stein, found in an oasis a room in a temple grotto in which were layers of manuscripts in bundles to a height of

F. W. K. MÜLLER

ten feet above the floor; altogether they filled a space of about five hundred cubic feet. Dr. Stein ascertained that the accumulation of the manuscripts and the walling up of the grotto took place shortly after A.D. 1000, presumably because of the dangers of war. In the ruins of an old fort Dr. Stein made further rich discoveries. All kinds of rubbish which covered the floor of the room in which changing garrisons lived and maintained their headquarters, issued passes, and so on, until the ninth century of our era, yielded valuable material. German expeditions conducted by A. von Le Coq and another German scholar have sent back hundreds of chests full of archæological and linguistic treasures from various parts of the country. The French emissary Pelliot brought back a considerable number of manuscripts to Paris, and so it went. In these innumerable discoveries all the peoples who dwelt or travelled in the country during the first thousand years of the Christian era were linguistically represented, as connecting roads between China and the western countries ran through this region. Chinese, Thibetan, Syrian, Iranian, and Turkish (Uighurian) were included.

The harvest was of great importance for India, for many important Indian manuscripts came to light. In general, the oldest Indian manuscripts we have come from Eastern Turkestan; they date from the first centuries of the Christian era. In India itself there were no manuscripts older than the eleventh century. Climate and insects are responsible for the destruction of whatever was not renewed by constant copying. The oldest known before the discoveries in Eastern Turkestan were two written palm leaves from the year 609, which were preserved in Japan. We shall not consider further these Indian manuscripts or their significance for the history of the alphabet and the history of literature.

But the Brāhmī system of writing was used in Chinese Turkestan for other languages than Indian. It was used for two foreign languages, as R. Hoernle first pointed out. The exact determination of these two languages so unexpectedly revealed has cost scholars a good deal of trouble. One of them obviously belonged in the southern part of the country, where the discoveries were made chiefly in the district of Khotan, while the other belonged in the northern part, where the discoveries were made principally in the region about Turfan. The southern language was investigated by the German Leumann and the Norwegian Sten Konow, not to mention others. It has turned out to be an Iranian language with many loan-words from Indian. We may safely call it *Sakian*. Besides Parthian and Sogdian [1] it is the third otherwise wholly unknown Iranian language discovered in Chinese Turkestan.

The other of the two languages which use the Brāhmī script, the language of the north, was called *Tokharian* by F. W. K. Müller, a scholar who has done much in working over the great store of linguistic material from Eastern Turkestan. This name has been objected to time and again, but there are many arguments for its correctness, despite the fact that what we knew previously of the Tokharians through the Greeks points toward a region farther west.

Tokharian is plainly an Indo-European language, but belongs to

[1] See pp. 29, 185.

none of the groups hitherto known. Remarkably enough, it resembles the western Indo-European languages, especially Italic and Celtic, more than the eastern, and shows no particular agreement with its nearest neighbors, Iranian and Indian. Tokharian occurs in two dialects, which differ markedly from each other. We shall designate them as East Tokharian, belonging about Karashar, and West Tokharian, belonging near Kutcha. The eastern dialect was the first

SYLVAIN LÉVI

to become better known, for in 1908 the Germans Sieg and Siegling published a grammatical sketch, accompanied by a brief specimen. They printed a volume of texts in 1921. The western dialect, which proves to be in a much older stage, we know through the labors of two French scholars, Sylvain Lévi and A. Meillet.

As for the date when the languages flourished, Sylvain Lévi has determined that some of the West Tokharian texts date from the seventh century after Christ. Through Chinese sources, the history of the Kutcha people can be followed from the first century before Christ to 800 after Christ. They played a prominent part in civilization, and distinguished themselves especially in music. Through them Buddhism seems to have been brought to China about the first century after Christ. By the year 1000 their cultural period was over: the Turks ruled.

It has been possible to achieve a fairly good understanding of Tokharian with relative quickness, partly because the meaning of many words was found plainly indicated in Sanskrit, and partly because some of the texts were translations of Indian works already known, often of Buddhist content. When all the texts have been published and worked over, we may hope to acquire a rather complete knowledge of this remarkable language, rediscovered after a thousand years of oblivion.

Tokharian writing shows a little peculiarity which is of universal interest; that is, the way in which it indicates syllables with a special ə-like vowel which was very common in Tokharian, but was not present in Indian. In agreement with the whole system of the Indian alphabet, one would naturally expect that a new vowel-mark would have been introduced for syllables containing the ə vowel. To a certain degree this actually happened. Just as, for instance, the basic character for the syllable ča acquires the meanings čā, či, ču, and so on, by the addition of various Indian vowel-marks, so in Tokharian it acquires the meaning čə by the addition of a newly invented Tokharian vowel-mark (two dots, like those above German ä). But in most cases the syllables containing the ə vowel are expressed by a separate basic character. Thus the basic character ka, through addition of the Indian vowel-marks, acquires the meanings kā, ki, ku, and so on, but the syllable kə has a wholly different basic character. This is really a relapse to the pre-alphabetical syllabic systems of writing. How this method of procedure was developed is too far afield from the present subject to discuss here. But such a relapse is always possible, as long as an alphabet has not attained a clear analysis of the syllables into vowels and consonants. This very relapse is illuminating in regard to the actual character of the Semitic alphabet.

The Old Turkish "Runes." The Hungarian "Runes"

As early as the beginning of the eighteenth century, under the rule of Peter the Great, some rune-like inscriptions were discovered in Southern Siberia along the upper course of the Yenisei. A great many scholars busied themselves with these inscriptions, and made the most varied conjectures about their language, but they had been published so imperfectly that no deciphering was possible. In 1887 and 1888 two expeditions were sent by Finland to Siberia. As a result, a valuable edition of the inscriptions appeared in 1889, and the Finnish scholar O. Donner published a word-index to them. Meantime, in 1889 similar inscriptions had been discovered beyond the Russian boundary in Mongolia, near the river Orkhon, and not far from the ruins of Karakorum. Here were found two very large stones with inscriptions partly in unknown characters (very long), partly in Chinese (shorter. On one of the stones the Chinese text was virtually illegible). The Orkhon inscriptions were published in both Finland and Russia in 1892; in the Finnish edition a word-index and a translation of the legible Chinese inscription were added. At the outset, it was clear that the Chinese text could not be a translation of the main inscriptions; but it did serve at least as a means of dating the monuments. It informed us that one of the stones was erected A.D. 732 in memory of a Turkish prince who had died in the previous year. The Chinese had much intercourse with these "Turks" — we know of no other name for this people than the word now employed as a designation in common for the whole group of languages — from the middle of the sixth century until 745, when they were conquered by another Turkish people, the Uighurians. The other stone was dated A.D. 735, and was erected, as we now know, in memory of the brother of the prince who died in 731 — namely, of the chief ruler of the Turks, Bilgä Kagan. Toward the close of the century a stone presumably fifteen years older was found, about three hundred kilometers to the east. It was the tombstone of the minister of Bilgä Kagan, Tonyukuk.

The historical situation into which the 732 stone introduces us must naturally direct our thoughts to the conjecture that the principal language of the inscription was Turkish. But this was not certain in advance; as a matter of fact, there was a number of other possibilities, and in the beginning of the nineties scholars were still completely baffled by the problem.

But in 1893 the Danish scholar Vilhelm Thomsen succeeded in reading the inscriptions completely. A careful examination enabled him to determine several facts important for deciphering them: the order of the lines, the direction within the lines, the internal system of the script, which characters indicated vowels, and so on. But for actual reading a key was necessary. Thomsen naturally tried to find in the unknown text some of the proper names which occurred in the Chinese. But he sought long in vain, and for a very good reason: most of the names are not there. One of them does occur, obviously: that of the prince for whom the monument was erected in 732. But even after Thomsen had discovered the group of characters in which this name was to be sought, he found it impossible for a long time to make the characters agree. The fact is that the Chinese rendering of foreign names is necessarily very inaccurate, and it is difficult to determine the pronunciation of the Chinese characters in the eighth century. According to the Chinese rendering of the prince's name (in modern pronunciation *K'we-te-kin*) scholars had conjectured the Turkish form *Kök-tigin*: but finally the word turned out to be *Kül-tigin*. In addition to his name, Thomsen found also the Turkish

VILHELM THOMSEN

word *täñgri*, "heaven," in a group of characters which occurred often in the places where one might expect to find the Khan's title ("the celestial Khan"). The two words together contained all the characters necessary for reading a word occurring very frequently

$$\text{Ϛ ϒ Ν h}$$
$$k \quad r \quad ü \quad t$$
$$(4 \quad 3 \quad 2 \quad 1)$$

türk, the name of the people whose prince Kültigin was. Now progress was rapid. The language proved to be the oldest and purest Turkish dialect we know. The day on which Thomsen succeeded in deciphering the writing was November 25, 1893. At the meeting of the Copenhagen Academy of Science on December 15 Thomsen announced his discovery. He had determined all the characters, and determined them in such a manner that there has been nothing to correct since. The entire deciphering was completed at one stroke. Then followed his edition of the Orkhon inscriptions, a model from the point of view of philology and linguistics. It contains a transcription of the text, and a translation with notes and word-index, and two introductory essays: one on the system of writing together with an investigation of the origin of the alphabet, and a second including the necessary historical orientation. As an illustration of the size of the Orkhon inscriptions with their information about the warlike deeds of the Turks, it will suffice to remark that the texts alone fill twenty octavo pages in Thomsen's edition.

Kül-tigin's "Turks" were not the only Turkish tribe to use "runic" writing. The Yenisei inscriptions, the script of which gives the impression of being older and closer to the original than that of the Orkhon inscriptions, belong presumably to another tribe, possibly to the Kirghiz. The Uighurians also used this system. In addition to the two stones mentioned above, a third was found near Orkhon, not so old by a hundred years and badly damaged, with an inscription in three texts, the languages of which were determined after the discoveries in Chinese Turkestan. The first text, which is written in "runes," is Uighurian; the second, Sogdian, is written in the Sogdian script which the Uighurians later adopted; the third is Chinese. The characters on this monument have rounded forms which indicate that the runic alphabet had been used in books as well. And among the numerous Turkish manuscripts which came to light with the great discoveries in Chinese Turkestan there actually are some written in the runic alphabet. It was, then, a national Turkish alphabet; but in the course of time the Turks forsook their national script.

This national alphabet, the best the Turks have ever had, was undoubtedly developed from an Aramaic source, apparently without an Iranian intermediary. How early it developed we do not know, but there is no reason for going much farther back than the sixth century after Christ. The rune-like form with vertical or oblique lines predominating — there are some curved lines, also, but very few horizontal ones — may have been influenced by the writing material first used; presumably it was wood. In its internal system the writing shows clearly its relationship to the Semitic alphabet with its vowel-neutral syllabic characters. Vowel-characters were known, but were used only to a limited extent. The idea was certainly taken from the Semitic reading aids (*matres lectionis*), but the Turks invented one or two new characters in order to express the Turkish wealth of vowels more satisfactorily. Nevertheless, the vowel-characters are insufficient, and a remedy was sought by varying most of the "consonantal characters" (syllabic characters) according to the vowel of the syllable. The words *alty* "six" and *kälti* "come" are written thus, with different *l*- and *t*- characters:

$$ \text{Γ ⟐ ⌐}\qquad\qquad \text{Γ h Υ ⅂} $$
$$ y\ t\ l\qquad\qquad\quad i\ t\ l\ k $$

The aid to the proper reading of the vowels contained in these different "consonant-characters" is considerably augmented by the phenomenon in Turkish known as *vowel harmony*, which requires vowels of the same kind in all the syllables of a word: either pure back vowels like *a, y, o, u*,[1] or pure front vowels like *ä, i, ö, ü*. These double [2] "consonant-characters" were created partly by using the superfluous abundance in the Semitic alphabet — *t* in *alty* is Semitic *tēth*, *t* in *kälti* Semitic *tāw* [3] — partly by inventing new characters. One is tempted to say that it was done by a stroke of genius, but one must not forget, nevertheless, that it is one of the relapses to the pre-alphabetic principles to which we referred on p. 196 above.

It is very remarkable that a vowel at the beginning of a word can be left undesignated, for instance the *a* in *alty* "six." But that this is no argument against the originally Semitic source of the script becomes clear when we consider that the same peculiarity occurs in the Tuaregian system of writing (see above, p. 121). There this rule occurs in connection with another rule that the names of the characters must end in the characteristic consonant: *yab, yah, yaw, yet* = *b, h, w, t*, etc. It is easy to suppose here that the Turks also replaced the old Semitic names of letters which were so lengthy with names like *al, äl, at, ät*. And one of the manuscript finds in Chinese Turkestan has confirmed this conjecture. We cannot go into more detail as to the manner in which these names arose.

---

[1] Students of Turkish linguistics use the letter *y* for a vowel similar to the one in English *but*, originally much more closed.

[2] In the case of the *k* syllables there were even five characters.

[3] The Turks could not hear the difference between the two Semitic *t* sounds, but they could hear that they influenced the following sounds differently. The case was in a way repeated later with the adoption of the Arabic alphabet; the Osmans, for instance, write *taš* "a stone" with the character *tēth*, but *täpä* "a hill" with *tāw*.

Vilhelm Thomsen's name, which is so intimately associated with the Turkish "runes," is also associated, by a curious accident, with a decisive event in the investigation of another system of writing, to which the name of "runes" has likewise been given, but which belongs far from the chief cities of the "Turks" and Uighurians.

A German scholar, who was preparing an edition of Hans Dern-schwam's manuscript description of a journey undertaken in Turkey and Asia Minor in 1553–55, found in it a copy of an inscription in Constantinople, in rune-like characters. It had been on an oblong white stone near the ground in the outer wall of a stable belonging to an inn where the ambassadors of the European powers were quartered and guarded while they waited — often for some time — for an audience with the sultan. The buildings were destroyed by fire in 1865 and later completely demolished, so that now there is very little probability that the inscription will ever come to light again. The rune-like nature of the characters prompted the editor to send a photograph and an inquiry to Copenhagen in 1913. These came into the hands of Vilhelm Thomsen. Although he was ill, he was able to say at once what sort of writing it was, and to give a preliminary interpretation. Members of a waiting embassy had in-scribed it in their native Hungarian language in the year 1515, as a diversion and relief from their impatience. They chose to write it in a script which they knew would be incomprehensible. At the most dangerous place, where the Turkish sultan is named, they took care to make it even more incomprehensible by using a rare character and an abbreviation.

This incomprehensible script was in an alphabet used by the Szeklians,[1] a Hungarian tribe in Transylvania, about whose age and authenticity scholars had been in great doubt during the nineteenth century. Now the doubt is completely dispelled, and the discovery of the Constantinople inscription contributed substantially toward dispelling it. It has prompted inquiries and investigations which are recorded in a stately tome published in 1915 by the Hungarian scholar Sebestyén.

The first references to the existence of such a system of writing are in the chronicles of the thirteenth century. The evidence of the fifteenth century is plainer, and the sources of this century expressly state that the letters were usually cut in wood, whence, obviously, is

---

[1] The Hungarian name of the tribe is *Székely*. Pronunciation: *sz* like *s*, *é* a long *e*, *ly* a palatal-ized *l*.

to be explained their rune-like appearance. The oldest specimen is a copy of a medieval perpetual calendar which was found in Transylvania in the seventeenth century. The copy is preserved in Bologna, but until very recently it was forgotten. In addition to the Constantinople inscription, two church inscriptions, from 1501 and 1668, are known, and there are various old copies of the alphabet itself. In the seventeenth century the writing was still sufficiently alive for a Calvinistic superintendent in Transylvania to propose that it be adopted for daily use in order to put an end to the confusion in spelling, though he complained that at that time there were but few who understood the old writing.

As a rule, Szeklian is written from right to left. A remarkable peculiarity is that the vowel *e* is not indicated, even at the beginning of a word. The word *ezer* "thousand," is written

$$\text{Ͷ Ꞵ}$$
$$r \quad z$$

The letter *e* is obligatory only at the end of a word. The other vowels are always written with their own individual characters. The names of the characters are *a*, *eb*, *ec*, *ed*, and so on; they end with the consonant they designate. There are two *k* characters, *ek* and *ak*: the *ak* character includes a preceding *a*.

The reason Vilhelm Thomsen was able to determine instantly the nature of the Constantinople inscription was that he had already been face to face with the alphabet when working on the Old Turkish inscriptions. Hungarian scholars had attempted to find similarities between the Yenisei-Orkhon alphabet and the Szeklian even before the Turkish inscriptions were deciphered. In his work on the Orkhon inscriptions, Vilhelm Thomsen declared that the points of conspicuous resemblance between the alphabets were too slight to prove relationship. This scepticism, however, does not now seem justified.

It is noteworthy that the Hungarian scholar P. Király de Dada, against whom Thomsen's remark was directed, did not go altogether astray in his comparisons. Every one familiar with the study of alphabets knows how extremely rash it is to attempt comparison between characters whose meanings are not known. This kind of comparison can lead to valid results only when two very closely related alphabets are compared. And, indeed, after the deciphering of the Old Turkish inscriptions, it became clear that most of Király de Dada's comparisons were meaningless, for the characters he had compared designated entirely different sounds. But in some cases he had hit upon Turkish characters with the same meaning as the Hungarian, although he relied exclusively on similarities in form.

If now, when the Turkish inscriptions have been deciphered, we compare the symbols in the two alphabets (Turkish and Szeklian) with reference to their meaning, we cannot fail to be struck by the frequency with which the symbols thus compared show similarity in form. When we add the direction of writing and a certain agreement in internal principle, it becomes very difficult to believe that all this is due to accident.

In addition, historical considerations strongly recommend the acceptance of a relationship. The idea that the Szeklian alphabet may have been a purely artificial secret writing can no longer be accepted. It must be an ordinary system, developed historically and naturally. But it cannot have developed from the systems of any of the surrounding European peoples, and therefore it must either have been brought from the Asiatic home of the Magyars or have been taken over from one of the peoples with whom they came in contact during their migration to Europe. In the latter case, only a Turkish people can be considered. Finally it is worthy of mention that the Hungarian word for "to write," *ír-*, is borrowed from Turkish *jaz-* (Hungarian *r* from Turkish *z* is regular).

Hence there is a strong probability that the Szeklian alphabet is a continuation of the Old Turkish, and thus a new feature is added to the picture of the dissemination of the Turkish alphabet.

THE COUNTRIES OF THE GREEK ALPHABET

In the regions dominated by the Greek alphabet the nineteenth century has had problems to solve similar to those which we have observed in Asia and Africa. Unknown varieties of writing have been found and deciphered; unknown languages have risen from their graves. And even in the case of the Greeks themselves, inscriptions have yielded rich material (and imposed many new problems) for both philology and linguistics, and for the history of writing, also.

Greek Discoveries

The discoveries of papyri in Egypt about the close of the century have played an important part in Greek philology. Papyri, most of which are found in excavating old rubbish heaps, are our oldest

THE OLD TURKISH AND THE SZEKLIAN ALPHABETS

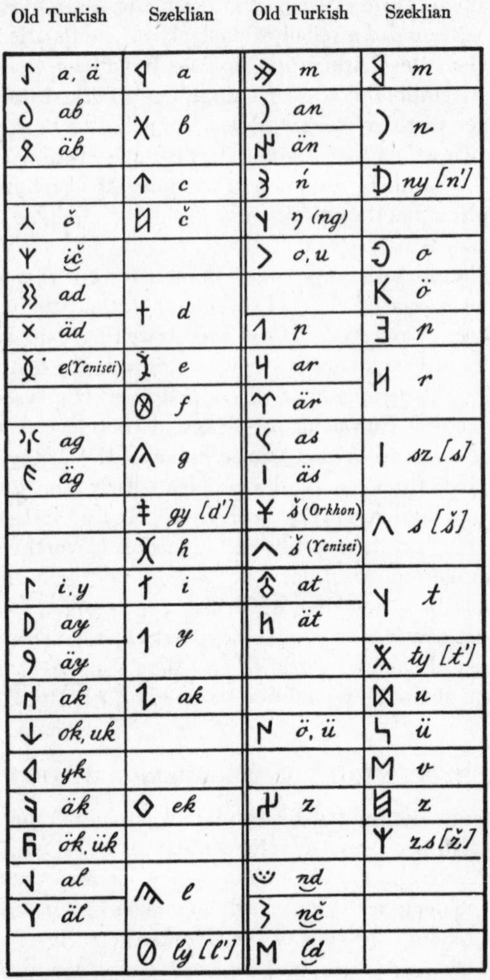

Old Turkish	Szeklian	Old Turkish	Szeklian
ſ *a, ä*	ᕾ *a*	⋙ *m*	৪ *m*
⊃ *ab*	X *ß*	) *an*	) *n*
४ *äb*		ᴎ *än*	
	↑ *c*	३ *ń*	Ð *ny [n']*
⅄ *č*	ᴚ *č*	⅄ *η (ng)*	
�год *ič*		> *o, u*	Ɔ *o*
⅀ *ad*	† *d*		K *ö*
× *äd*		⅂ *p*	Ǝ *p*
ꙮ *e(Yenisei)*	⅄ *e*	ч *ar*	ᴎ *r*
	⊗ *f*	⋎ *är*	
⏉ *ag*	ᴧ *g*	⊻ *as*	∣ *sz [s]*
ᕤ *äg*		∣ *äs*	
	‡ *gy [d']*	⅄ *š (Orkhon)*	ᴧ *s [š]*
	X *h*	ᴧ *š (Yenisei)*	
Γ *i, y*	↑ *i*	⍟ *at*	Ч *t*
Ð *ay*	⅂ *ỵ*	h *ät*	
9 *äy*			X *ty [t']*
N *ak*	Ɫ *ak*		⋈ *u*
↓ *ok, uk*		Ṉ *ö, ü*	Ⴑ *ü*
◁ *yk*			M *v*
� *äk*	◇ *ek*	↲ *z*	⅄ *z*
ꓤ *ök, ük*			⅄ *zs [ž]*
↓ *al*	ᴧ *l*	ꙷ *nd*	
Y *äl*		३ *nč*	
	Ø *ly [l']*	M *ld*	

Greek manuscripts. While the oldest Greek literary codex which we knew before, a manuscript of Homer, did not antedate the fifth or sixth century after Christ,[1] some of the papyri take us back to 300 B.C., and we have a great many from the first centuries of our era.

[1] Some Biblical codices date from the fourth century.

Many of these papyri are literary in content, and several of them awakened the greatest interest on their appearance, because they made us acquainted with authors whose works were thought to have been completely lost, or of whom we had only the merest fragments. Others are documents and private papers of all sorts which give us a remarkable insight into the most varied kinds of life among the Greeks in Egyptian provincial towns. Most of these documents are carefully dated, and dates are of course of vast importance. Not all of these papyri are in Greek; other languages are represented, though not to so great an extent — Latin, Coptic, and Arabic. From the Jews in Elephantine in Upper Egypt we have a number of Aramaic papyri.

While the papyri take us back only to the Hellenistic period after Alexander the Great, the inscriptions go back much farther, to the eighth century before Christ. The immense significance which the study of inscriptions [1] has had for our whole knowledge of Greek antiquity can be set forth here only in its main outlines. Although most of the fifty thousand inscriptions are brief, and although each one, if taken by itself, seems of slight consequence, in the main they make up a considerable body of information. And, as a matter of fact, longer and more important inscriptions have been found. Keen interest was aroused in 1885 by the publication of an inscription about six hundred lines long from Gortyna in Crete, dating from the fifth century before Christ and containing a number of regulations concerning domestic rights; among many other interesting passages there is a section on "sole heiresses," daughters who, when there were no sons, inherited their parents' fortune, but in return were bound to marry one of their father's brothers.

Linguistically the inscriptions are of great importance because they supply direct evidence of the language of antiquity in many parts of the country and in widely varying periods. On the basis of inscriptions from Athens and Attica, K. Meisterhans wrote a relatively complete exposition of Attic grammar, which in several respects supplements or corrects the literary tradition which has been handed down through so many intermediaries, but supports this tradition in all essentials. Still greater is the importance of the inscriptions for our knowledge of the ancient Greek dialects. The information about them in the literature is very insufficient, and the manuscripts are less trustworthy than the manuscripts of Attic literature, for obvious

[1] Among its founders the philologist Böckh may be named. See above, pp. 84 ff.

reasons. In the inscriptions we have much richer and better material, and they are the principal basis for that knowledge of the ancient Greek dialects which was gained during the nineteenth century (cf. pp. 84 ff., 89 ff., above).

Finally, the inscriptions yielded us an unexpected abundance of material for the history of the Greek alphabets.[1]

The oldest Greek inscription is from Attica, and dates from the eighth century before Christ. But the most ancient form of the alphabet is found in inscriptions from two of the farthest south of the Cyclades, Melos and Thera (=Milo and Santorini), and from Crete. The inscriptions from Thera go back to the seventh century before Christ, but are very brief: names of divinities cut in stone, epitaphs of the shortest kind, consisting almost exclusively of proper names, and — a very impressive phenomenon from that period, when writing was scarce — rock inscriptions consisting of proper names with additions which place them in the same category with the perverse scribblings of street urchins. Somewhat later are the old inscriptions from Melos. Here we have a text which extends to two lines of verse recording a gift to a temple. Latest of all are the corresponding inscriptions from Crete, where the old form of the alphabet maintained itself for an exceptionally long time. From here we have such detailed and interesting texts as the great legal inscription of Gortyna. Strangely enough, an additional source of information about the appearance of the most ancient Greek alphabet is a number of reproductions of the alphabet itself, which have been found in Etruria. An example is a vase from the city of Caere.

By means of these sources we can determine that the oldest forms of the Greek letters from *alpha* to *tau* are virtually identical with the most ancient Semitic characters (compare the table above, p. 179). The direction of writing was, as with the Semites, from right to left, or from right to left and back like a furrow: first a line from right to left, then the next back from left to right, while the letters themselves shift in direction: in the first line ꓭ was written, in the second B, and so on. But in course of time the direction from left to right prevailed.

The internal principle of this script, however, differed radically from the Semitic basis. The Greek system is from the first a vowel

---

[1] Most thoroughly studied by A. Kirchhoff in *Studien zur Geschichte des griechischen Alphabets* (1863 and 1887).

and consonant system. As characters for the vowels, the Semitic *'alef*, *hē* and *'ayin* were used, since they were not needed as consonant signs because Greek was not so rich in gutturals as the Semitic, the only Greek guttural being *h*, which was designated by the Semitic *ḥēth*. In the Greek pronunciation of the names of these three Semitic characters the gutturals disappeared completely, but the last one seems to have exerted an influence with which we are well acquainted in modern Semitic languages: it gave a following *a* a deeper sound. Thus the names began, to the Greek ear, with *a*, *e*, *o*, and were used as the characters for these sounds. Nor did the Greeks need the Semitic *yōd* as a consonant character, since they had no consonantal *y*. In their pronunciation of the name of this letter they substituted a vowel *i* for the consonant *y* and used the character as a sign for *i*.

In its fully developed form the Greek alphabet has five letters after *T* (tau) for which there are no corresponding letters in Semitic:

    Υ ypsilon (older upsilon)
    Φ phī   (phē)
    X khī   (khē)
    Ψ psī   (psē)
    Ω ōmega (å̄mega, with a long open sound as in Eng. *paw*).

The inscriptions teach us that the first of these five characters belonged to all forms of the Greek alphabet, that the last originally belonged to a single alphabet which finally extended over the whole of Greece (the Ionian alphabet), and finally that the three characters in between were absent in the oldest period in Melos, Thera, and Crete, but otherwise had a very wide and very early dissemination in all parts of Greece, though not everywhere in the same application.

Y belongs to all the Greek alphabets as a fifth vowel character beside *A*, *E*, *I*, and *O*. The Greek vowel system could not be well expressed with less than these five. Actually the five were not sufficient, as there were two kinds of *e*, a closed *e*, *ē*, and an open *ǟ*, and two kinds of *o*, a closed *o*, *ō*, and an open *å*. But the Greeks continued for a long time to indicate these two different kinds of *e* and *o* by the same characters. Finally the Ionians hit upon a remedy by inventing the character Ω for the *å̄* sound and by taking the ancient *häta* (which they pronounced without the *h*) into use as the designation for the *ǟ* sound.

Of the letters Φ, X, Ψ only Φ had the same value throughout ancient Greece. The meaning of the other two characters varied; thus X meant *kh* in the Eastern Greek alphabets,[1] but in the Western Greek alphabets it meant such a *k* sound plus *s*, of which the Latin X is an example today.

[1] A *k* sound different from that of Greek *K*; Greek χ and *K* differed from each other much as English and French *K*, only still more strongly.

The provenience of the letters Υ, Φ, X, Ψ is disputed. Some scholars regard them as transformations of other letters in the alphabet, just as Ω is a transformation of O; others suppose that they were borrowed from some other system of writing. In that case we should have to think of a script which was known and used by the Greeks before the adoption of the Semitic alphabet. It is worthy of remark that the syllabic characters of Cyprus for *u* and *ksa* resemble closely Greek Υ and X (cf. the table, p. 169). There is really nothing improbable in the idea that the Greeks, who took over the alphabet from the Phœnicians, were previously acquainted with the syllabic system which we know from Cyprus from a relatively late period, but which necessarily must have existed much earlier, and might well have had a somewhat wider use than simply in Cyprus. This hypothesis also casts light upon other characteristics of the formation of the alphabet by the Greeks. The Cyprian characters for the syllables *a*, *e*, *i*, *o* and *u* might have been one of the stimuli which called forth from the Greeks the inspired idea of introducing vowel-characters into the Semitic alphabet.

That the alphabet in Greece is much older than the oldest preserved inscriptions may be regarded as virtually certain. The reason that it still has such a fresh appearance in seventh-century Thera is the same that enabled it to retain a similar appearance much later in Crete: the development had been retarded. Colonists from Chalcis in Eubœa took the alphabet with them to Southern Italy in the eighth century before Christ in its special West Greek form, and at the same time a Greek alphabet including the additional characters φ, etc., was being written in Phrygia. This presupposes a development which must have required some time. The date for the first adoption of the alphabet from the Phœnicians cannot therefore be placed later than 900 B.C. Perhaps an even earlier date would really be more probable.

The Greek Alphabet among Foreign Peoples

From the Greek alphabet a whole series of national alphabets descends. We can distinguish between two periods of dissemination, a pre-Christian and a Christian. In the first the alphabet was disseminated through ordinary intercourse — partly unchanged, partly adapted to the foreign languages — in Asia Minor and Thrace, in Italy, Gaul, and Spain. In the second period it was taken over by various foreign peoples as the medium of a Christian literature: by the Copts in the third century, by the Armenians and Georgians in the fifth, by the Slavs in the ninth, and even by the Goths in the fourth, though in a very individual way (see p. 235).

The peoples who took over and applied the Greek alphabet along with Christianity have preserved their languages, for the most part, and continued the use of the alphabet to the present day (this can be said with some truth even of the Copts). They themselves, then, have told us the meaning of their letters.[1] But of the peoples about the Mediterranean, who had learned their alphabet from the Greeks in pre-Christian times, only one was able to continue its method of writing through the centuries: the Romans. The Roman empire went to pieces, but the Latin language lives on in the whole group of Romance languages, and the Latin alphabet in conjunction with Christianity has conquered half the world.

But the other peoples who wrote in ancient times, each with its own form of the Greek alphabet, have disappeared linguistically, or (I refer to the Mediterranean people farthest to the west) have at least forgotten their national alphabetic tradition. These peoples were rediscovered in the nineteenth century through inscriptions, and, although the discoveries were not accompanied by such dramatic suspense and did not yield such surprising results as those we have chronicled above, yet they were important enough in themselves.

We have inscriptions in the following groups of languages:

(1) Lycian, Carian, Cretan
(2) Lydian, Lemnian, Etruscan
(3) Phrygian, Thracian
(4) Venetic, Messapic
(5) The Italic languages (Latin and Faliscan, Oscan-Umbrian; perhaps also Siculian and Ligurian)
(6) Gaulish
(7) Iberian

In this classification two offshoots of the Latin alphabet are not included, as they lead us far to the north and to other civilizations. They will be discussed later (pp. 229 ff.).

1) *Lycia*, the westernmost province on the southern coast of Asia Minor, or, more accurately, the broad peninsula between the two bays of Adalia and Macri, was in classical times the center of an important civilization which left behind it various monuments, among them a number of inscriptions. The first two Lycian inscriptions became known in Europe in 1811, and a series of expeditions during the first half of the century soon increased the number. Moriz Schmidt published an edition of all the inscriptions known up

[1] For the Goths this does not apply literally; cf. above, pp. 31 ff.

to 1868. In the seventies and eighties the Austrian government sponsored expeditions to Lycia, and a new edition, containing one hundred and fifty inscriptions, mostly from the fifth and fourth centuries before Christ, appeared in 1901.

Moriz Schmidt laid the foundations for the scientific investigation of Lycian, but the greatest progress in understanding the language was made in the last decade of the nineteenth century, and is due

ALF TORP
[After *Festskrift til Professor Torp*, Christiania, 1915]

especially to the Frenchman J. Imbert, the German Rudolf Thurneysen, the Norwegians Sophus Bugge and Alf Torp, and to the Dane Vilhelm Thomsen, who contributed more than any other person to an understanding of the peculiar and involved construction of Lycian.

Most of these inscriptions are epitaphs from rock graves. If one considers how much labor it cost to hew graves out of the solid rock and what care and skill were applied in this labor, one will readily understand why the epitaphs are invariably intended to prevent improper use of the graves. They state precisely for whom the grave is intended, and specify punishments for those who disturb the quiet of the tomb.

The interpretation of these inscriptions was no light task. It was difficult enough in the first place to determine the meaning of the characters. For although the alphabet is of the Greek type, it was adapted in such a peculiar way and amplified by so many novel characters that it became an entirely new thing. However, we have some bilingual inscriptions in Lycian and Greek which have helped

THE XANTHOS STONE
[After *Tituli Asiae minoris*, I]

not only in the reading but also in the interpretation. We now understand the epitaphs very well on the whole; but the other texts remain obscure. Thus, from the town of Xanthos we have a long inscription cut on the four sides of a great hewn stone. It certainly marks a grave, but its contents are historical. The text includes, besides the Lycian, a Greek poem of twelve lines which is undoubtedly related to the subject matter, and although we can recognize in the Lycian itself a long series of proper names, and can even determine that an event occurring in 412 B.C. is mentioned, of which we have an account in Thucydides, we can translate scarcely one sentence correctly. We may plead in excuse the fact that the stone is somewhat dam-

First inscription

ebeññẽ	xupã	me-ti	prñawate	Pumaza	Erteliyeseh	tideimi
this	grave	(and)	built	Pumaza	Erteliyes's	son

hrppi	ladi	ehbi	Uwñte	xumetiyeh	zzimazi	se	tideime	ehbiye
for	wife	his,	Uwinte	xumetiye's	grand-daughter (?),	and	children	his.

Second inscription

Purihimeti-ti	prñawate	Masasah	tideimi
Purihimeti	built,	Masasa's	son,

xupã	ebeññẽ	hrppi	atli	ehbi	se	tideime	ehbiye
grave	this	for	self	his	and	children	his.

TWO LYCIAN INSCRIPTIONS

aged; but what would we not give to understand this great inscription as completely as we understand the Old Turkish inscriptions from the Orkhon river!

The Xanthos stone has special importance for us because it contains, besides the inscription in ordinary Lycian ("Lycian 1"), another in a different dialect ("Lycian 2"), which in many respects seems to be of an older type. Where this dialect was spoken we cannot tell. It occurs only on the Xanthos stone and on a sarcophagus from another city. In both cases the text in Lycian 2 seems to be in metrical form. Obviously, it was an older dialect which maintained itself in poetical use at a time when a later form had not only become the current spoken idiom but was also employed as a written language for prose and practical matters.

There has been much discussion as to the family to which the Lycian language belongs. Probably it is Indo-European, with which it agrees morphologically, so far as we know it; but the vocabulary is very unfamiliar. The question is somewhat the same as in the case of the Hittites (see above, p. 165), and Lycian is probably quite closely related to Hittite. I have pointed out above (p. 16) that the place-names and proper names make such a relationship possible, and the language of the inscriptions does not contradict this impression. But it must not be expected that the resemblances between the Hittite language of about 1500 B.C. and the Lycian inscriptions of the fifth and fourth centuries before Christ will be very striking. Our fragmentary knowledge of the two languages makes it almost impossible to select the corresponding elements. The different systems of writing may also obscure some of the similarities. And in addition there is a lapse of a thousand years and a distance in location which even as early as 1500 B.C. may have produced an appreciable difference in dialect.

We have Carian inscriptions to the number of about seventy, some found in Caria itself (the southernmost province on the western coast of Asia Minor), some in Egypt as far south as the boundary of Nubia. When King Psammetichos made an expedition to Elephantine about 600 B.C., a troop of his mercenaries, among whom were Carians and Greeks from Asia Minor, proceeded up the Nile as far as they could by water. On the way back they carved a short description in Greek of their deeds on a colossus near the rock temple in Abu Simbel, and some of them seized the opportunity to immortalize their own names, the Greeks in Greek and the Carians in Carian. This remarkable monument was discovered by Lepsius in 1845.

The Carian inscriptions have been discussed especially by Sayce, by P. Kretschmer, and by the Finn J. Sundwall. But they are brief and difficult to work with. We are still in the dark as to the alphabet. Still, it may be said that in spite of many peculiarities this seems to depend upon the Greek, and that the language must be very close to Lycian.

From the town of Praisos in Crete we have an inscription (see above, p. 171) in ancient Greek letters written furrow-wise (from right to left and back) in a non-Greek language. There are also two later inscriptions from the fourth century before Christ in the same language. We understand absolutely nothing of all these, but have to rely on Herodotus, who says that the pre-Greek population of Crete was related to the Lycians.

2) *Lydia*, the central province on the western coast of Asia Minor, was, according to Herodotus, the native land of the remarkable Etruscan folk in Italy, and this testimony has become more and more strengthened in the light of modern linguistics.

The Etruscans played a very important part as a great power and as disseminators of culture in Italy. Many of the Italian tribes received their alphabet through them. But much points to their having been foreign invaders. To be sure, they were not wholly without kinsmen in the peninsula: the Rhaetians (see above, p. 91) were linguistically close to the Etruscans, according to the testimony of classical authors, which is confirmed by inscriptions found in Rhaetian territory, as was pointed out by Carl Pauli in 1885. But this kinship gives no hint as to the original home of the Etruscans. On the contrary, we may suppose that the Rhaetians were simply one branch of the Etruscans who were forced up into the Alps from their homes in the south by the Gaulish invasion of Italy. The Etruscans themselves regarded the city of Tarquinii (in Southern Etruria, near the sea) as the starting-point of their civilization, and they pretended to know also how long — how many "ages" — their nation had existed. Their reckoning of time was a little peculiar. Each "age," Latin *saeculum*, closed with the death of the man who had lived the longest of those who were alive at the beginning of the "age." This is not very easy to make out; the Etruscans believed, however, that the gods announced the beginning of each new *saeculum* by miracles. If we collect what information we have about these "ages" we reach the conclusion that the Etruscans began to reckon at about the year 1000 B.C., which does not differ materially from the date which modern archæologists regard as that of their immigration.

The Greek name of the Etruscans, *Tyrs-ēnos*, *Tyrrh-ēnos*, seems to point directly to Asia Minor, for the Greeks used the ending *-ēnos* only with Asiatic names, as Saussure pointed out in 1898. Moreover, the Greeks mention the Tyrrhenians as not only in Italy, but also in various parts of their own land: for instance as earlier inhabitants of Athens and of the island of Lemnos, south of Thrace.

Vel Seϑre puia-c
"Vel Seϑre and wife"

Fasti Aneinei   Velcznaś   Titial   śec
"Fasti Aneinei, Velczna's (and) Titia's daughter"

TWO ETRUSCAN INSCRIPTIONS

However, no amount of study of the information contained in the Latin and Greek classics will solve the riddle of the Etruscans.[1] Our hope must rest in the inscriptions.

The Etruscans have left us several thousands of these — a large part of them extremely monotonous reproductions of mere names, often very arbitrarily abbreviated. The oldest can be dated in the seventh and sixth centuries before Christ, but most of them are later. The longest and most noteworthy were found in the nineteenth century. Great interest was awakened in the nineties by the discovery of an Etruscan inscription on a roll of linen wrapped round an Egyptian mummy whose last resting-place is the museum at Agram.

Various scholars, particularly in the last quarter of the nineteenth

[1] Such a study was carefully made by Carl Ottfried Müller in his thorough work *Die Etrusker*, 1828.

century and at the beginning of the twentieth, have energetically attempted to penetrate the language of these inscriptions. The Germans W. Deecke and Carl Pauli, and the Norwegian Alf Torp should be mentioned especially. A collected edition was begun by Pauli in 1893 in collaboration with the Swede O. A. Danielsson, and

O. A. DANIELSSON

was continued after Pauli's death by Danielsson and the German Gustav Herbig, but it is not yet complete. And in spite of all the work that has been done, our knowledge of Etruscan is still very imperfect.

The alphabet presents no great difficulties. It is the Greek alphabet, not with additions, as in Lycian, but with the omission of several characters which the Etruscans could not use. The only added character is *8*, meaning *f*, a sound which abounded in Etruscan but was lacking in Greek. We can read the inscriptions, then, well enough, but we understand only the shorter ones, particularly the conventional epitaphs. Of the longer texts we can merely guess the contents, and understand fragments here and there. The results so far are a rather thorough knowledge of the Etruscan system of names, and a much more modest insight into the general vocabulary. We know the meaning of a small number of Etruscan words, perhaps a hundred, and a good deal about the inflection of nouns, but very little about the verbs. As for the numerals, we are fortunate enough to have two dice on which the numbers from one to six are written in letters, but thus far no one has succeeded in determining with any certainty the order of these six numerals. From Etruscan dice with the numerals themselves we know that there were definite rules for the arrangement of numbers on dice. The opposite sides must have either two successive numerals, as 1–2, 3–4, 5–6, or two numbers whose sum is seven, as 1–6, 2–5, 3–4. On the dice which have the names of the numbers written out, we have the following opposites:

$$max — zal$$
$$\vartheta u \quad — hu\vartheta$$
$$\acute{s}a \quad — ci\,^1$$

Within this scheme scholars have attempted to determine the correct order of the numerals by inferences drawn from inscriptions where the same numerals or corresponding multiples of ten appear in a comprehensible context. As yet we have no certain results.

Along with the work of interpretation, inquiry has been made into the question of the relationship of Etruscan to other languages. It is easy to understand why scholars have guessed that Etruscan is an Indo-European tongue, for in some features it actually resembles Indo-European. But it cannot be denied that in this connection some investigators have employed defective methods and have indulged their imagination in altogether too lively a fashion. W. Deecke's attitude toward the problem was peculiar in that he finally adopted the theory against which he himself at first had directed a crushing critique. We can now say with certainty that Etruscan is not Indo-European. The numerals themselves prove it: all Indo-European languages agree plainly with one another in the numerals from two on, but Etruscan differs. Deecke thought he could get a glimpse of the similarity when he arranged the words for the numerals in the following way:

$$max \quad \vartheta u \quad zal \quad hu\vartheta \quad ci \quad \acute{s}a$$

But this order is impossible because of their positions on the dice. The closest approach to Deecke's arrangement which the dice permit is:

$$max \quad zal \quad \vartheta u \quad hu\vartheta \quad ci \quad \acute{s}a,$$

¹ χ and ϑ were certainly pronounced like k and t in English; z like German $z(ts)$; $\acute{s}$ was a special sound which we cannot determine accurately. $c = k$.

an arrangement which actually has had, and still has, its advocates. If one wishes to perceive here some similarity to our family of languages, one is compelled to accept a mass of sound-changes and other alterations for which it would be difficult to find parallels even in the most recent languages of the family. The Indo-European hypothesis therefore had to disappear. On the other hand, after a plea made by Vilhelm Thomsen in 1899, scholars have lately directed their attention toward certain similarities between Etruscan and the Caucasian languages.

The Caucasian hypothesis recommends itself also because it can easily be brought into agreement with the information concerning the origin and race of the Etruscans left by classical authors, and so far consistently supported by the discoveries of inscriptions.

In 1886 it became known that an extremely interesting discovery had been made on the island of Lemnos (see p. 215). Two French scholars had found a large stone, almost a meter long, near a country town an hour and a half's journey from the coast. Upon it were a picture of a warrior with a lance in his hand, and an inscription in an old Greek alphabet but in an unknown tongue. Apparently the inscription should be dated about 600 B.C. As for the language, the French scholar Bréal, as well as Sophus Bugge and Carl Pauli, quickly pointed out the striking likeness to Etruscan. Although no satisfactory translation has yet been made, we can scarcely doubt that the observation of the three scholars is correct. The Tyrrhenians of Lemnos mentioned by the Greeks were therefore really related to the Etruscans of Italy.

In connection with the information of Herodotus concerning the relationship between the peoples of Lydia and Etruria, recent discoveries have made an independent opinion possible. For a long time it seemed that the voice of Lydia would remain silent in the great chorus of the national voices of antiquity. Two inscriptions were found, one in Pergamos, north of Lydia, and one in Ephesus, near the southern boundary of Lydia, but they were not understood. It was the keen-sighted scholar Sayce who first explained (in 1895) an inscription on a rock near the Nile as Lydian. But no one felt sure that this could be relied on, and, moreover, the inscription contained, according to Sayce's essentially correct interpretation, only a man's name, *Alus*, in addition to his father's name. But finally

INSCRIPTION ON THE FRONT OF THE LEMNOS STONE

[After Pauli, *Eine vorgriechische Inschrift von Lemnos*]

The letters are:

(Reading upward and around the corner from right to left)   *holaie ː z ː naφoϑ   ziazi ː*

(Above, from right to left)

1.   *ː mara.z ː mav*

(Next line, from left to right)

2.   *sialχvei.z ː ari ː z*

(Next line, from right to left)

3.   *evisϑo ː zeronaiϑ*

(Next word from left to right)

4.   *zivai*

(At the left; from bottom to top)

       vamalasial ː zeronaimorinail
       aker ː tavarzio

On the right-hand side of the stone there is another inscription which contains very much the same words as the front, and makes it probable that the lines above should be read in the order 3, 4, 2, 1.

American excavations in the ancient capital of the Lydians, Sardes, brought to light decisive material. Some thirty inscriptions were found, including an epitaph in two languages with eight lines of Lydian and eight lines of Aramaic. This bilingual text was such an excellent starting-point for the deciphering that by its help we can work our way through some of the shorter inscriptions in Lydian alone. The study of the material was turned over to the Semitic scholar Enno Littmann, who published in 1916 a first instalment of the inscriptions, mostly epitaphs, among them a very pretty one in verse on a plaque of fine white marble. The second instalment was edited in 1924 by W. H. Buckler. It includes a new edition of the inscriptions treated by Littmann and all those discovered elsewhere than at Sardes: fifty-one inscriptions, all told. Some of these are dated: the Lydian-Aramaic is from the tenth year of King Artaxerxes' reign (there were more than one Persian king of this name; the year 394 B.C. must be meant), another is from the fifteenth year of King Artaxerxes, two others are from Alexander's fifth and twelfth years (this seems to be Alexander the Great).

As a specimen of the Lydian alphabet the Lydian part of the Lydian-Aramaic epitaph is reproduced on the previous page. With the assistance of the Aramaic text not only can the value of most of the letters be determined, but the meaning of the words as well. It must suffice here to transcribe the three lowest lines. They should be read from right to left. The letters represented as *ạ* and *ẹ* indicate nasalized vowels, λ a sort of *l* sound:

aktin	*nạhis*	*helλk*	*fẹnsλifid*	*fak-mλ*	*Artimuś*
If then	anyone	on anything	does damage	so him	Artemis
Ibśimsis	*Artimu-k*	*Kulumsis*	*aaraλ*	*biraλ-k*	*kλidaλ*
of Ephesus	and Artemis	of Koloe	from house	and home,	from land
kofuλ-k	*hiraλ*	*helλk*		*bilλ*	*vẹbahẹnt*
and water,	from possessions	(and) everything		his	shall drive forth.

From this we can say that Lydian in the fourth century before Christ was very far from Etruscan. Nevertheless there are such obvious points in common that we must admit that the story of Herodotus bears the seal of truth. Lydian has simply preserved a much older and more primitive appearance than Etruscan. Thus we can conceive of the Tyrrhenians as a viking people (related to the Lydians) who, coming from Asia Minor in very remote antiquity, settled in many places on this side of the sea (in Athens, for instance) and finally founded in Italy a large and powerful empire to which immigration may have continued throughout a considerable period.

If we inquire to which of the cuneiform languages Lydian-Lemnian-Etruscan may be related, the most probable reply must be: Van and Mitanni (see above, p. 150).

The Lydian alphabet is the Greek alphabet with certain omissions and additions. Some characters remind one of Lycian — a fact which is not so very remarkable, for although Lydian and Lycian were not closely related,[1] they were in any case neighboring languages. But the character *8* is remarkable: as in Etruscan, it seems to mean *f*. Since we cannot believe that the Etruscans brought their alphabet with them from Asia Minor — they unquestionably learned to write from the Greeks in southern Italy — the agreement in the character *8*, if it is not purely accidental, must obviously be explained by the hypothesis that the Etruscan character was taken over from Lydian, which would imply that the Etruscans remained in some communication with their native land.

3) *Phrygia*, east and north of Lydia, is the principal home of a third group of languages in Asia Minor. While the Lycian group appears to be Indo-European with many foreign features, and the Lydian group seems to be non-Indo-European with some characteristics reminiscent of our own family, the Phrygian group is clearly Indo-European of the same type as the well-known Indo-European languages.

The earliest records we have from Phrygia are some few inscriptions in an old Greek alphabet similar to that on the stone of Lemnos. The oldest of these date perhaps from the eighth century before Christ. We understand but little of them. But from a much later period, the first centuries of our era, we have about eighty inscriptions written in the contemporary Greek alphabet. We understand much more of them; for instance, a closing formula: "He who does harm to this grave will be cursed." For this we have a Greek key. And the certain understanding of this sentence gives us a clear conception of the Indo-European character of the language.

The first to begin to penetrate the Phrygian inscriptions was Moriz Schmidt, in 1869. But most of them were discovered and published later, largely by the Englishman William M. Ramsay, who travelled in Phrygia in the early eighties. A successor of Ramsay is W. M. Calder, who travelled there in 1908 and 1910.

[1] This is the opinion maintained in the present book.

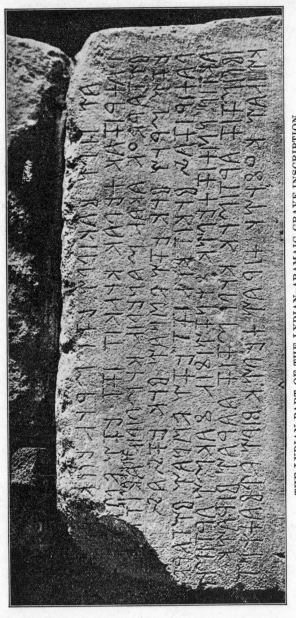

THE LYDIAN PART OF THE LYDIAN–ARAMAIC GRAVE INSCRIPTION

[After Littmann, *Lydian Inscriptions*]

Herodotus informs us that the Phrygians emigrated to Phrygia from Thrace, and that the Armenians in turn were descendants of the Phrygians. This does not seem to be a random shot. Certainly we have but a poor result when we compare our fragments of Phrygian with Armenian. In the whole Phrygian formula for ensuring the quiet of the grave there is not a single word which reminds us of Armenian, with the exception of the word for *this*, and even this word is not more reminiscent of Armenian than of Slavonic or Baltic (Lithuanian and Lettic). It is also quite clear that the oldest form of Armenian is far more decayed than the language of the latest Phrygian inscriptions. But perhaps we should find more points of agreement between the two languages if we knew Phrygian a little better. In any case it is quite certain that both belong to the same regular type of Indo-European and contrast in the same way with all the other ancient languages of Asia Minor, the Lydian and Lycian groups. Nor can we find anything improbable in Herodotus' theory of immigration. On the one hand, we know from cuneiform inscriptions that a foreign population, possibly related to the Lydians and to the Mitanni people, still dwelt in what later became the Armenian district near Lake Van [1] as late as the seventh century before Christ; and from the little we are able to infer from the store of names surviving from antiquity, some sort of connection between Phrygia and Thrace seems thoroughly credible. But the soil of Thrace has long stubbornly denied us inscriptions in the native tongue. Now at last we have a single one on a gold ring found in 1912 in a grave mound in the country town of Ezerovo, near Philippopolis. It is in the Ionian alphabet, and dates from the fourth or fifth century before Christ. Though still virtually unintelligible, it awakens the hope that more may be found.

4) *Venetic and Messapic*, the languages of the eastern coast in ancient Italy, have been discussed above on p. 91. We have many short Venetic inscriptions in the North Etruscan alphabet from the fourth to the second centuries before Christ, and also many Messapic inscriptions, most of them brief, dating from 450 to 150 B.C. Carl Pauli, W. Deecke, Alf Torp, and O. A. Danielsson have taught us something of their contents. A very short Illyrian inscription, found quite recently in the neighborhood of Scutari in Albania, may prove

[1] See above, pp. 73 f., 150 f., 163.

From right to left: *foied uino pipafo (pafo) cra carefo*

"Today shall I drink wine, tomorrow, lack."

FALISCAN INSCRIPTIONS

[After *Corpus inscriptionum Etruscarum*]

From right to left:

Manios	med	fhe	fhaked	Numasioi
Manios	me	has	made	for Numasios

TWO OF THE OLDEST LATIN INSCRIPTIONS

[After Dessau, *Inscriptiones Latinae selectae*, and Zvetaieff, *Inscriptiones Italiae inferioris dialecticae*]

This inscription runs round a triple vase in two lines from right to left, the tops of the letters pointing downward. It begins on the vase which is toward the front in the drawing. The upper line ends just under the first letters of the beginning of the line; the second line, however, does not extend all the way round, but ends on the reverse side of the vase on the left. The inscription contains some corrected mistakes, and also, quite certainly, some that are uncorrected. It is difficult to interpret. It seems fairly clear, however, that it is a love-charm. In Thurneysen's version, it reads thus (uncertain words are in parenthesis; those that are wholly doubtful are omitted):

iouesăt	deiuos	qoi		med	mitat,	nei	ted
(help will)	the god	that one who		me	sends,	if not	thee

endo	cosmis	uirco	sied	asted	noisi	opetoitesiai
against	gentle	a girl	is	and thee		

pacari	uois.
(be favorably looked upon)	thou wilt.

duenos	med	feced	en	manomeinom	dženoi
a good (man)	me	has made	for	good (intention	for a good man):

ne med	maaostatod.
not me	(a bad person shall give).

of some importance for settling the question of the interrelations between Messapic and Illyrian.

5) From the rest of Italy we have a meager supply of inscriptions in Ligurian, in the North Etruscan alphabet, abundant material for Umbrian and Oscan, very scanty materials for Siculian, and no great store of Faliscan inscriptions, but naturally an abundance of inscriptions in Latin itself. All of these languages are discussed above (pp. 92–98). In here classifying them in the *Italic* group, we do so with certain reservations for Siculian and especially for Ligurian.

The smaller fields — Ligurian, Siculian, and Faliscan — have been studied by several scholars already mentioned: Pauli, Torp, Danielsson, Kretschmer, Herbig, Thurneysen, Deecke.

The Latin inscriptions have had much the same importance for Latin philology as the Greek inscriptions have had for the Greek field. They have also been of great importance for the history of the language, although in this respect they cannot be compared with the Greek inscriptions. And finally they have thrown light upon the development of the Latin alphabet. The plan of the present work does not permit us to dwell on this subject, to mention when the most interesting inscriptions were discovered — all of the oldest first came to light in the nineteenth century, more accurately from 1880 on — or to describe in detail the progress of investigation. F. Bücheler was an indefatigable interpreter of Old Latin inscriptions; Thurneysen's acuteness has also thrown light upon the subject.

The most important Oscan and Umbrian inscriptions were known before the beginning of the nineteenth century. Seven bronze tablets with a very long Umbrian inscription (between four and five thousand words), containing directions for a series of religious ceremonies, were found in 1444 near the city of Iguvium (now Gubbio). Originally there were nine tablets, but two of them were lost soon after the discovery. Presumably they date from the third or second century before Christ, and they are the chief source of our knowledge of Umbrian. The remaining Umbrian inscriptions, of which some take us back to a period older than the oldest of the tablets from Iguvium, are very few and quite brief. Oscan inscriptions are much more numerous. The two most important, an agreement between the towns of Abella and Nola, and a fragment of the laws of the town

MAP

OF

ANCIENT ITALY

of Bantia, were discovered in 1745 and 1793. But their interpretation belongs to the nineteenth century (see page 94, above).

The study of the Oscan-Umbrian inscriptions was a task of a very peculiar nature. It cannot be compared with the interpretation of texts written in ancient pre-alphabetical systems whose word-characters furnish a guide to the contents, or with those cases in which bilingual texts exist, for no such assistance was available for Oscan-Umbrian. The results are not comparable to those arrived at elsewhere in the interpretation of very brief inscriptions whose contents were so far indicated by external circumstances that a comparison with distantly related languages (for instance with the Indo-European family in general) was a sufficient guide; for in such cases (in Messapic, for example) texts of greater scope and more varying content have nonplussed scholars. The longer Oscan and Umbrian inscriptions, on the other hand, have been translated completely and with almost entire certainty. And finally, we can draw no comparison with the Old Turkish inscriptions, where the deciphering of the characters was the most difficult undertaking, whereas the interpretation of the text, once it could be read, was supported by closely related key-languages, because its deviations from the known forms of Turkish did not exceed what can be termed a dialectal difference. The difference between Oscan-Umbrian and Latin was much greater: it may be likened to the difference between Old English and German. And yet it was comparison with Latin, together with a profound study of the texts themselves, which revealed their secret.

The service thus rendered by Latin to Oscan-Umbrian has been richly repaid, for it is impossible to overestimate the light which these newly discovered languages throw upon almost every aspect of the history of Latin. Oscan, with its abundance of ancient forms which are far older than the Latin forms, is especially valuable. Umbrian is much more decayed.

Oscan and Umbrian have special alphabets, based mainly on Etruscan; but we possess also Oscan and Umbrian inscriptions in the Latin alphabet. In the extreme south, Oscan was written in the pure Greek alphabet.

6) Just as various are the methods of writing among the *Gauls*. We have some few Gaulish inscriptions from Italy, among them one in Latin and Gaulish. In these the North Etruscan alphabet is used, although it is very deficient in characters. They date from the close

of the second century before Christ. From what is now France we have a number of inscriptions from the time of the Roman emperors, in the contemporary Latin or Greek alphabet: Greek in the south near the Mediterranean, Latin elsewhere. With but one exception,

V.	*Aadirans.*	*V.*		*eítiuvam*	*paam*
V.	Adiranus	V.'s son		money	which

vereiiaí,	*Pompaiianaí*	*trístaamentud*
to youth	the Pompeiian	by will

deded	*eisak*	*eítiuvad*
gave,	for the	money

V.	*Viínikiís*	*Mr.*		*kvaísstur*	*Pomp-*
V.	Vinicius	Mr.'s son		quaestor	the Pom-

aiians	*trííbom*	*ekak*	*kombennieís*
peian,	building	this	the popular assembly's

tanginud	*opsannam*	*deded*	*ísídum*	*profatted*
decision	to erect	gave,	the same	approved it.

"The money which V. Adiranus, V.'s son, bequeathed to the association of young men of Pompeii, for this money V. Vinicius, the son of Mr., Quaestor in Pompeii, contracted the erection of this building after the decision of the popular assembly and inspected (and approved) it likewise (after completion)."

OSCAN INSCRIPTION FROM POMPEII

[After Zvetaieff, *Inscriptiones Italiae inferioris dialecticae*]

the Gaulish inscriptions are all very short, and it is sometimes difficult to understand them. The single exception is the fragments of a calendar from the first or second century of our era, written on bronze tablets which were found in 1897 in the little town of Coligny, in the Département d'Ain. If the calendar had been complete we might have learned a good deal from it; but what we have is one hundred and twenty-one fragments. With great difficulty it was shown after a fashion how they went together; the result, however, was not a unit, but forty-five pieces, some consisting of a single bit, others of several. Thus the instruction we derive from reading them is considerably diminished, and it is still further diminished by the fact that most of the words are abbreviated, as seems to have been customary in calendars at that time. In spite of their scantiness the Gaulish inscriptions have given us a knowledge of old Celtic inflectional endings with which we should not willingly dispense. The vocabulary, however, or rather that part of it whose meaning we can determine, is quite meager.

7) On *Iberian* inscriptions see page 124, above.

Offshoots of the Latin Alphabet

From the Latin alphabet the Irish Ogham alphabet and the Germanic runic alphabet are descended.

Historical conditions were much the same for both of these. Both arose among peoples who were the immediate neighbors of the Romans, but not their subjects, and both arose in heathen times. Thus they are due to the influence of neither the Roman state nor the Roman church, but are the result exclusively of the free interchange between neighbors. Furthermore, a common external condition prevailed with runes and Ogham: the writing was, as we know from the literature, first of all devised to be cut in wood. Even the rôle played by this form of writing in the lives and ideas of the folk was the same with the Irish and the Germans. It was not common property. The science of runes was a great privilege. Likewise Irish saga finds it natural that an especially distinguished man should be called upon to reveal the secret (*rún*, the same word as Old Norse *rún*, "*rune*") of an Ogham inscription. The system is not a simple means of communication, but possesses great magic power. It was discovered by a divine being: for the Scandinavians by Odin, the god of wisdom; for the Irish by Ogma, who is not a late Irish mythological figure, since the name is identical with that of the Gaulish god of eloquence, *Ogmios*, who is mentioned by a Greek author in the second century after Christ. The alphabet of both peoples is arranged in a remarkably irregular way, and is divided into groups (families) with an equal number of characters in each. Sometimes the Scandinavians employed this system to resolve the characters into mere parallel branches on a vertical line. The number of branches to the left and right determined the group of each letter and its position therein.

i   s   a

(third, fifth, and fourth runes in the second group)

Among the Irish this procedure became a fixed rule: the letters always consisted of parallel lines exclusively. The names of the letters were neither among the Irish nor among the Germanic peoples the short Latin names, but long names which were also words in the language. Moreover, there is a remarkable coincidence in the letter *b*, which is called "birch" in Irish (*beith*), in Old English (*beorc*), and in Old Norse (*bjarkan*). Neither the Ogham nor the runic alphabet was ever completely forgotten. It played too great a part in the imagination of the folk. Yet, it was only the scholarship of the nineteenth century which threw light upon the oldest monuments in these kinds of writing.

Obviously, no direct relationship between runic and Ogham can be thought of. In the first centuries of the Christian era there was no connection between the Irish and the Germanic people. One might indeed suppose that the similar psychological atmosphere which surrounds the systems is purely accidental — an outcome of parallel historical conditions; but it is perhaps not too bold to explain the resemblance by the hypothesis that both peoples learned to write from the Gauls, who were neighbors of the West Germanic tribes, and with whom the Irish had constant maritime intercourse by way of the commercial centers at the mouths of the Loire and the Garonne.

Stones with Ogham inscriptions are found all over Ireland, and in Wales and Cornwall as well, but here the language betrays the fact that they are from the hands of Irishmen (see above, p. 55). Finally, we have Ogham inscriptions from Scotland. They are difficult to understand, but there is no doubt that they emanate from the immigrant Irish population which gave the country its name (see p. 55). The writing, then, is a special Irish system.

The Ogham inscriptions extend over a period of several centuries, but to date the beginning of the period exactly is extremely difficult. That we must go back to a time prior to A.D. 500 is certain on linguistic grounds, but how much farther back we should go it is not easy to ascertain. The most cautious scholars content themselves with the fourth century, but those who conjecture the second century

OGHAM STONE FROM DROMLUSK
[After Macalister, *Studies in Irish Epigraphy*]

may come closer to the truth. In any case the Ogham period begins in the heathen period; but Ogham monuments continued to be set up in Christian times, so that we find stones decorated with the Christian cross, and stones with double inscriptions, partly in Ogham and partly in the Latin alphabet which came in with Christianity.

The inscriptions are extremely brief, usually containing little more than a proper name in the genitive: "So-and-so's (stone)." Save for proper names, then, the stones afford only a small vocabulary. But their linguistic value is far from negligible. One of the recent scholars who have done most to extract this gain is John MacNeill, who was imprisoned in 1916 for suspected participation in the Sinn Féin disturbance.

OGHAM STONE FROM FAUNKILL AND THE WOODS
[After Macalister, *Studies in Irish Epigraphy*]

The Ogham alphabet has the following appearance:

The line upon which the characters are placed is the corner of the stone.

There has been no lack of fantastic conjecture regarding the origin of this remarkable script. It is clear at once that Ogham cannot have been an independent Irish invention. A knowledge of the principle of the alphabet must be presupposed, and the particular alphabet in question cannot have been, say, the Phœnician — a conjecture which would also be quite absurd from historical and geographical points of view. The resolution of the syllables into vowels and consonants makes it possible to think only of the Greek or the Latin alphabet. The preponderance of external evidence points most naturally and probably toward the Latin, and indubitable internal evidence points in the same direction: note, for example, the character for *q*, which is applied in the same way as Latin QV. But obviously one cannot expect to recognize the Latin letters in the Ogham characters. It is, indeed, conceivable that *l, d, g, o* are written with two lines because the corresponding Latin letters may be said to consist of two lines: L D G O. But it cannot be regarded as a rule that the number of strokes in the Ogham characters depends upon the appearance of the Latin letters., In many cases, apparently, it depends upon the position of the character in the alphabet, and not vice versa, and the order seems again to be determined by various considerations: on the score of phonetics (hence *u* after *o*, *i* after *e*, *t* after *d*, *q* after *c*, which always meant *k*), of tradition (thus *a* is the first vowel, *b* the first consonant), perhaps also of a certain striving for symmetry between the various divisions (the labial *b* at the beginning of the first division corresponds perhaps to the labial *m* at the beginning of the third division; *s* and *n* at the end of the first division correspond perhaps to *z* and *r* at the end of the third division).[1]

One cannot reasonably use the names of letters (such as *beith, luis*, and so on) as an argument against a Latin origin. Certainly they differ sharply from the short Latin names (*be, el*, etc.), but they are to be explained simply by the fact that the Irish were like some children of today who forget the short meaningless names but can easily remember that "*A* stands for Ann" and so on. And even though a few of the long names depend upon the names of Greek letters (*beith* on Greek *bēta*, for instance), there is no reason for contending that this points away from Latin. The Irish may very well have become acquainted with the Greek names at second hand, for these were not forgotten in the Latin world.

The oldest runic alphabet was used throughout the whole Germanic territory, and it fortunately happens that we have the alphabet itself represented in no less than three instances: on a gold bracteate found in 1774 near Vadstena, in Sweden; on a silver buckle

[1] Quite recently the Norwegian scholar Carl Marstrander has shown that the order of the Ogham characters was determined to a very great extent by the signification of their names. All these names are originally names of trees. But in the Old Irish laws the trees were divided into four classes according to their different values: "chieftain" trees, common trees, shrub trees, and bramble trees. The fine for damaging a tree depended upon the class to which the tree belonged. Now Marstrander has proved that the names of the first family of the Ogham alphabet all designate common trees, the names of the second family chieftain trees, and the names of the third and fourth families designate shrub or bramble trees.

found in 1829 near Charnay, in Burgundy; and on a stone found in 1903 in Kylver, in Gotland. The three specimens supplement one

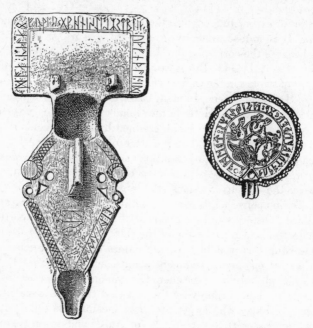

THE CHARNAY BROOCH AND THE VADSTENA BRACTEATE

[After *Aarbøger for nordisk Oldkyndighed*, 1874]

another so well that there can be no doubt of the order of the alphabet and its divisions. It consisted of twenty-four characters in three groups:

ᚠᚢᚦᚨᚱᚲᚷᚹ : ᚺᚾᛁᛃᛇᛈᛉᛊ : ᛏᛒᛖᛗᛚᛜᛟᛞ

f u þ a r k g w   h n i j ᴇ p z s   t b e u l ng o d

(ʀ)

Archæological discoveries prove that this oldest runic alphabet was the common property of all the Germanic nations. Movable articles with runic inscriptions on them, especially weapons and ornaments, have been found in Scandinavia and elsewhere on the

---

[1] The runic characters for *j* (English *y*) and *ng* have many varying forms and have given rise to much discussion. Scholars are mostly inclined to think that ◇ is the proper form of the *ng* rune.

Continent, and in England, also. Some come from the Goths, such as the inscriptions on a gold ring from Pietroassa, Rumania; others come from the Germans. Two inscriptions have been found in the neighborhood of Harlingen, in the Dutch province of Friesland. The most remarkable of the Scandinavian inscriptions upon movable articles is that on the Golden Horn found in 1734 at Gallehus, near

"I.H.H. MADE THE HORN"
INSCRIPTION AND FIGURES ON THE TOP PART OF
THE GOLDEN HORN FROM MØGELTØNDER
[After Wimmer, *Les monuments runiques du Slesvig*]

Møgeltønder, Jutland, only a few steps away from the place where a peasant girl had found a similar horn without an inscription in 1639. In 1802 both horns were stolen from the Royal Museum in Copenhagen and melted, so that now we have only the old copies and descriptions to go by. Fortunately the inscription was so clear that we are scarcely in doubt concerning a single letter. In Norway and Sweden, but not in Denmark, there are also stones inscribed in the ancient runic alphabet.

On the Continent, the runes quickly went out of use except in Scandinavia. In the case of the Goths, Bishop Ulfilas exchanged them for an adapted form of the Greek alphabet, although his adaptation was made with constant reference to the runes, and characters which were lacking were borrowed from the runic alphabet. Elsewhere the Latin alphabet prevailed. We can almost see the process taking place on a gold medallion from Friesland, which bears both a runic inscription and one in Latin letters.

Runic writing maintained itself much longer in England, where the number of runes was increased by various new characters, and in Scandinavia, where the development proceeded in an exactly opposite direction: one after another of the old characters was given up, until finally, about 850, the alphabet consisted of only the following sixteen:

ᚡᚢᚦᚨᚱᚡ : ᚼᚾᛁᛆᛋ : ᛏᛒᛚᛘᛦ
f u b a r k　h n i a s　t b l m ʀ

This striking development is due partly to changes in pronunciation which forced the Scandinavians to choose between inventing several new characters and contenting themselves with using the same character for several different shades of sound. They chose the latter alternative, and went much farther in this direction than there was any need of doing. They wrote *kunukR* for *konungR* "king," *trikR* for *drængR* "hero," *buta* for *bōnda* "peasant" (accusative case), *kubl* for *kumbl* "grave mound," *kuþr* for *gōðr* "good," and so on. One cannot avoid seeing something psychological in this, a sort of indolence. Obviously the whole development was possible only under definite social conditions, when little was written except fixed formulas, and there was no demand that what was written should be easily read by any one. It is peculiar, also, that the old characters for *a* and *j* changed their meaning under the influence of changes in the pronunciation of the names of the letters: in old times we have **ansuR* "god" and **jāra* "year," which later become *ặss* (with nasalized *ā*) and *ār* (without *j*-). This also indicates a period when little writing was done, when the letters and their names were well known, while there was no fixed tradition of orthography, so that whenever a word was written the writer had to undertake the syllabic analysis anew from the beginning, so to speak; when ideas of the individual letters and their names were much more firmly fixed than ideas of written words as wholes. Such a period was very different from our own day, when, if a writer spells a word a little differently from current usage he is likely to precipitate another Battle of the Books.

Most of the Danish runic inscriptions are written in this abbreviated alphabet; but a few of them, dating from the first half of the ninth century, still show some of the older characters. Norwegian and Swedish runic monuments from the same period employ the same short alphabet, but it was never used by other than the Scandinavian peoples.

However, this alphabet did not maintain itself unchanged. From bout the year 1000 a movement in the opposite direction can be traced, a movement toward an increase in the number of characters. A dot is added to the sign for *k* when it means *g*, and a similar dot is put in the middle of the line for *i* when it means *e*; *u* is changed to *y* by the addition of a dot, and so on. These are called "pricked runes." In this and similar ways a runic alphabet was attained in the thirteenth century with quite as complete an equipment of characters as the Latin. But by that time the tale of runes was already told: the Latin alphabet had been adopted, and prevailed everywhere.

SOPHUS BUGGE

In runic scholarship during the nineteenth century the Scandinavian monuments play the most prominent part. The Scandinavian inscriptions in the ancient runes are very old, so old that they exhibit a much earlier form of the language than the oldest manuscripts, and are the oldest inscriptions in any Germanic tongue. Their precise date is difficult to determine. Some runologists have been content with assigning the oldest monuments to the fourth century, but archæologists have been willing to concede a considerably greater age, at least an additional century. The extremely ancient form of the language is the reason why scholars groped blindly after their interpretation as long as they attempted to use the Old Norse literary language as a key. Sophus Bugge took the first steps toward their correct interpretation in 1865 by utilizing the older forms of words made available by the methods of comparative linguistics.

The year 1874 is marked by an important advance in runic scholarship, an investigation by Wimmer into the origin and development of runes in the North. Wimmer put an end once for all to the earlier

LUDVIG WIMMER

fantastic conceptions of the origin of runes, and pointed out that they could descend only from one of the Græco-Italic alphabets. He insisted also that we must seek the prototype of the runes neither in a Greek alphabet nor in any of the ancient non-Latin alphabets of Italy, but must go to the Latin itself. His penetrating and careful investigation resulted in the conclusion that runic writing was based on the Latin alphabet of the first imperial period, with which the Germanic folk became acquainted either directly or through Gaulish intermediaries.

Wimmer's results render possible the conjecture which I threw out concerning a certain indirect connection between runes and Ogham, in that the Germanic folk and the Irish may have had the same teachers. It must not be forgotten, however, that a highly regarded authority has recently attempted to shake Wimmer's theory, and has maintained that the runic alphabet did not arise among a West Germanic tribe neighboring the Gauls, but among the Goths, and that it at least partly depends upon the Greek alphabet. The hypothesis, however, of a Greek or partly Greek origin rests upon insufficient evidence, and cannot be supported convincingly from the point of view of the history of alphabets, either in the form in which it has been advanced, or in any other conceivable form.

In addition to the works mentioned, both Sophus Bugge and Wimmer contributed in many other ways to runic scholarship. As editors also they have taken high rank, Bugge by publishing the inscriptions of Norway in the ancient runes, Wimmer by publishing the Danish runic monuments in the later runes. Among the Swedish runic scholars can be named, of the more recent workers, Otto von Friesen and Axel Kock. The German runic monuments were discussed by R. Henning in 1889, and by Wimmer in 1894.

Ogham and runic writing are the only two offshoots of the Latin alphabet, unless one includes Frashəri's Albanian alphabet (see above, pp. 71 ff.). It would fall outside the plan of the present work to sketch the expansion of the Latin alphabet throughout the world. During this expansion it has maintained itself, unchanged, like the Arabian alphabet, throughout its whole territory. It was enriched, as time went on, by the differentiation between *u* and *v*, *i* and *j* (in the sixteenth and seventeenth centuries) and by certain local extensions in different nations, such as Swedish *å*, Danish *ø*, the Czech characters invented by John Huss, such as *š*, *ž*, *č*, and so on. During the Middle Ages two deviating shapes of letters were developed, which now again are giving way. On the Continent there is the angular or "Gothic" type, which each country has called its own („Danish letters", „Swedish letters", „German letters"), but which at present only Germany continues to use. In England and Ireland there is the so-called Anglo-Saxon type, which is still used in Ireland, and naturally is called Irish type.

VII

THE METHODS OF COMPARATIVE LINGUISTICS
A SURVEY OF THEIR DEVELOPMENT

AFTER a bird's-eye view of the achievements of linguistic science in the nineteenth century, we turn once more to the beginning of the century in order to learn how the method has developed which knits this science together: the method of comparative linguistics.

The method was developed in the nineteenth century, but the soil capable of giving it growth had been tilled by preceding centuries and by the work of collection in the eighteenth century. Scholars had attained so comprehensive a knowledge of the world of languages that it was no longer possible to fail to distinguish the difference between the old fancies of common Hebrew origin or the like, and actual investigation of relationships. It was perceived that the conclusions of these visionaries must be false; but wherein the error consisted was as yet only partly understood. It was plain enough, perhaps, that their treatment of sounds was wild, but just where the principal defect lay was not so clear. No method for the investigation of sounds was dreamed of. On the other hand, scholars had opportunity again and again to observe that languages which were reasonably suspected of being related, actually agreed in their inflectional systems, and hence they came to set up agreement in inflectional system as a criterion of linguistic relationship.

It was the establishment of this fundamental principle in method which pulled etymological scholarship out of the bog where it had stuck fast since classical times, and rendered the existence of comparative linguistics possible. It is, indeed, a matter of course that he who follows this principle will never be exposed to the danger of comparing unrelated languages; and since he is seeking where there is something to be found, he will really make discoveries, even though his mind still relies in details rather on intuition than on the clearness of his theories.

As early as the eighteenth century many intelligent men like Ludolf and Hervas referred to the significance of inflectional forms in proving relationships among languages. By an accident the new principle was first applied in a practical way in the Finno-Ugric field by Gyármathi in 1799 (see above, p. 105). But it was not Gyármathi's work which provided the point of departure for the new linguistics. For many reasons, it was impossible for linguistics to develop first in the Finno-Ugric field. The Finno-Ugric languages were too far beyond the horizon and interest of most European scholars, and, besides, the problems to be solved were too difficult, because the languages are very distantly related, and lack old documents to a very considerable degree. Their problems were therefore not adapted to the feeble powers of the infant science.

Nor was the Semitic family adapted to become the first field cultivated by comparative linguistics. This family possesses in abundance what the Finno-Ugric family lacks — ancient monuments. If we include archæological discoveries and inscriptions which came to light in the nineteenth century, it surpasses even the Indo-European family of languages in age. But it is a disadvantage that the oldest surviving forms of languages, Assyrian and Hebrew, — of which, moreover, only Hebrew was known at the beginning of the century, — are not especially ancient and original in appearance, but are much developed and decayed, so that they are not nearly so ancient in form as Arabic, which is actually much younger. Besides, neither of these languages is now the native tongue of any European nation. Finally — and this is the most essential point — the Semitic languages could not stimulate awakening linguistics with surprising problems, as the Indo-European languages could. The relationships are altogether too easy to see, too directly manifest. They could not incite scholars to investigation at a time when there was no interest in seeking conformity to laws in the evolution of languages, simply because there was no suspicion of the existence of such laws. At the beginning of the nineteenth century, when the subtleties of linguistic science were unknown, men were hardly in a position to perceive that any problem existed in this regard.

The modern period of linguistics, therefore, began only when Rask and Bopp in 1814 (1818) and 1816 methodically pointed out the relationship among the languages which are the most distant from one another in the Indo-European family.

By the labors of Rask and Bopp the spade was thrust into a soil which was more fit than any other for linguistic cultivation. In the age of its languages, its wide dissemination and rich variation, and its profound but not unrecognizable divisions, the Indo-European family is unique. And the problems concerning it easily attracted general interest, since languages of that family were the mother tongues of the nations which have been and still are the leaders in the development of civilization and scholarship. In this field, then, comparative linguistics advanced rapidly and without interruption. The century during which this science has been in existence has been so rich in results and in development that it is wise to divide it into periods. Hence we shall discuss two periods, each of which is characterized by a different degree of clearness in method.

The first period, in which the chief works are Bopp's comparative grammar (1833 and following) and Schleicher's *Compendium der vergleichenden Grammatik der indo-germanischen Sprachen* (1861–62), had at first, especially in the case of Bopp himself, essentially no other method than that implied in the proposition concerning the significance of grammatical forms for comparison. Rask is the only one of the early investigators who was awake from the first to another principle in method — the significance of the laws of sounds. As Rask's ideas were taken over by Grimm, and every increase in the number of correct etymologies showed in itself the evolution of sounds more clearly, the new principle gradually grew stronger and stronger. In Schleicher's *Compendium*, which is the final step in the development of this period, it plays a very prominent part; but still no one, not even Schleicher, objected to unmotivated exceptions in these laws. In this period no one attained any clear idea of the life and development of language. Scholars indulged in figures of speech which were finally taken seriously. In all seriousness Schleicher conceives of language as an organism, and reckons linguistics as one of the natural sciences. The ancient languages, which were the cardinal points of departure for comparison, were regarded quite differently from the modern. Schleicher even maintained that the evolution of language took place only in prehistoric times, while historical times have known only linguistic decay. Sanskrit was an object of especially exaggerated importance throughout the whole period, in spite of efforts to relegate it to its proper position.

The insufficient basis in method explains many of the mistakes made by the first students of comparative linguistics. In his principal work Rask committed the error of doubting the relationship between Celtic and Germanic (or, to use modern terms, of doubting that Celtic belongs to the Indo-European family). Since he knew Celtic only through the forms extant in his time, he could find no profound similarities in the inflectional systems, and resemblances in vocabulary he did not consider as of decisive weight, from the point of view of his method: they might be due to loans.

Yet Rask soon rectified this error. Bopp made the far more serious mistake of regarding the Austronesian (see above, p. 129) languages as Indo-European. Here there was no similarity in the inflectional systems. Bopp, however, did not stop here, as Rask did in the case of Celtic, but attempted to carry out a comparison of the vocabulary. For this undertaking he had no other method than the complete lack of method inherited from the preceding centuries. The results are easily conceivable.

As an example of the early scholars' confusion about sounds, we may refer to what Bopp says about the numerals *eleven* and *twelve*, which have the following forms in Gothic and Lithuanian:

Gothic	*ain-lif*		*twa-lif*
Lithuanian	*vienúo-lika*		*dvý-lika*

These numerals are obviously compounds, of which the first elements are *one* and *two*. The last elements Bopp wished to explain from the well-known Common Indo-European numeral for *ten*, Greek *déka*, Latin *decem*, which in Gothic is *taihun* and in Lithuanian *dešim-t*. The last element in *eleven* and *twelve*, then, was supposed by Bopp to be, in other words, the same as the last element in *thirteen, fourteen, fifteen*, etc. (Gothic *fimf-taihun*.) Bopp does not ponder a moment over this extreme variation in sound development. "That one and the same word used in different applications may be changed in the course of time into different forms, a phenomenon of which innumerable examples can be adduced, requires no further support," he explains. Nowadays we always demand a knowledge of the conditions which called forth a varying development. He is only surprised that he has so long overlooked the fact that such is the origin of *eleven* and *twelve*. Even Schleicher, who — quite differently from Bopp — had an eye for regularity in the development of sounds, in this case supports Bopp's explanation by referring to the fact that a change from *d* to *l* is known in other languages. Nothing shows better how far Schleicher was, in spite of all the progress that had been made, from a clear conception of the historical character of laws of sounds: the process must be pointed out not in *other* languages, but in the language under consideration. Moreover, it is not merely the *l* which is wrong here: every single sound in Lithuanian *-lika* is unfit for comparison with *dešimt* (the circumstance that *-lika* has some degree of similarity to Greek *déka* naturally does not help), and with regard to the Germanic languages the case is not much better. Rask also was far from clear as to the regular conformity to law in the evolution of sounds; but his sober judgment protected him from excessively wild flights of the imagination, such as Bopp's interpretation of *eleven* and *twelve*. On the last element of these numerals Rask remarks in his chief work (p. 253) that they belong with Old Norse *leifa* "to leave," Lithuanian *lik-ti* "to leave"; *eleven* is thus properly "one left, one remaining" (after ten). This explanation is correct.

The other period of the development of comparative linguistics begins about 1870. A series of splendid discoveries made by scholars of various nationalities accounted for the most striking cases of apparent irregularity in the Indo-European laws of sounds. The proposition that such laws admit no exception was then advanced, and became the subject of a lively discussion. A thorough-going study of the life and development of language began. It brought phonetics (the description of the sounds of language) and the modern languages into the center of interest. Scholars now occupied themselves not merely with the older periods, in far distant perspective: they now wished to see languages in the actual process of growth. It is natural that this new point of view brought about a more and more energetic interest in the inclusion of syntax in the field of comparative linguistics. Sanskrit receded a little from its position in the foreground, since it was clear, in the light of the new discoveries, that it could not in all respects lay claim to the most primitive appearance, but that in particular instances it is not so old as its sister languages, notably Greek.

Conceptions of the Indo-European *ablaut* (vowel shifts, vowel alternations: cf. above, pp. 39–42), which in the period of Bopp and Schleicher were not advanced beyond the discoveries of the Indian grammarians (p. 22) — and which almost always went astray when they varied from the Indian doctrines — were subjected to a thorough revision which led in an entirely different direction from Grimm's ideas of the symbolism of sounds. It is now possible for us to say that we have some idea how most of these ancient vowel-shifts arose. Like so many recent vowel-shifts, they were the result of changes in sounds: but such changes whose results were already in existence in the parent language must naturally be older than the parent language itself. Thus we have a glimpse of an even more remote period than that to which the comparison of the separate Indo-European languages takes us back. This comparison gives us the picture of a parent language which to a great degree resembles the oldest historical forms of our family, Sanskrit and Greek. But the alternations teach us that certain sound-changes took place in what we may call the prehistorical period of this parent language: if we attempt to do away with these earlier sound-changes, the picture alters completely. The difference is much greater, for instance, than that between the language of Cynewulf and the language of Chaucer. The language in which these sound-changes had not occurred resembled Greek and Sanskrit no more than a larva resembles a butterfly. We shall have to consider as much of this larva as we can when the question of the relationship of our family of languages with other families arises.

With the development which has taken place since the seventies, it can be said that comparative linguistics has now attained full maturity and a clear consciousness of its methods and undertakings: a fact which naturally does not exclude the possibility, now as before, of both good and bad work.

Since it has become clear that the evolution of sounds conforms to laws, nobody has doubted what Rask already suspected — that, if there is an agreement controlled by definite laws of sounds among the central elements of the vocabulary of two languages, this agreement is just as satisfactory a proof of relationship as an agreement in the inflectional system.

That agreement in the inflectional system is an especially clear and striking proof of kinship, no one denies. But it is only an anachronism in theory, which has no significance in actual practice, when such an agreement is still designated as the only valid proof. No one doubted, after the first communication about Tokharian (see above, p. 194), that the language was Indo-European, although at that time virtually no similarities in inflection had been pointed out. Such similarities have since been shown, but even where they are almost obliterated, proof of kinship could be adduced from the vocabulary and from sound-laws. Hardly any one will assert that it would be impossible to recognize the relationship between, say, English and Italian, even without the help of other related languages or of older forms of those two languages themselves, although agreements between the inflectional systems are practically nonexistent.

From the modern point of view it must be said that proof for relationship between languages is adduced by a systematic comparison of the languages in their entirety, vocabulary as well as grammar. The reason why earlier scholars felt they should disregard the vocabulary was that they knew of no method of systematic comparison in this field.

The agreements in phonology and morphology which are to be recognized as decisive for relationship must, however, be etymological, in that they point back to the original *identity* of the words and inflectional forms, not merely to *parallelism*.

For instance, nothing whatever is proved about the relationship between Finno-Ugrian and Turkish when one points out a clear parallelism in the inflection of nouns:

HUNGARIAN	*Singular*		*Plural*	
	hajó	ship	hajók	ships
inessive	hajó-ban	in the ship	hajók-ban	in the ships
elative	hajó-ból	out of the ship	hajók-ból	out of the ships
illative	hajó-ba	into the ship	hajók-ba	into the ships
approximative	hajó-hoz	toward the ship	hajók-hoz	toward the ships
dative	hajó-nak	for the ship	hajók-nak	for the ships [1]

OSMAN	*Singular*		*Plural*	
	kúš	bird	kušlar	birds
locative	kuš-da	in the bird	kušlar-da	in the birds
ablative	kuš-dan	from the bird	kušlar-dan	from the birds
dative	kúš-a	for the bird	kušlar-a	for the birds

Here we have the same system: a number of clearly defined case endings which are added in exactly the same way to a basic form for the singular and plural. The system is quite different from the unanalyzable entanglement of the designations for number and case in the old Indo-European languages, as for instance in Latin:

nominative	*dominus*	*dominī*
accusative	*dominum*	*dominos*
dative	*dominō*	*dominīs*
genitive	*dominī*	*dominōrum*

But in spite of all the parallels in the systems of Hungarian and Osman, there is not a single pair of identical endings in the two languages. And we can find quite similar inflectional systems in entirely different fields, in some of the younger Indo-European languages, for instance. Thus, we have the following inflection in modern Armenian:

	hay	Armenian	*hayer*	Armenians
instrumental	*hay-ov*	with an A.	*hayer-ov*	with A.
dative-genitive	*hay-u*	for an A., of an A.	*hayer-u*,	for A., of A.
ablative	*hay-ē*	from an A.	*hayer-ē*	from A.

And in East Tokharian (see above, p. 195), nouns are inflected after an analogous system. Precisely this noun inflection was one of the first bits of intelligence which came to light when the new-found

---

[1] The Hungarian language has some twenty cases, most of them absolutely different from the Indo-European cases. The meaning of those here cited will be seen from the translation.

language was communicated. Any one could see that it deviated from the old Indo-European inflection both in principle and in the etymological material of the endings. In material, however, these endings agreed just as little with those non-Indo-European languages with whose principles they seemed to agree. Hence, quite properly, the endings exercised no influence upon the verdict as to the relationship of East Tokharian. In this case the etymological agreement (controlled by sound-laws) with Indo-European in the integral part of the vocabulary — for instance, in the whole system of numerals — was regarded, with good reason, as convincing. And now, by the help of West Tokharian, we can show how this remarkable inflectional system was built up on the ruins of Indo-European inflections. We can do the same thing for modern Armenian by the help of Old Armenian. A common linguistic type is not an indication of kinship, since such types may suffer change (cf. above, p. 100).

It must not be overlooked that the Tokharians were, and the Armenians both were and are, the neighbors of the Turks. And although the Armenian as well as the Tokharian inflectional system was constructed from native material, it is not impossible that this proximity may have favored some of the native possibilities of development in Tokharian and Armenian at the expense of other possibilities. The first germs of the peculiarities of morphology are to be sought in certain syntactical customs, certain tendencies in construction, which may very well pass from one neighboring language to another, even though there is no relationship. In this way, for instance, certain striking similarities among widely differing languages in the Balkan Peninsula may be explained: the use of suffixed articles in Albanian (see above, p. 70), Rumanian, and Bulgarian; the loss of the infinitive mood in modern Greek (they say "I can that I walk," instead of "I can walk"), in Bulgarian, Albanian, and Rumanian, and so on. Agreement in principle, without agreement in material, may also have very great interest, but no inferences as to relationship can be drawn from it. Such inferences *are* drawn now and then in our own time, but not by well-trained scholars.

In the case of the phonological system, also, it holds good that an agreement must be etymological in order to prove relationship. Mere similarity in sound, or in habits of sound, without etymological correspondence can at most prove only ancient proximity. No more than this is proved by the fact that vowel-harmony appears in both Finno-Ugrian and Turkish, which two groups of languages permit the first vowel in a word to determine the coloring of those succeeding (cf. above, p. 200):

Osman   *kuš* bird, *kuš-da*, *kuš-dan*, *kuš-a*, *kuš-lar*, *kuš-lar-da*, etc.
          äv house, *äv-dä*, *äv-dän*, *äv-ä*, *äv-lär*, *äv-lär-dä*, etc.
Hungarian *hajó* ship, *hajó-ban*, *hajó-ba*, *hajó-hoz*, *hajó-nak*, etc.
          kéz hand, *kéz-ben*, *kéz-be*, *kéz-höz*, *kéz-nek*, etc.

These very striking resemblances between Finno-Ugrian and Turkish (-Mongolian) are often incorrectly cited as proof of relationship. Vowel-harmony is not an inherent principle in certain languages, but is the result of a development of which we have examples in the most widely differing languages. Those habits of pronunciation which are the germs of the evolution of sounds can be passed very naturally, like so many other habits of pronunciation, from one language to another, but in this case just as well to an unrelated as to a related language. The sole requisite is neighborly intercourse. As an actual proof of kinship between Finno-Ugrian and Turkish (between Uralian and Altaic) these agreements in principle in the habits of sounds suffice just as little as the agreements in inflection. Only etymological identity in the root of the word or in the endings, proved by the help of definite correspondences in sounds, has conclusive force in the problem of the relationship.

The Older Period of Comparative Linguistics

Chronologically, the first of the great specialists in comparative linguistics in the century is Rasmus Kristian Rask (1787–1832). His chief work, *Investigation on the Origin of the Old Norse or Icelandic Language*,[1] may well be called a comparative Indo-European grammar in embryo. The book owes its title and its plan to the fact that it appeared in a prize competition conducted by the Danish Academy of Science in 1811. Rask sent in his work from Iceland in 1814 — he lived there from 1813 to 1815 — and after the granting of royal support in 1817 for its publication the book appeared in 1818, while Rask was away on his long journey (1816–23), the ultimate goal of which was India.

The subject set for the competition was as follows:

"To investigate and illustrate, with appropriate examples, by means of historical criticism, from what source the ancient Scandinavian language can most surely be derived; to state the character of the language and its relations, from ancient times and throughout the Middle Ages, to Scandinavian and Germanic dialects; and to

[1] *Undersögelse om det gamle Nordiske eller Islandske Sprogs Oprindelse.*

determine exactly the fundamental principles upon which all derivations and comparisons in these languages should be built."

Seldom has a prize competition had a more splendid result, and we may perhaps admit that the question was well conceived and sensibly formulated. But it is doubtful whether the formulation corresponded to Rask's natural conception of the subject. In any case there is something in the choice of words ("from what source

RASMUS RASK
[After *Danske Stormænd fra de senere Aarhundreder*]

the ancient Scandinavian language can most surely be derived") which recalls the old unhistorical view of the relations between languages (cf. above, pp. 2 ff., 7 ff.), — precisely the view which it is the merit of comparative linguistics to have abandoned. In his investigation Rask faithfully retains the phraseology of the subject set, but after arguing in detail that Greek is the oldest and most primitive of the languages related to Old Norse, he warns us expressly in his conclusion against the belief that Old Norse is descended directly from Greek. Greek is merely the oldest survival — we should say "continuation" — of the extinct language from which Old Norse is descended.

Rask examines all the languages neighboring Norse in order to determine whether they are related, and where he finds relationship he follows the trail farther, even when it leads to distant fields. He recognizes as related those branches which are now called Germanic, Baltic, Greek and Latin (these two he groups together, like all his contemporaries), Armenian; and he concedes the possibility that the two branches which were very little known, Indian and Iranian, may be related. On the other hand, Eskimo, Celtic (here Rask erred), Basque, Finno-Ugrian, and Semitic are unrelated. Farther than India we need not go in our search for languages related to Old Norse, "for the chain is closed on the one hand by the monosyllabic languages, on the other by the Malay and Australian groups, which are again bounded by the ocean, but both of these immense families of languages are very different in every way from the Gothic, Thracian,[1] and Indian groups."

The scheme of relationships which Rask drew up is both very complete and astonishingly correct. What was lacking he soon supplied. As early as 1818 he perceived that Celtic is Indo-European, and abandoned his reservation with regard to Indian and Iranian.[2] But in 1818 he bracketed Armenian with Iranian and still excluded Albanian from our family. These two errors he abandoned also. His final views on Albanian and Armenian we have already discussed (see pp. 67, 73, above).

Rask's great merit lies not only in the correct determination of linguistic relationships, but also — and here the merit is even greater — in his careful reasoning in substantiating them. An excellent preface to this is the introduction, in which he discusses the proper linguistic method. In agreement with the opinions of the dawning age, he asserts that in the comparison of languages the grammatical side especially must not be forgotten; "for experience demonstrates that agreement in words is extremely uncertain. Through the intercourse of different peoples, an incredible number of words may pass from one language to another, however different the two may be in origin and type.... Grammatical agreement is a much more certain indication of kinship or of original identity, because a language which is mixed with another seldom or never takes over morphological

---

[1] That is, Græco-Latin. This very unfortunate terminology comes from Adelung. See above, p. 10.

[2] *Samlede Afhandlinger*, II, 281.

changes or inflections from it.... This kind of agreement, which is
the most important and the most certain, has nevertheless been
almost entirely overlooked hitherto in the derivation of languages,
and this oversight is the principal error in most previous discussions
of this subject; for this reason earlier work is so uncertain and of so
little scientific value." But directly after this statement of the case
for the grammatical side, there follows a passage which shows that
Rask was quite clear as to the fact that there might be some firm
point in method to hold to, besides the inflectional system: "A
language, however mixed it may be, belongs to the same branch of
languages as another when it has the most essential, concrete, indispensable words, the foundation of the language, in common with
it.... When agreement is found in such words in two languages, and
so frequently that rules may be drawn up for the shift in letters [1]
from one to the other, then there is a fundamental relationship between the two languages; especially when similarities in the inflectional system and in the general make-up of the languages correspond
with them." This sounds quite modern, aside from the method of
expression. Here Rask points out clearly the significance of laws of
sounds as a proof of kinship, although he adds that they are especially convincing when supported by similarities in grammar. Thus
in Rask we find the whole kernel from which modern methods have
developed; but it would naturally be unreasonable for us to expect
to find the method developed with perfect clearness in the work of
this early representative of modern linguistics. It would be easy to
prove that Rask still did not perceive the full historical regularity
of the laws of sounds.

The book contains many evidences of Rask's efforts to find and
apply such laws, and of his talent in doing so. With him this principle was not mere theory, but real practice. Thus in his treatment
of Slavonic he perceived one of the most important laws of the
group — a law which Bopp announced seventeen years later with
all the joy of discovery.[2] The most complete chapter in the book is
the one on "Thracian." Here Rask compares Greek and Latin with
Germanic, and begins with the following characteristic words, which

---

[1] The use of *letter* for *sound* is found also in Grimm and Bopp.

[2] This is the change from *s* to a sound like German *ch*, by which many well-known ancient
words have developed a greatly changed appearance. Slavic *jucha* "soup" is thus actually
the same word as Latin *jūs* "soup" (in Danish the Latin word was borrowed, but via French
jus, and has the form *sky* "gravy"; the Germans borrowed the Slavic word in a contemptuous
connotation: *Jauche* "dung water, pus").

clearly refer to the discussion of method in the introduction: "If we compare, then, the Thracian class of languages, of whose principal stock and offshoot [1] we have so many invaluable ancient remains, with Gothic and Lithuanian, from the point of view of grammar and individual words, the well-informed investigator will discover not merely many words which resemble one another to a certain extent in form and meaning, but such numerous resemblances that rules for the changes of the letters can be drawn up, and almost the entire structure of the languages proves to be the same in both." The conception concisely expressed here is then developed in a brief survey of sound-changes (pp. 167–171), a grammatical comparison (pp. 171–275), and a vocabulary (pp. 275–300) of three hundred and fifty-two words in all, to which must be added forty-eight adjectives, pronouns, and numerals compared in the grammatical portion. Rask chose and arranged the words in the list "according to the meaning, in order to show how the most important and most necessary words in language, words which indicate the first objects of reflection, are the same in both branches of languages."

Although very few pages remain for the phonology, these few are of immense significance. They contain a treatment of those laws which first revealed to the interested public a glimpse of an unexpected regularity in the development of sounds — those laws, namely, which we now group together under the name of the Germanic consonant shift. Among others Rask gives the following examples (in parentheses I add supplementary instances from his vocabulary):

$p > f$: Gr. *patér* (L. *pater*), O.N. *faðir* "father"

$t > þ$: Gr. *treĩs* (L. *trēs*), O.N. *þrír* "three"

$k > h$: L. *cornū*, O.N. *horn* "horn"; L. *cutis*, O.N. *húð* "skin"

$d > t$: Gr. *damáō* "I tame" (L. *domō*), O.N. *tamr* "tame"

$g > k$: Gr. *gynê*, O.N. *kona* "woman"; L. *gena*, O.N. *kinn* "cheek"
      Gr. *génos*, O.N. *kyn* "family"; Gr. *agró-s* (L. *ager*), O.N. *akr* "field"

Gr. φ (*ph*, L. *f*) $> b$: Gr. *phēgós* "oak" (L. *fāgus* "beech"), O.N. *bók* "beech"
      Gr. *phérō*, L. *ferō* "I carry," O.N. *bera* "to carry"

Gr. ϑ (*th*) $> d$: Gr. *thyrā* (L. *forēs*), O.N. *dyrr* "door"

Gr. χ (*kh*) $> g$: Gr. *khytó-s* "poured," O.N. *gjóta* "to pour," Gr. *kholê*,
      O.N. *gall* "gall" (L. *hostis*, "stranger, enemy," O.N.
      gestr "guest")

Rask adds that other changes occur within words:

[1] That is, Greek and Latin.

$k > g$: L. *macer*, O.N. *magr* "thin"; L. *taceō* "I am silent," O.N. *þegja*,
         þagða "to be silent, I was silent"
$t > ð$: L. *pater*, O.N. *faðir* "father"; L. *frater*, O.N. *bróðir* "brother"

After what has been said, it must be quite clear that Rask fully
perceived the significance of these laws, the earliest Indo-European
sound-laws of major importance. Indeed, he appeals expressly to
the regular agreement in such laws as proof of relationship. The
treatment of these laws is so clear and so complete that it was not
until the seventies that scholars were able to advance a considerable
step beyond them. Rask is confused on but one point, the original *b*:
it actually follows the same direction as *d* and *g*, and thus becomes
the voiceless sound *p*. But *b* was very rare in Indo-European, and
Rask did not find good examples. Although he makes the correct
comparison of Greek *kánnabis*, Old Norse *hampr* "hemp" in another
place in the book, he assumes here that *b* most often remains, and
cites some incorrect examples.

Rask also perceived a second and later shift by which High German became distinguished from the other Germanic languages. For
this High German shift he gives the following examples in one of his
early chapters, where he characterizes the Old Norse language in
comparison with those most closely related to it:

pf from *p*: G. *Kupfer*, O.N. *koparr* "copper"; G. *Pforte*, O.N. *port* "gate"
z from *t*: G. *Zoll*, Eng. *toll*; G. *zittern*, O.N. *titra* "tremble"; G. *setzen*,
         Eng. *to set*; G. *reizen*, O.N. *reita* "to tease" (*s* from *t*: G. *gutes*,
         Goth. *godata* (neuter of) "good," p. 189);
ch from *k*: G. *weichen*, O.N. *víkja* "to yield"; G. *sich*, *mich*, O.N. *sik*, *mik*
         "(him)self, me."

As is to be expected, this is a very incomplete treatment, yet
within the very restricted limits of this chapter it is not so inconsiderable, after all.

But although it is proper to single out Rask as the first of the
moderns who had his eyes open to the significance of laws of sounds,
it must be added that he did not perceive the complete regularity
of development in this regard. He does not try to find the reasons
for the exceptions to his main rules,[1] and therefore his own laws did
not put him on his guard against certain comparisons which we now
regard as quite invalid, because they are the result of accidental

---

[1] He does not say a word, for instance, about why the second *t* in Old Norse *titra*, German
zittern, did not follow the same path as the first. The fact is that *tr* never goes to *zr* in High
German; cf. *treten*, *Winter*, English *tread*, *winter*.

similarity or loan. But his sober caution always restrained him from going far in the wrong direction.

Regarded as a first sketch of comparative Indo-European grammar, Rask's *Undersögelse* has its obvious faults, as well as its merits. Among minor faults are the mistakes he made both in the phonology and in the comparison of inflectional endings. They had their causes in the spirit of their time. More significant are the unfortunate conditions which the prize competition imposed upon him: he was forced to compare the related branches of languages one at a time with Old Norse, whereas he should have compared them all at once. This was remedied to a certain extent by Rask's often including in the main section on the "Thracian" languages even Lithuanian and Slavonic, which had been treated earlier. But this section cannot be set apart and regarded as complete in itself, as J. S. Vater attempted to do in 1822 by publishing it alone in German (*Über die thrakische Sprachclasse*). Even if this translation had been faultless, as it is not, it would have done more harm than good by depriving the Danish edition of readers without compensating them for their loss. And a fatal shortcoming was that Rask had not yet included Sanskrit in the comparison.

No doubt many of these errors would have disappeared if Rask had returned to the subject and prepared a new treatment. Such a project may indeed have been in his mind. In the preface he expresses the hope that after he has completed his journey to the East he "may be enabled to prepare a more satisfactory continuation of this investigation." But no second edition appeared. The remainder of Rask's brief and restless life was filled with other enterprises. It fell to the lot of a German scholar to write the first detailed Indo-European grammar, and this did not come until after Rask's death.

This German scholar was Franz Bopp. Bopp studied Sanskrit at Paris, and, as the first fruits of his studies, published a book in 1816 which, according to its title, treats the verbal inflection of Sanskrit in comparison with Greek, Latin, Persian, and Germanic.[1] Actually, however, it is only the first half of the book (157 pages) which treats this subject, the remainder being taken up by translations from Sanskrit.

As the title indicates, Bopp's work embraces two branches of languages which Rask did not discuss, but on the other hand, Bopp

[1] *Über das Conjugationssystem der Sanskritsprache....*

does not include two branches which Rask included, Slavonic and Baltic. Bopp's two additional branches are Sanskrit and Persian. But they play very different parts in the plan of the book. Bopp really knew Sanskrit, and its inclusion points forward to a new era. But of the ancient Iranian languages he could not know anything in 1816. What he treats is simply Modern Persian, and the inclusion of this language points not forward, but backward — back to the

FRANZ BOPP
[After Lefmann, *Franz Bopp*]

ancient fancy of a special relationship between Persian and Germanic (see above, p. 7), for Bopp treats Persian and Germanic under one heading. Certainly his eye for relationships was none too keen here. He allowed himself to be deluded by certain superficial resemblances whose purely accidental character becomes evident from a slightly more thorough study of Modern Persian itself.[1]

A no less powerful reminder of the good old times is Bopp's attitude toward phonology. It is not separately included in his comparison, which is concerned only with morphology (the inflection of verbs); and when in the course of his work he touches upon phono-

[1] Bopp very soon gave up this misapprehension as to Persian.

logy, he shows a complete lack of understanding. The relation between German *schwitzen* and English *to sweat* he explains by the
supposition that a derivatory *s* is added in German to the root in *-t*.
He had no stronger impression of the great regularity of what we
now call the High German sound-shift. The changes in sounds with
which he reckons defy all rules. It disturbs him not at all to find the
same starting-point leading to two different results. Sound-changes
are a kind of liberty which a language may or may not use, at will.
In his estimation, such changes are arbitrary and accidental. He
uses figurative and vague expressions which, if taken seriously, would
convey no intelligible meaning. In brief, there is not the faintest
tendency toward anything new in phonology.

Thus, the merit of the book lies exclusively in the field of inflections. And here, again, we must say that the most significant matter
is not what Bopp regards as the goal of the investigation. He wished
to point out the origin of inflections in the light of the new sun from
the East. This is an ambition which could be only partly successful
with the means available. And certainly he who seeks in the direction which Bopp followed in this youthful work will not go far. He
was dominated by one great idea which he thought he could work out
everywhere: the idea that every verb-form contains the concept
"to be," and that in all sorts of verbal endings one may expect to
find elements with this meaning. In all *s*-endings he sought the
root *es-*, *s-* (Latin *es-t* "he is," *s-unt* "they are"). Nowadays we
cannot agree with a single one of these explanations of the *s-* endings,
and his central idea must be dismissed as completely mistaken. It
rests upon a mixture of logic and grammar which has nothing to do
with modern linguistics. But if it was this idea which prompted
Bopp's pen, it did have its uses, no matter how mistaken it was. For
this comparison of the principal languages of the western world
(Germanic, Latin, Greek) with Sanskrit, which Bopp included in his
little essay, was a necessary condition for the progress of comparative
linguistics. Without Sanskrit it was possible to advance a long step
forward, as Rask showed. But it may be questioned whether it was
possible to go appreciably farther than Rask. If it was impossible at
that time, then it must be admitted that Rask's work did not contain
sufficient incentive to create the science of comparative linguistics.
On the other hand, Sanskrit had an unsurpassed power of stimulating
investigation. A mere acquaintance with this language had revolutionary effects, not only because it was something new, something

which lay well outside the old circle of knowledge, something to which scholars came unhampered by the old misconceptions, which were not easy to shake off when Greek and Latin were discussed — but also because Sanskrit is so extraordinarily perspicuous in structure. Just as its clear structure had brought about the admirable clarity of Indian grammar, so it produced comparative grammar when it acted upon the minds of European scholars. Although Rask's work was in many respects more mature and more thorough, Bopp's book, in spite of its many shortcomings, could not fail to provide a much stronger stimulus to further research, stronger even than the stimulus which Rask's work could have provided if it had been written in a world language. Bopp's little essay, therefore, may be regarded as the real beginning of what we call comparative linguistics.

In contrast with Rask, Bopp returned repeatedly to the subject and elaborated his investigations. As early as 1821 he announced that he had in mind the production of a complete work on "all the languages related to Sanskrit." This plan began to bear fruit in 1833 — after Bopp had published several aids to the study of Sanskrit — when he began to issue his great *Vergleichende Grammatik des Sanskrit, Zend,*[1] *Griechischen, Lateinischen, Litthauischen, Gothischen und Deutschen.* This work appeared in several parts in 1833, 1835 (here Old Slavic is included), 1837–52, and in all contains fifteen hundred pages. Meantime, in 1838, Bopp adduced grammatical proof for the Indo-European character of the Celtic languages (see above, p. 57), and after going astray during the forties on Austronesian and Caucasian, he published in 1854 his treatment of Albanian discussed above on p. 71. Toward the end of his life he issued his comparative grammar in a new edition (1857–61). A third edition appeared after the author's death, in 1868–70, and a French translation was made by M. Bréal in 1866–74.

It is evident from the date of the first edition that Bopp was able to use the works of other scholars, such as Rask, Grimm, and Dobrovský. As a matter of course the treatment is not only more complete in his comparative grammar than in his *Conjugationssystem*, but is also the result of maturer ideas. But his original peculiarity is still clearly perceptible. In his comparative grammar there is virtually no phonology. Not yet did he understand that this subject could be treated scientifically, and accordingly, his practice with regard to

[1] The treatment of the Avesta language is one of the great merits of this work.

sound-changes remains quite arbitrary. The morphology, however, which takes up the principal part of Bopp's work, seems relatively modern. Systematic comparison of the inflectional endings of all the Indo-European languages, when it is carried out with the acuteness in analysis which is precisely Bopp's strong point, must lead to a large number of correct results. That he regards "the investigation of the relationships of languages not merely as an end in itself, but also as a means of penetrating the secrets of the evolution of language," that is, the secrets of the origin of inflection, does no serious harm. In this respect he is less one-sided than in the work of his youth, and allows himself to be guided more by actual observation, and less by a preconceived theory.

Besides Rask and Bopp we must name also Jacob Grimm among the founders of comparative linguistics.[1] In conformity with Grimm's own choice of words, he has often been designated as the founder of historical rather than comparative linguistics, and he has been contrasted with specialists like Rask and Bopp. But this is no way to get at the root of the matter. Grimm's *Deutsche Grammatik* is itself comparative, although he compares only nearly related languages, or different stages of the same language. His comparison is that of the Germanic languages with one another. He himself expressly maintains in the preface to the first volume (1819) that he has had to forego comparison of non-Germanic languages, and he refers for this sort of thing to Rask's *Undersögelse* and Bopp's *Conjugationssystem*.

But the fact that the circle of comparison is narrower in Grimm's case than in Rask's and Bopp's did not prevent him from influencing the development of the comparative method. The field cultivated by Grimm was not a remote, tightly inclosed one which could not be seen from the highroad of comparative linguistics. No one interested in comparative Indo-European linguistics could ignore the Germanic languages. They were too near, their evidence was too important, and their contribution to the collective picture of the whole family was too significant. Rask had taken Germanic into account, but he had confined himself too exclusively to Old Norse, and a single representative was not enough to enable one to recognize the characteristics of the whole Germanic group. The scholar who wished to compare this branch with others had to have a clear under-

[1] Cf. above, pp. 37–42.

standing of the mutual relationships of the individual languages, and he who would compare the Germanic languages with one another had to look beyond the limits of the individual branch to discover the common source. Thus it was a matter of course that a superior worker in the comparison of the Germanic languages could not remain indifferent to comparative Indo-European linguistics.

In his *Undersögelse* Rask had made a number of correct observations on the relations among the main languages in our branch, but he undertook no thorough comparison. This explains one of Rask's chief errors, the excessive importance which he ascribes to Old Norse and modern Icelandic, which he identifies too closely with Old Norse. This explains also several mistakes in details as to which Grimm has the correct view. Thus we can see clearly how necessary Grimm's work was in the development of comparative linguistics as a science.

But Grimm also had something to learn from Rask. This becomes clear on comparison of the first and the second edition of the first volume of Grimm's grammar. The first edition appeared in 1819, and was completed before Grimm had read Rask's *Undersögelse*. The second appeared in 1822, and shows plainly that Grimm, who of course could read Danish, had not remained uninfluenced by Rask.

In the first edition, Grimm, like Bopp, considers only morphology. Omitting phonology, he begins with the inflections, and when he speaks incidentally of changes in sounds he shows little advance over Bopp. Especially when he touches upon some of the words which may be used to illustrate the Germanic sound-shift, it is evident that Grimm has no suspicion either of regular conformity to law in the development of sounds or of the historical character of sound-laws. When he saw that Latin *qu-* in the interrogative pronoun (*quis* "who?" etc.) corresponds to Germanic *hw-* (later *w*; German *wer*), he did not infer that an original *kw-* shifts to *hw-* wherever it occurs in Germanic. On the contrary, he inferred, as scholars had been doing for centuries, that now and then, by some caprice, *kw-* in any language is changed to *hw-* or *w-* and he felt justified in using this observation to assert relationship between Latin *vacca* "cow," and German *Kuh*, two words which have nothing whatever to do with each other.

In the second edition all this is changed, no doubt as a result, in part, of Rask's influence. Rask's *Undersögelse* thus occupies a twofold position in the development of nineteenth-century science. If we take the date at which it was submitted to the Academy of Science (1814), it is the earliest of the fundamentally important treatises, and with this position accords the fact that its failure to take account of Sanskrit represents a stage to which Bopp's *Conjugationssystem* (1816) rises superior. But if we reckon from the date when it begins to exert an influence outside of Scandinavia, it takes its place after Bopp's book and the first edition of Grimm's *Deutsche Grammatik*, and with this position agrees Rask's advanced method, beyond which Grimm's second edition, influenced by Rask, shows further progress.

We have already discussed (pp. 37–42) the elaborate phonology of nearly six hundred pages by which Grimm introduced his second edition. Here it will be appropriate to add a few words on his discussion of the laws of change in sounds which he found already sketched by Rask — the consonant-shift in Germanic. The High German consonant-shift is developed much more completely than in Rask's book, but not altogether without errors. The Old High German dialectal variations were too involved for Grimm, and he could not master them. Of much greater importance, however, is the "Common Germanic" sound-shift, which Grimm discusses in a way which contrasts startlingly with the utter confusion of the first edition. He gives a long series of examples, not only those found in Rask, but also many others, most of them correct. In reality he advanced beyond Rask in but one respect: he perceived that *b* was not present initially in Indo-European, and that this is the reason why initial *p* was not originally present in Germanic,[1] and he assumed correctly that wherever Indo-European *b* was found in some other position, it must have become Germanic *p*; yet he has no other correct example for this change than Rask's: Greek *kánnabis*, Old Norse *hampr* "hemp."

Rask mentioned the fact that other changes occur *within* words, but he deals with this point very briefly, because his starting point was Old Norse, where this peculiarity is not striking. On comparison of all the Germanic languages, however, these apparent irregularities

---

[1] It is doubtful that initial *b* was totally lacking in Indo-European, but at any rate it was very rare. Most of the Germanic words that begin with *p-* are of foreign origin. Some such words are hard etymological nuts, like Danish *pige* "girl," English *play, plough*; but in any case they are not ancient words.

Grimm was not the first to recognize that the old *b* shifted to *p* in Germanic. It had been pointed out in the short but clear treatment of the Germanic sound-shift which Rask's follower, Jakob Hornemann Bredsdorff, gave in his little essay *Om Aarsagerne til Sprogenes Forandringer* ("On the Causes of Change in Language"), 1821, pp. 21–22.

become very obvious, and they are most conspicuous in Old High German. In some words medial *k*, *t*, *þ* become Germanic *h*, *þ*, *f*, just as they do when initial, whereas in others Germanic *g*, *d*, *b* appear:

Old Latin	*dacru-ma* tear	Latin	*macer* thin
O.H.G.	*zahar*		*magar*
O.N.	*tár*		*magr*

Latin	*fräter* brother		*pater* father
Gothic	*brōþar*		*fadar*
O.E.	*brōþor*		*fæder*
O.H.G.	*bruoder*		*fater*
Mod.H.G.	*Bruder*		*Vater*
O.N.	*brōðir*		*faðir*

Latin	*nepōs* grandson		*aper* boar
O.H.G.	*nevo* nephew		*ebur*
Mod.H.G.	*Neffe*		*Eber*
O.E.	*nefa*		*eofor*
O.N.	*nefi*		*jǫfurr* prince

In German the difference between these two forms *h* : *g*, *þ* : *d*, *f* : *b* is preserved in spite of all subsequent changes. But in Old Norse, *þ* and *d*, *f* and *b* coincided when medial between vowels, and *f* and *b* coincided in Old English also.

Now Grimm could not, like Rask, dismiss these irregularities in a brief note, but had to make an effort to discuss them somewhat thoroughly. But he was quite unable to explain them; and for this he certainly cannot be reproached. With the knowledge then extant no penetration could have solved the riddle. But he may well be censured for not seeing that all three changes play in a single category. He tried to explain away *h* : *g* and *þ* : *d* separately, each in a different mistaken way, while he shut his eyes to the third case, *f* : *b*.

Thus Grimm's treatment of the Germanic sound-shift makes no progress beyond Rask's, save in a single isolated point, other than by its more impressive form. Nor did Grimm see the great significance of these laws any more clearly than Rask. For Rask they were the corner-stone in the proof of the relationship between Græco-Latin and Germanic; Grimm lays special stress upon their significance for strict etymology ("Strenge der Etymologie"). He gives a few examples of cases which do not agree with the sound-shift, and indicates that they depend either upon loan or upon purely accidental similarity, but he abolishes the method inferred from the sound-shift almost completely by declaring at once that though the sound-shift is the great rule, it is never carried out consistently; words remain in the old stage; the stream of evolution has flowed past them; [1] he then cites a long series of supposed examples where this sound-shift or both sound-shifts failed to take place. Evidently, then, the great regularity of laws made as strong an impression on Grimm as it did on Rask, but Grimm is just as far as Rask from holding that the newly discovered laws admit no exceptions. Such an assumption conflicted too strongly with previous modes of thought. Still, the more extensive treatment in Grimm may be reckoned as a virtue. And Grimm has still another merit: here, as in so many other cases, it was he who gave to the phenomenon the name which it has retained: the Germanic sound-shift (*Lautverschiebung*). By this means, and by its insertion in Grimm's great phonology, the discovery was assured of all the attention it deserved.

As the next chief representative of the growing significance of phonology within the field of Indo-European linguistics we must name August Friedrich Pott. His principal work, *Etymologische Forschungen auf dem Gebiete der indogermanischen* [2] *Sprachen* (1833–36), is, according to its plan, a comparative Indo-European grammar with special emphasis on phonology — a Common Indo-European phonology which attempts to do for the whole family what Grimm's phonology had done for Germanic. Besides the phonology and the material on derivation and inflection (the chapters on declension and conjugation are very short, because these subjects had been already treated by Bopp), the book contains a section somewhat outside of the grammatical programme which may be called an attempt at an etymological dictionary: a comparative treatment of three hundred and seventy-five verb-roots which are common to Sanskrit and others of the chief languages of the family.

The prominent position given to phonology in the plan of the

---

[1] "Die lautverschiebung erfolgt in der masse, thut sich aber im einzelnen niemahls rein ab; es bleiben wörter in dem verhältnisse der alten einrichtung stehen; der strom der neuerung ist an ihnen vorbeigeflossen."

[2] The designation "Indogermanic" for our family of languages was never used by Bopp; he argued against it. It seems to have originated with Julius von Klaproth, *Asia Polyglotta*, 1823. It has never become current outside of Germany.

book is emphasized further by the mottoes on the title-pages of the first and second volumes, both of which point to the pretensions and significance of phonology. These mottoes are a summons to conflict. Pott anticipates that his preoccupation with sounds will be attacked as soul-destroying and unworthy of a philologist. His *Introduction* begins with a passionately figurative protest against the application of the words "The letter killeth, but the spirit giveth life" to phono-

AUGUST POTT

logical study. And Pott shows not only enthusiasm but mature understanding of sound-change. On this subject he makes many penetrating remarks — for example, on the difference between such similarity in sounds as may be almost complete and yet quite accidental, and agreement according to fixed laws — "etymological parallelism in letters," which may be absolute even where no direct similarity can be seen. Among his examples for the first kind, Pott cites English *bad* and modern Persian *bad*, both meaning the same thing. Here the similarity is complete, but relationship is out of the question, as a single glance at the older Iranian forms proves. As an example of the second kind, he cites modern Persian *xvāhar*, Ossetic *xo* [1] "sister," and English *sister*. Here the similarity is non-existent, but etymological identity can be proved to the smallest detail. And in particular he maintains the historical character of the laws of sounds, asserting repeatedly that phonology is the surest and most important key to etymology.

Yet Pott, like his predecessors, has no idea that these laws admit no exceptions. Hence, along with a quantity of material useful for historical phonology, his book contains much that is worthless. And bad organization, continual digressions, polemic, and the habit of jumping from one subject to another, make it hard reading nowadays.

Pott does not attempt to reconstruct the Indo-European phonological system. In his tabular survey of the consonants he starts invariably from the Indian system, with but one exception, and the same is true of his comparative list of verb roots. Indeed, he goes so far as to omit roots found in some of the main languages of the Indo-European family but lacking in Sanskrit. Thus near was Pott to identifying Sanskrit with the parent language, although in other respects he understood admirably how to apply the historical point of view to the problems of linguistic relationships. For instance, he protests vehemently and with excellent arguments against the old idea that Latin is descended from Greek.

A new edition of Pott's *Etymologische Forschungen* came out in 1859–76 in ten volumes.

From Rask by way of Grimm's second edition to Pott there is a straight line of advancement toward better and better understanding of the regularity with which changes in sound conform to law. The movement was continued by a younger generation whose most conspicuous representatives are Georg Curtius, Schleicher, and Fick, but it did not assert itself definitively before 1870. Both Curtius and Schleicher announce as their programme in almost the same words "the strictest observation of sound-laws," "strict adherence to sound-laws." But Curtius differentiated between "regular or thoroughgoing sound-changes" and "irregular or sporadic sound-changes," and hence he was far from demanding complete adherence to laws, although it may be regarded as a step forward that he segregated the "irregular" changes and thus left less chance for confusion. And Schleicher's laws, also, were sufficiently flexible to permit him to take over some of Bopp's worst misapprehensions.

[1] *x* = German *ch*.

Curtius is especially important because of his activity as a teacher, and because he made known the results of comparative linguistics to a wider public. But he performed at least one more substantial service for the progress of the new science. It was he who began (in Germany) the demolishing of Grimm's teaching concerning the three basic vowels *a*, *i*, and *u*,[1] for in 1864 he proved at length that Gothic *a*, *i* and *u* did not form the oldest Germanic vowel-system, but that Germanic had from the first a vowel *e* in the same cases as Greek and Latin, etc.: *e* in Old English *etan* "to eat" is, in spite of Gothic *itan*, historically identical with *e* in Latin *edo* "I eat."[2] Thus it became clear that *e* was common to all branches of the Indo-European family save Indian and Iranian. The splendor of the Gothic triad had passed, but nevertheless scholars continued to believe in the Indian triad. They continued to suppose that *a* in Sanskrit *ad-mi* "I eat" was older than the corresponding *e* in Latin and Greek, and so on. And this distribution of *a* and *e* now became the strongest support for a two-fold division of the whole Indo-European family which had been already advocated. On the one hand were Indian and Iranian, which had preserved the old system of *a*, *i*, and *u*; on the other were all the other languages, which not independently but in common had split the old *a* into the two vowels *a* and *e*. Thus the conviction arose that the oldest and most profound division in our family of languages was between an Asiatic and a European (or, as was soon perceived, a European-Armenian) group, a conviction which proved persistent even after its original basis had disappeared.

Of greater importance than Curtius was August Schleicher, whose distinguished work in Slavonic and Baltic I have already mentioned. For comparative Indo-European his activity lay not so much in creative work as in organization. His chief contribution in this field was his excellent *Compendium der vergleichenden Grammatik der indogermanischen Sprachen*.[3]

Schleicher's book is very different from Bopp's. While Bopp's *Vergleichende Grammatik* really contains no phonology, in Schleicher's *Compendium* the phonology occupies the entire first volume. The

[1] See above, p. 39.

[2] This had already been announced in Denmark in 1860 by E. Jessen, in the *Tidskrift for filologi og paedagogik*, I, 218.

[3] 1861–62, second edition 1866, third and fourth editions (after Schleicher's death), 1871 and 1876.

material is cited in short, clear paragraphs in a well-arranged, sensible treatment which shows the strongest possible contrast to the method of Pott, Schleicher's predecessor in this field. And the volume seems rather modern, for, naturally enough, it treats only of the phenomena which Schleicher felt able to arrange under rules. But Schleicher's appreciation of the regular development of sounds did not prevent him from admitting wild interpretations. These are not

AUGUST SCHLEICHER

found in the phonology, however, but occur here and there in the morphology. Such, for instance, is the desperate explanation of the numerals *eleven* and *twelve* which Schleicher took over from Bopp.[1] We may add that in retaining this explanation Schleicher showed a sort of rigid conservatism which recurs so often in his work that it must be regarded as one of his characteristics. The explanation had already been refuted, clearly and conclusively, by C. W. Smith, in a periodical of which Schleicher himself was co-editor. Similarly, we find in the morphology a no less desperate explanation of our numeral for *one thousand*, Gothic *þūsundi*, which he breaks up into *þū-sundi* and is content to regard as a compound of *ten* and *hundred*, that is,

[1] See above, p. 243.

as derived from the two words which in Gothic are *taihun* and *hund.*[1]
The whole word, according to Schleicher, is "an irregularly changed
formation which has escaped the usual laws." In the phonology
there is not a hint of the changes in sounds which would be required
to justify such etymologies. The Old Adam has been cast out from
the phonology, but still frolics at will in the morphology.

Schleicher contributed especially to the progress of method by his
precise reconstructions. On the basis of comparisons between the
surviving Indo-European languages, he reconstructed both the
phonological system and the individual words and forms of the
parent speech. The necessity for such reconstruction was pointed
out as early as 1837 by Theodor Benfey in his review of Pott's
Etymologische Forschungen, but Schleicher was the first to carry it
out in practice. He applied this method in the first edition of his
Compendium without any remark whatever, but in the second edition
he gave the reasons for it at some length, emphasizing the fact that
on the one hand reconstructions place the most recent results of
research concretely before the eye, and that on the other hand they
make it perfectly plain that Sanskrit is not identical with the Indo-
European parent language. Both of these observations are correct
and appropriate. To reconstruct the forms which are regarded as
the original or primitive Indo-European forms is really the shortest
method of indicating later changes in the individual languages. This
method has also the great advantage of making clear at once to
beginners and non-specialists — in whose case the childhood mal-
adies of linguistics might otherwise be repeated — that no one of the
languages compared is regarded as the source of all the other Indo-
European languages. It may be added that the necessity of reconstruction compels the student to give his undivided attention to
every detail in the development of sounds. Therefore the method has
maintained itself to this day, and must be regarded as indispensable.
Reconstructed forms are usually indicated nowadays by an asterisk
placed before them (for example, Indo-European **eḱwo-s*, or more
exactly **äḱwå-s* "horse"), so that they may not be confused with
historically authentic forms like Latin *equu-s*, Greek *hippo-s*, Sanskrit
aśva-s, Avesta *aspa-*, Old English *eoh*, Old Irish *ech*, West Tokharian
yakwe, East Tokharian *yukə*, etc. This practice, too, goes back to
Schleicher.

[1] He had already used the first of these two words as the explanation of *ain-lif* "eleven"
and *twa-lif* "twelve."

When Schleicher speaks of reconstruction, however, there is something in his choice of words which sounds strange to the ears of modern scholars, and this impression is augmented when one learns that he attempted to write a whole fable in the Indo-European parent language. In spite of all his caution, Schleicher had much greater confidence than we now have in the power of linguistics to reproduce this tongue which disappeared thousands of years ago. We have held to a full belief in the utility of reconstructions *as formulas*. The formula *ek̑wo-s* tells us at a glance, for instance, a great many things about the forms of the word for *horse* in the various Indo-European languages: it tells us that there is virtually nothing in the form of the Indian *aśva-s* which we can regard as wholly primitive: each of the two identical vowels had originally its own coloring, the first like *e* (cf. *e* in Latin *equu-s*), the second like *o* (which Greek *híppo-s* has best preserved), and both the consonants were at first different in quality from what they are in Indian. In the same way the formula with its five characters tells us many things about the presumable development of the other languages that it would take much longer to express in words. But if we are asked whether *ek̑wo-s* is identical with the pronunciation of the noun which the linguistic ancestors of our race used thousands of years ago in their original home, we must reply only that we cannot be sure.

We have altogether too many examples how far the results we get from the comparison of a number of related languages can be from the actual common original of the languages, to reply otherwise. The comparison of all the living forms of the Germanic word for *horn* (German *Horn*, Dutch *hoorn*, English *horn*, Danish *horn*) can lead us only to the basic form *horn*, never to the Golden Horn's *horna*.[1] A comparison of German *senden*, Dutch *zenden*, English *to send*, Danish *sende*, or of German *älter*, English *elder*, Danish *ældre* must lead inevitably to parent forms with an *e*-colored vowel in the first syllable, and yet we know that this syllable still had *a* at a time when our branch had long since broken up into distinct languages (cf. Gothic *sandjan* "to send," Old High German *altiro* "elder"). A form beginning in *æld-*, which would be the result of a reconstruction founded on a comparison of the modern languages, certainly does not underlie German *älter*: *d* changed to *t* earlier than *a* became *æ*. The ending in *elder* we should refer to a parent form with *r*, if we were to rely on the comparison of the living languages, but the actual consonant

[1] See p. 235.

was z at a time when these languages were still united (cf. Gothic *alþiza*). If we will only stay away from Sardinia we can wander throughout the world of Romance languages without being shaken in our belief that the first syllable in the word for *heaven* (Italian *cielo*, French *ciel*) and the second syllable in the word for *ten* (Italian *dieci*) began originally with a sibilant (*č*). Only in Sardinia can one hear such forms as *kelu* "heaven." Some years since it was also dangerous to go to the island of Veglia, on the coast of Croatia, for here one ran the risk of hearing *dik* "ten." But that danger is now past since the last speaker of Dalmatian, Anton Udina, was blown up (see p. 93). And the time will come when Sardinia also will be purified. Then there will be no living language to gainsay the *č* pronunciation; and yet we know with absolute certainty that the pronunciation included a *k* sound as long as the unity of the Romance languages remained unbroken.

Whence do we get the impression that similar traps are not laid for us when we compare the oldest Indo-European languages? May not they also have developed parallel-wise in many respects, after their actual unity had long been destroyed? Or may not some dialects which deviated from the general parallelism have been lost without a trace, leaving behind them a uniformity which deceives us with respect to the age of individual features? It is not only possible, but highly probable, that we make many mistakes in our reconstructions of Indo-European forms — mistakes which we cannot hope that our successors will be able to correct, simply because they are incurred under the necessities of logic; it is highly probable that in our reconstructions we include sounds of entirely different ages which never existed contemporaneously. We must relinquish the hope of writing fables in the parent language, and must admit that we cannot reconstruct whole words, but only the older stages of the individual sounds of words, and that we do not know how old these reconstructed stages are. Nevertheless, we permit ourselves to put the reconstructed sounds together into syllables and words, and to assert hopefully that these reconstructed forms come much closer to the original historical starting-point than any of the forms in the individual languages. But whether they themselves ever had historical existence in a definite place and definite period we do not know. We pass them on, then, as nothing more than formulas, a sort of common denominator for all the varying forms of the separate languages.

But in return we demand that the formulas be worked out with strict exactness in accordance with the forms in the individual languages. They must contain no more and no less than the historical forms warrant. Schleicher, however, occasionally intermingled various preconceived theories. When we see that *mother* in Latin is *māter*, in Greek (Doric) *mātēr*, in Sanskrit *mātā*, accusative *mātar-am*, and that in Lithuanian it is *mōtē* "woman," accusative *mōter-į*, we infer that the word was originally **mātē* and under inflection showed the stem **māter-*. From this we can explain all of the forms (including the Greek and Latin, where *-r* has crept into the nominative); for every single sound in the formula **mātē* we have historical authority. But Schleicher reconstructed **mātar-s*, a formula which contains both more and less than the forms in the individual languages. It contains an *-s* for which there is no historical authority, and it contains a short vowel in the second syllable, whereas all the historical forms have or had a long vowel. Schleicher *could* perpetrate this because his sound-laws were so flexible. It cost him nothing to assume the dropping of an *s* and partly of an *r* too, or the lengthening of a short vowel in the individual languages, although this did not agree especially well with what we know of the evolution of the sounds of these languages. And he was *compelled* to do it because he conceived that the parent language of our family was something entirely original, primitive, wherein no "decay" had taken place, but where all the words were still completely "undamaged." In such a language the nominative case of the word "mother" naturally had to consist of a stem and the usual nominative ending in *-s* without any irregularity. In Schleicher's formula there is reflected a lack of clearness with regard to the conditions of the development of sounds, and an unhistorical conception of the parent language, which, no matter how old the period may be to which it belongs, must have passed through a development of perhaps more than a hundred thousand years, with decay and new formations as in historical times. Thus the new method was far from perfect in the hands of its founder.

Schleicher assumed the following system of phonology for the Indo-European parent language:

Original vowel ("grundvokal"):	*a*	*i*	*u*
First "increment" ("erste steigerung")	*aa(ā)*	*ai*	*au*
Second "increment" ("zweite steigerung")	*āa(ā)*	*āi*	*āu*

Consonants:

		r	*n*	*m*
(*j* like *y* in English *yard*)		*j*	*v*	*s*
		k	*g*	*gh*
		t	*d*	*dh*
		p	*b*	*bh*

A glance shows that this is a system of divisions in threes or multiples of three exclusively, and Schleicher himself calls attention to these "peculiar numerical facts" in which he, as a disciple of Hegel, apparently saw a recommendation for the system. Upon us this has rather a contrary effect. Even if we can bring ourselves to believe that Schleicher arrived at his system of phonology honestly, and that his philosophical joy over the triads came *after* the fact, we cannot escape a suspicion that here and there the facts may have been forced a bit in connection with this system of threes. In general, however, Schleicher's system may pass as an expression of the current opinions of his time. Not only for Schleicher, but for all his contemporaries, Sanskrit was of sufficient importance to assure the acceptance of the triad *a, i, u* in spite of the protest of the languages of the European branches. And scholars were very willing to bracket *r* and *l* together on the score of Indian and Iranian, although they are plainly distinct in the other branches. Thus Schleicher attained the threefold scheme *r, n, m*, which, however, labors under the defect that it is not actually threefold, but consists of one sound of one type and two sounds of another. The next threefold scheme labors under the same defect: *s* belongs in an entirely different berth from *j* and *v* (especially in view of the fact that there was no *v* in the parent language, but *w*). And finally, Schleicher's threefold scheme of the stops was built more upon Greek than upon Sanskrit. As we have already seen in Rask's system of sound-shifts (p. 252), Greek actually has a threefold system of stops:

k	*g*	*kh*
t	*d*	*th*
p	*b*	*ph*

But Sanskrit has a fourfold system:

k	*g*	*gh*	*kh*
t	*d*	*dh*	*th*
p	*b*	*bh*	*ph*

In general, corresponding to Greek *kh, th,* and *ph,* Sanskrit shows the remarkable sounds *gh, dh,* and *bh;* for example, Sanskrit *stigh-nō-ti* "he walks, strides forward," Greek *steichō* "I walk," Old English *stígan* "to ascend." But there are other cases, although they are much rarer, where *kh*, *th* and *ph* occur also in Sanskrit: Sanskrit *śaykha-s* "shell," Greek *kóncho-s*. In 1862 the famous mathematical and linguistic scholar Grassmann proved that this plurality of sounds in Sanskrit must be an inheritance from the parent language, so that Schleicher might at least have made a correction in his system in his second edition; but he made no such correction.

Most extraordinary is the method by which Schleicher has carried out his threefold plan in the vowel system. The two "increments" serve the purpose of explaining the Indo-European vowel alternations (Grimm's *Ablaut*), and the scheme fits well enough in cases like

O.N. *aka* (original vowel *a*) "to drive": preterite *ók* (increment)
Goth. *bitans* (" " *i*) "bitten" : " *báit* (")
Goth. *biudans* (" " *u*) "offered" : " *báud* (")

But there are a great many other vowel alternations inherited from the parent language which cannot be forced into Schleicher's system. And the system has the defect that it employs long *ā* twice, whereas long *ī* and long *ū* have no place at all, although in many instances they agree in occurring throughout all the old Indo-European languages. Schleicher's ablaut system is really an unsuccessful adaptation of the less symmetrical system of the ancient Indian grammarians, which was based on much keener observation.

Just as Schleicher created a clear and precise method of expression for phonology in his reconstructed forms, so he set forth his ideas on the relationships of the Indo-European languages clearly by drawing up a genealogical tree.[1] This method of procedure had the great advantage of excluding at first glance certain of the false conceptions of previous times, such as the notion that Sanskrit is the parent language, or that Latin is descended from Greek. But here Schleicher did not build permanently. For the genealogical tree is really not fitted to give correct ideas about the relationships of languages. Such a tree always shows complete linguistic unity up to a certain date, and from that date on, complete linguistic separation. This conflicts not only with modern experience with dialects, but also, as we shall see in the next section, with the way in which the individual similarities and dissimilarities among the Indo-European branches actually occur.

The last name in the group of scholars who close the first period of

[1] See below, pp. 311 ff.

comparative linguistics is that of August Fick. Whereas Schleicher died before the new era came, and Curtius, as we shall see, steadfastly opposed the new ideas, Fick's destiny was to live to see the new era and adopt its ideas and methods. Yet his chief work was produced before the transformation, and even in its later editions it retains to a certain extent the atmosphere of the old days, in spite of all the modernizations made.

AUGUST FICK
[After *Indogermanisches Jahrbuch*, v]

In its first edition this work bore the title *Wörterbuch der indogermanischen Grundsprache in ihrem Bestande vor der Völkertrennung* (Göttingen, 1868). Here the title itself points toward Schleicher's confidence in reconstruction. In succeeding editions this was changed to *Vergleichendes Wörterbuch der indogermanischen Sprachen*. The second edition appeared in 1870–71; the third, in four volumes, in 1874–76. Since 1876 is the most decisive year for the transformation of Indo-European linguistics, even the third edition is now antiquated. In 1890 a fourth edition began to appear, in which several other scholars took part besides Fick.

The second edition, still in one volume, consists of seven sections.

In the first section appears the vocabulary of the Indo-European parent language before the initial division of the folk into an Indo-Iranian half and a European half. The second and third sections contain the vocabulary of the Indo-Iranian period and of the Common European period. As for the further division of the European half, it must be remembered that at that time scholars did not have to deal with all the branches of languages which we must now study. Not only were Armenian and Albanian included later in the comparison, but Celtic as well was then a field extremely difficult of access. Schleicher had treated it grammatically in his *Compendium*, but Fick had to forego a lexical treatment of it. For those branches of languages whose treatment was possible, Fick adheres to the division into a Southern European (Græco-Italic) and a Northern European (Germanic-Baltic-Slavonic) group, whose vocabulary is set forth in the fourth and fifth sections, while the last two sections treat the two subdivisions of the Northern group, the Common Balto-Slavonic language, and the Common Germanic language. The reconstruction of the numerous prehistoric forms (Common Indo-European, Common Indo-Iranian, Common European, and so on down to Common Germanic) proceeds according to the genealogical-tree theory. The tree is, indeed, different from Schleicher's, but the fundamental idea is the same. Fick continually works with the division of an originally uniform language into two groups which have nothing to do with each other after the division. This point of view makes it possible to apply the principle which he expressed by the motto on the title-page:

"Durch zweier Zeugen Mund wird alle Wahrheit kund." [1]

If a word is found in the two branches, then it was also to be found in the original language which divided into these two branches. If, on the contrary, a word is not found in both branches, one has no right to assume its existence in the original of the two branches. Therefore Fick assumes as Common Indo-European a word which is found in at least one of the Indo-Iranian dialects and in at least one of the European languages, regardless of which one, whereas, on the other hand, a word which is found in all the European branches cannot pass as Common Indo-European unless it is found also in Indo-Iranian. The vocabulary of the subordinate common languages is determined similarly. For Common European there must be the

[1] This refers to the legal rule that agreement between the statements of two independent witnesses is supposed to be a sufficient proof of truth.

double evidence of a word's occurrence both in one of the Southern languages and in one of the Northern; for Common Germanic the words must occur on both sides of the line of division which Fick drew through this branch.

In the course of time Fick's system was forced to undergo changes. But his initial division of the Indo-European family into an Indo-Iranian and a European branch is still maintained in the fourth edition, and the method of determining the Common Indo-European vocabulary is the same. A witness from each side is invariably the necessary and satisfactory condition for recognizing that a word descends from the parent language of the family. In this respect the book now seems old-fashioned. Today we assume no wider division between Indo-Iranian and the other branches than between these branches themselves, and we no longer know any simple and mechanical method of determining the age of a given word. We must examine each case individually with due attention to various kinds of probability, and very often we cannot go beyond uncertainty. But in general we are willing to regard a word as inherited from the parent language if it occurs in all of the branches but one, even if this one be Indo-Iranian. On the contrary, Fick would exclude such words. Yet he recognized a word as Indo-European although it occurred in only two branches, provided one of them was Indo-Iranian. With this we cannot agree. No doubt cases are easily conceivable where the evidence of two branches would be sufficient to justify our attributing Indo-European age to a word. But in such cases the languages must belong to opposite extremes of the family, and there must have been no special intercourse between them. It is not sufficient for us that they fall on different sides of Fick's main line of division. We know of too many cases of special intercourse across that line. A word which we find only in Indo-Iranian and in one of the languages farthest east of the "European" group naturally *may* be descended from the parent language, but we must also take into account the possibility that it did not develop until later, after the Indo-Europeans had spread over a wide territory, and that it never belonged to the entire territory.

Evidently it was Fick's intention to remedy in the fourth edition the incompleteness excusable in the earlier issues, and to include in his work all the Indo-European languages. He succeeded in inducing Whitley Stokes to study the Celtic vocabulary in a special volume. But no collaborator was to be found for Armenian or Albanian.

Moreover, the ancient vocabularies of these two languages cannot be reconstructed according to Fick's method. Here there are not two witnesses to examine. Armenian from the first is a single language, and likewise Albanian, if some small dialectal variations are excepted. A vocabulary could be drawn up of words which Armenian or Albanian has in common with other Indo-European languages, but in this way the original plan of Fick's work would have been completely abandoned. He planned not a series of parallel treatments of the lexical heritage of the various languages from the parent speech, but a collective treatment of the Indo-European vocabulary itself.

It is not possible now to rejuvenate this work of Fick's, conceived in the mode of thought prevailing before 1870, and to bring it up to date completely. But this fact cannot lessen Fick's honor in having made the first great effort toward a collective treatment of the Common Indo-European vocabulary: the first, and until now the only attempt in this direction. Our times boast information many times more abundant than that accessible when Fick's dictionary was begun. But thus far there has been virtually no effort made to organize it in any other form than in etymological dictionaries of the separate languages, dictionaries in which one is often nearly smothered with detail. Nevertheless, a comprehensive Indo-European dictionary with Fick's clearness but without Fick's errors ought some day to be written. But it cannot be built on Fick's invariable two-way division. In a single section it must contain all the ancient words which can be found in more than one branch, with the exception of those which occur only in two very closely related branches. We should have to give up the attempt to specify what belonged to the whole Indo-European field, and what was current in only one portion of it, what originated in the still undivided parent language, and what first developed after the language had attained a wide dissemination and had split up into dialects. In our reconstruction of vocabulary we must practise great caution, just as we must in reconstructing the forms of sounds.[1] Any one who desired a survey of the vocabulary which can be found in all or most of the branches, or, *vice versa*, of the vocabulary which is known from only a restricted portion of the field, would then have to extract it himself from the dictionary, although much help could be afforded by proper indices.[2]

[1] See pp. 268 ff.

[2] In 1926 a comparative Indo-European dictionary by the late Alois Walde began to appear. It will be up to date and extremely useful, but without the greatness of conception of Fick's.

The close of the earlier period of comparative linguistics (the period prior to 1870) which brought with it the comprehensive works of Curtius, Schleicher, and Fick, brought also the first periodical specially devoted to comparative Indo-European linguistics, the *Zeitschrift für vergleichende Sprachforschung*, edited, from 1852 on, by Adalbert Kuhn,[1] who was prudent enough to limit its field to the three best-known branches of the family, Germanic, Latin, and Greek. The other branches found space in another publication, *Beiträge zur vergleichenden Sprachforschung*, which Kuhn edited in collaboration with Schleicher from 1858. It was not until 1876, in the new period of comparative linguistics, that the two were united. Together they have had vast importance in organizing collaboration among the various scholars in this extensive field.

The New Period of Comparative Linguistics

The reason no one up to and including Schleicher had attained a clear grasp of the regularity of the evolution of sounds lay in the quality of the equipment of detailed results with which scholars had to work. This equipment offered a number of examples of regularity, but at the same time the most striking irregularities. Where scholars assumed an Indo-European k as the starting-point, they found in Sanskrit sometimes k, sometimes $č$, sometimes $ś$, in Latin c (pronounced k), qu, in Greek k, p, t; it all seemed confusion. Sanskrit k, $č$ and $ś$ might correspond to Latin c; Greek k, p and t seemed to correspond just as well to Sanskrit k as to Sanskrit $č$, and so on. Nobody knew why f and b, $þ$ and d, h and g alternated in Germanic.[2] And with the vowels the matter became frantic. Schleicher proposed three Indo-European vowels, a, i and u; i and u certainly caused no trouble, for they appeared fairly constantly as i and u in all the oldest languages; but the development of Schleicher's Indo-European short a was all the more complicated. It occurred in the individual languages as a, o, u, e and i, apparently so helter-skelter that it was extremely difficult to fix upon any regular correspondence. One can get an idea of the confusion by glancing at the following table, in which I have arranged the varying vowels in four sections, in anticipation of modern knowledge. The vowels which appear in the same sections may correspond to one another. The a which in the case of Latin is included in parentheses in the first, second and fourth sec-

---

[1] The title is often abbreviated as "Kuhn's *Zeitschrift*."

[2] See above p. 261.

tions is still an unsolved difficulty, which, however, when it is isolated, no longer confuses the general picture; such cases as Latin *quattuor* are meant:

Indo-European (Schleicher).............................*a*

Sanskrit.............	*a*	*a*	*i, a*	*i, u, a,* no vowel
Greek...............	*e*	*o*	*a*	*a* (dialectal *o*)
Latin...............	*e, i* (*a*)	*o, u,* (*a*)	*a*	*e, i, o, u* (*a*)
Celtic...............	*e, i*	*o, u*	*a*	*e, i, a*
Gothic.............	*i*	*a*	*a*	*u*
O.N., O.E., O.H.G....	*e, i*	*a*(or umlaut)	*a*(or umlaut)	*u, o* (or umlaut)
Lithuanian..	*e*	*a*	*a*	*i*
Slavonic.............	*e*	*o*	*o*	*e, ĭ,* no vowel

In order to understand completely how confusing this multiplicity was, the reader should ignore this division into sections. The result will be that all the vowels correspond with one another after a fashion. If one observed that in Latin *ferō* "I carry" the *e* corresponded to the *e* in Greek *phérō*, the next moment one was confronted with Latin *tenuis* "thin": Greek *tanaós* "long," or Latin *centum* "hundred": Greek *he-katón*, or inversely Latin *quattuor* "four": Greek *téttares*. If one observed that Latin *o* and *u* corresponded to Greek *o* in *hortus* "garden": Greek *chórtos* "inclosure" or in Latin *sulcus* "furrow": Greek *holkós*, the next moment one might be confronted with Latin *cornus* "dogwood": Greek *krános* or Latin *ursus* "bear": Greek *árktos* (in Sanskrit *ṛkṣa-s* without any vowel whatever).

Curtius had made a small beginning in bringing order out of chaos by pointing out that in words where Latin and Greek agreed on *e* (Latin *ferō* : Greek *phérō*), all the other European languages also had *e* from the beginning. In other words, he had collected the cases which are included in the first section of the table. But since he did not explain all the numerous exceptions, no wonder his discovery was regarded by Schleicher as insignificant.

The whole confusion of consonants and vowels was explained, however, in the course of the seventies, by a series of brilliant discoveries by the Italian Ascoli, the Danes Vilhelm Thomsen and Karl Verner, the French Swiss Ferdinand de Saussure, and the German Karl Brugmann. It became evident that most of the difficulties depended upon the fact that the starting-points for development had been determined wrongly and that reconstructions had been incorrectly made. Schleicher thought to bury the ghost of the overvaluation of Sanskrit, to bury it and drive a stake through it by his method of reconstruction; but, as it turned out, the ghost was in the stake itself. His reconstructions did not rest upon a sufficiently exact comparison of the individual languages. They were dominated by Sanskrit in connection with a naïve idea of the pristine character and great simplicity of the parent language.

Graziadio Isaia Ascoli, a man of extremely broad scholarship in the Indo-European family of languages, as well as in other families,

GRAZIADIO ASCOLI
[After *Miscellanea linguistica... Ascoli*, Torino, 1901]

opens the series of discoveries. In his *Corsi di Glottologia* (1870) he attacks the *k* problem which neither Bopp nor Schleicher had been able to solve because neither of them dared to think that Sanskrit was, in this instance at least, very far removed from the original state of things, and was by no means perspicuous. Ascoli both thought it and proved it. He pointed out clearly that in this respect Iranian was much older and clearer than Sanskrit, and thereafter it became quite plain to him that there was not merely *one k* series in the parent language (*k, g, gh*), but *three* entirely different series.

K and *ś* in Sanskrit reflected a difference which descended from the parent language; *c* and *qu* in Latin (with which *k* and *p* in Greek correspond) reflected a second original difference. But on one point Ascoli overshot his mark. He believed that Sanskrit *č* also reflected one of the shades in the original language. This was wrong, and with this mistake there entered an error in his calculations.

ESAIAS TEGNÉR (THE YOUNGER)

Sanskrit *č* is actually due to an Indian sound-law. It developed from *k* under the influence of the following vowel, approximately as Greek *t* from one of the *k-* sounds is dependent on the following vowel. But this Indian law could not be seen unless one dared assume that the vowel system in Sanskrit is quite the reverse of primitive, and that the Latin *e* in *que* "and" (Greek *te*) is older than the *a* in Sanskrit *ča* "and." Vilhelm Thomsen was the first to utter this revolutionary thought. Later the same discovery ("The Law of Palatals") was made by Verner, by Esaias Tegnér in Lund, by Saussure, and by the two German scholars, Hermann Collitz and Johannes Schmidt. The discovery was published in 1878.

The change from *k* to a *č*-like sound before front vowels is so common a phenomenon that now one almost wonders that it took so long to explain

Sanskrit *č*. But the sound-change was not so clear-cut as, for instance, in modern Swedish, where any one can see at once the reason for the special pronunciation of *k* in *kind*, *kön*, etc.[1] The Sanskrit change took place in a very distant period and was obscured by later developments. Something similar happened in English, where no one can see directly why *chin* and *kin* are so pronounced: the first is Gothic *kinnus*, the second Gothic *kuni*. Or, more correctly, the Indian shift was much more obscure than the English, in many ways. And moreover, whereas no one is surprised at such occurrences in English, at that time such a thing was in no way expected in venerable Sanskrit. The Indian "Law of Palatals" was therefore a genuine discovery.

The mistake that Ascoli made, however, retarded appreciably a clear knowledge of the Indo-European *k* sounds. Some part of his results had to be discounted, and the discounting was done by guess before the discovery of the Law of Palatals. The guess went too far, so that scholars were content to accept two series of *k* sounds in Indo-European. The necessity of accepting three, therefore, had to be proved once more. This proof was not made until 1890, — by Bezzenberger, Hermann Osthoff, and Sophus Bugge.

As examples of the three series of *k* sounds which we now accept, the following may be cited:

Sanskr. *śatá-m* hundred, Gr. *he-katón*, L. *centum* (*k-*), Goth. *hund*
Sanskr. *ka-s* who, *katara-s* which of two, Gr. *pótero-s* which of two, L. *quis* who, O.E. *hwá* who
Sanskr. *kékara-s* squinting, L. *caecus* blind, Goth. *haih-s* one-eyed

Since we assume four sounds (*k*, *g*, *gh*, *kh*) in each series, we have twelve Indo-European sounds where Schleicher was satisfied with three. The large number of back-consonants with which we thus equip the parent language is perhaps a little surprising at first but in fact it is not at all striking either phonetically or historically. Both in front of and behind the place in the mouth where our customary *k* sound is produced, other *k*-like sounds, each with its own special shading, may be produced. In front of our *k* the "mouillé" *k* (with an *i* shading — cf. the so-called Southern pronunciation of words like *card*, *can't*) can be made, and far back in the mouth toward the uvula a *k* sound can be pronounced the shading of which is reminiscent of the Northumbrian burr (such a *k* sound is used by the Eskimos for instance). We are not accustomed now to use the back of the tongue a great deal for producing phonetic distinctions, but primitive customs of articulation were different. Scholars have not been altogether wrong in maintaining that the movement of the center of pronunciation from the back to the front of the mouth is a steady development in civiliza-

[1] Initial *k* in Swedish when followed by a front accented vowel is usually pronounced nearly like English *ch-*.

tion, a link in the "humanization" of language. Vice versa, the consequence is that the farther we go back in time the more ready we must be
to find precisely the shadings in pronunciation which can be produced
by the throat and the back of the tongue.

In 1875, before the "Law of Palatals" had been made public, Karl
Verner published his famous article, *An Exception to the First Consonant Shift (Eine Ausnahme der ersten Lautverschiebung)*. On
pp. 261 ff. above I have mentioned the irregularities in the Germanic sound-shift in the case of medial sounds, and have cited some
few examples (German *Bruder: Vater*, Gothic *brōþar: faḍar*, etc.).
The irregularities occur abundantly in the Germanic vocabulary,
and prevail from the earliest times throughout the inflection of
strong verbs. This last feature is most striking in Old High German,
although it is also quite evident in the other ancient Germanic
tongues:

O.H.G.	*slahan* to strike	:	*gislagan* struck
O.E.	*sléan*	:	*slegen*
O.N.	*slá*	:	*sleginn*
O.H.G.	*findan* to find	:	*funtan* found
O.N.	*finna* (*nn* from *nþ*)	:	*fundinn*
Mod.H.G.	*ziehen* to pull	:	*gezogen* pulled
O.E.	*téon*	:	*togen*
Mod.H.G.	*schneiden* to cut	:	*geschnitten* cut
O.E.	*sníþan*	:	*sniden*
Mod.H.G.	*sieden* to boil	:	*gesotten* boiled
O.E.	*séoþan*	:	*soden*
Mod.E.	*seethe*	:	*sodden*

And in the same way *s* interchanges with *r*:

O.N.	*kjósa* to choose	:	*korinn* chosen
O.E.	*céosan*	:	*coren*

This irregularity was indeed an abomination to scholars who had
anything to do with the older Germanic languages, but no one had
been able to explain it. Therefore the effect of Verner's article, in
which the solution of the problem was clearly given, was immeasur-
able. Now there were no more exceptions to the Germanic sound-
shift, and this absence of exceptions necessarily had quite as strong
an effect upon the whole conception of linguistics as the chief laws
applying to the sound-shifts had exerted in their time. Then,
scholars were beginning to understand that there *were* laws of
phonology; now, they were awaking to the fact that such laws
operate regularly. And to this effect Verner's explanation contrib-

uted: the cause of these changes was the position of the accent in
Indo-European, which is preserved in Sanskrit, but disappeared in
Germanic in prehistoric times. To the consonant-shift in Germanic
the shift in accent in Sanskrit corresponds exactly, as it manifests
itself in contrasts between single words (Sanskrit *bhrátā* "brother":
pitá "father") or in the contrast between the different inflectional
forms of the "strong" verbs (see an example on p. 286; Old High

KARL VERNER
[After *Nordisk tidsskrift for filologi*, third series, v]

German *werdan* and Sanskrit *vártē*). Verner's discovery suggested
how exhaustively one must study the phenomena, and how accurately one must discriminate, to understand the development of
sounds. It was, in fact, an emphatic warning not to regard any such
development as a mere whim of language.

The next year (1876) Karl Brugmann wrote an article entitled
Nasalis sonans in der indogermanischen Grundsprache, in which he
asserted that in the parent language of our family there must have
been syllables without vowels — syllables in which *n* or *m* had
syllabic functions. He also assumed syllables with syllabic *r(l)*. On

the basis of Brugmann's demonstration we today assume syllabic
n, m, r, l (*ṇ, ṃ, ṛ, ḷ*), as for instance in the following words:

Sanskr. *a-*, Gr. *a-*, L. *in-*, Goth. *un-* (negative prefix: Goth. *un-kunþ-s*,
    O.E. *un-cúþ*, unknown)
Sanskr. *śatá-m* hundred, Gr. *he-katón*, L. *centum*, Goth. *hund*, Lith. *šimta-s*
Sanskr. *ṛkša-s* bear, Gr. *árktos*, L. *ursus*
Sanskr. *vṛka-s* wolf, Goth. *wulf-s*, Czech *vlk*

The assumption of a syllabic *ṛ* in the parent language was not
entirely new. This sound was, indeed, preserved in Sanskrit and
also in the oldest Slavonic languages, as well as in some Slavonic
languages spoken today; and there had been hints from various
quarters that it belonged to the parent language (from Benfey in
1837, from Ebel in 1852). Naturally, Schleicher did not accept this
teaching in his *Compendium*, for it conflicted too strongly with his
theories: *ṛ* looks like a weakening of a more complete syllable, and
in Schleicher's opinion no weakening had taken place in the parent
language; that language knew only "the word still completely undamaged in all its parts." In the seventies several scholars had
touched upon the question again — G. Humperdinck in a school
programme (Siegburg, 1874), the famous Slavonic scholar Miklosich
in 1875, Brugmann's friend Osthoff in 1876. But the idea of a
syllabic *ṇ* and *ṃ* was quite new.[1]

Brugmann's article was not immediately accepted, as Verner's
was. On the contrary, it met with much criticism and opposition.
For this Brugmann was himself partly responsible. His article, in
sharp contrast with Verner's, is far from classical in form, and makes
very heavy reading. It must be admitted, also, that the conclusive
proof which can be adduced for the correctness of Brugmann's view
is not to be found in his article. But at least he had perceived the
truth and had so stated it as to convince others. Thus his discovery
did not have to lie in quarantine for twenty years, like Ascoli's. And
the significance of Brugmann's discovery can scarcely be overesti-
mated. It removed at one stroke all the irregularities in the fourth
section of the table on p. 278. After that it was not difficult, especially after the discovery of the "Law of Palatals" (p. 281), to make
headway with the remaining material — the first three sections of
the table — and to see that what was necessary was the assumption
of three Indo-European vowels: *e, o* and *a*.[2]

---

[1] Saussure made the same discovery while he was still in school.

[2] That is to say, an *e*-colored, an *o*-colored, and an *a*-colored vowel. We cannot give a com-

Brugmann's *ņ*, *ṃ*, *ḷ*, *ṛ* to a great extent broke the simple lines of Schleicher's system of Indo-European phonology, and these sounds are quite likely to puzzle those who are accustomed only to the pronunciation of the Western European (Germanic and Romance) languages. Certainly such sounds are not so very rare in English; in the last syllables of words like *heaven*, *cotton*, *chisel* we are not accustomed to pronounce a vowel plus *n* or *l*, but simply *n* or *l*. But our *ņ* and *ḷ* have no dignified place in the language, and we may be a little surprised to see them occur in formulas of our parent language on equal terms with self-respecting vowels like *e*, *o*, *a*, *i* and *u*. But we do not need to travel far before losing our surprise. As has been already indicated, some of the Slavonic languages have preserved Indo-European *ṛ* and *ḷ* to this day; indeed, they have partly developed such sounds, too, and in modern Slavonic languages we can hear them pronounced long and short and in various pitches just like vowels. We can even find a whole sentence without vowels, as in Czech *strč prst skrz krk* "stick your finger through your neck." Surely the greatest incredulity can demand no more.

The theory of syllabic Indo-European *n*, *m*, *l*, *r*, and with it the whole conception of the Indo-European vowel-system, reached completion at the hands of Saussure.

At the same time that the vowel-system of the parent language began to be cleared up, an understanding of the vowel-alternations inherited from the parent language also was achieved — the vowel-alternations which Grimm called **ablaut**.

On p. 272 above we have seen how Schleicher thought he had systematized these alternations. He regarded *a*, *i*, and *u* as the original vowels, and from them he derived *ā*, *ai*, and *au* by means of an "increment," and by means of a new "increment," *ā*, *āi*, and *āu*. The fresh discoveries, however, gave Schleicher's original stage and first "increment" a quite different appearance.

In the first place it was clear that *ei*, *oi* and *eu*, *ou* had to be substituted for Schleicher's *ai* and *au*. We see this clearly in the vowel alternation in Greek and Germanic verbs. In Greek the old diphthongs were simply preserved, while in Germanic they have been changed according to the laws of sounds. The changes of the diphthongs are especially great in English:

	ei		oi		i
Gr.	*péithomai* I obey	: perfect	*pépoitha* I trust	:	*e-pépithmen* we trusted

pletely accurate phonetic definition. But it is probable that the first two were very open sounds, closest to *ä* (as in English *man*) and *å* (more open than in English *not*), and the third was perhaps not a pure *a* but a sound similar to what phoneticians write as ʌ : the vowel in English *but*.

Goth.	*beidan*	:	preterite *baid*	:	*bidum*
	to wait		I waited		we waited

O.N.	*biða*	:		*beið*	:	*biðum*
O.E.	*bidan*	:		*bád*	:	*bidon*

	eu		**ou**		**u**
Goth.	*biudan*	:	preterite *baud*	:	*budum*
	to command		I commanded		we commanded

O.N.	*bjóða*	:	*bauð*	:	*buðum*
O.E.	*béodan*	:	*béad*	:	*budon*

But just as *ei* and *oi* alternated with *i*, and *eu* and *ou* alternated with *u*, it was seen that *en* and *on* alternated with *n̥*, *er* and *or* with *r̥*, etc.:

	en		**on**		**n̥**
O.N.	*finna*	:	*fann*	:	*fundum*
	to find		I found		we found
O.E.	*findan*	:	*fand*	:	*fundon*

	er		**or**		**r̥**
O.N.	*verða*	:	*varð*	:	*urðum*
	to become		I became		we became
O.H.G.	*werdan*	:	*ward*	:	*wurtum*
O.E.	*weorþan*	:	*wearþ*	:	*wurdon*
Sanskrit	*vártē*	:	perfect *vavárta*	:	*vavr̥timá*
	I turn		I turned		we turned

Eo and *ea* in *weorþan, wearþ* stand for *e* and *a* under the influence of the following consonant group *rþ*.

	el		**ol**		**l**
Goth.	*hilpan*	:	preterite *halp*	:	*hulpum*
	to help		I helped		we helped
O.H.G.	*helfan*	:	*half*	:	*hulfum*
O.E.	*helpan*	:	*healp*	:	*hulpon*

It was precisely these cases, with their *i-a-u* melody especially clear in Gothic, which had led Grimm to his short-sighted *ablaut* theory.[1] But Gothic *i-a-u* is not an old melody. How it sounds in the other Indo-European languages any one can easily figure out for himself with the help of the table on p. 278 (first, second, and fourth sections). From the alternation of *ar* and *r̥* which the Indians observed in their own language they followed the logical procedure of putting *r̥* in the same class as *i* and *u* in the ablaut table. Naturally Schleicher rejected this view. But after Brugmann's discovery there could no

[1] See above, p. 39.

longer be any doubt that not only ŗ and ļ but ṇ and ṃ played the same part in the Indo-European ablaut system as *i* and *u*.

On the other hand, it became evident that Schleicher's *a* belonged partly to the so-called first "increment," a fact which had been familiar to the Indians. Not only must *en* and *on*, *er* and *or*, etc., be arranged in the system in the same way as *ei* and *oi*, *eu* and *ou*, but it became evident that *e* and *o* in general had their regular place in the stage of the "first increment," whatever consonant followed them. For instance, there is an obvious parallelism between the two following Greek verbs:

ei		oi		i
péithomai	:	perfect *pépoitha*	:	aorist *e-pithómēn*
I obey		I trust		I obeyed

et		ot		t
pétomai	:	*pepótēmai*	:	*e-ptómēn*
I fly				

To Schleicher the two cases were entirely different. A form like *e-pithómēn* he had no objection to deriving from the parent language: it contained, indeed, the pure original vowel *i*. But *e-ptómēn* looked altogether too badly damaged to permit him to include it in his conception of the parent language, in which words were "undamaged in all their parts." It spoke so plainly of "decay" that Schleicher was compelled to regard it as having developed in historical times on Greek soil. But the truth is that no such dropping of vowels ever took place in Greece, and that a comparison of the languages shows plainly that forms like *e-ptómēn* are Common Indo-European, although the younger Indo-European languages have done away with most of them because of the inconvenient combinations of consonants.

When *e* and *o* thus took regular places in Schleicher's first stage of "increment," there was nothing left of his *a* in the so-called original stage except the cases in which Greek and Latin have *a*: the third section in the table on p. 278. That this *a* actually occurs parallel with *i* and *u* and with the ṇ, ṃ, ŗ, ļ discovered by Brugmann there can be no doubt. In this connection there are two different alternations:

ē		ō		a
Gr. *rhēg-ny-mi*	:	perfect *érrhōga*	:	aorist *e-rrhágēn*
I break		is broken		was broken

Goth. *lētan* : preterite *lailōt* : adj. *lat-s*
    to leave   left   lazy

        a   *ō*   *a*
Gr. (Doric) *phā-mí* :   *phōnē* : *pható-s*
      I say   voice   said

After all this, Schleicher's first and second stages (his original stage and first "increment") had changed character fundamentally. In the main our table must take the following shape:

i	*u*	*r̥*	*l̥*	*n̥*	*m̥*	*s*	*p* (or some other explosive)	*a*	*a*
ei, oi	*eu, ou*	*er, or*	*el, ol*	*en, on*	*em, om*	*es, os*	*ep, op*	*ē, ō*	*ā, ō*

A glance at this table will make it clear that it is impossible to conceive of the first stage as the original stage and the second as "increment." We must think of the second stage as the original, and the first as a result of its weakening. To these two stages we add a third, which exhibits a lengthening of our original stage (*ēi*, *ōi*, etc.). This lengthened stage corresponds to Schleicher's second "increment." This section, one-third of his system, can be permitted to remain substantially unchanged (but he himself had taken it over substantially unchanged from the Indian grammarians).[1]

This new conception of the Indo-European vowel-alternations was such a natural consequence of the discoveries of the seventies that we find it clearly enunciated by several scholars at the same time, and supported with the best proofs by Hermann Möller in 1878. But the most inspired treatment of Indo-European ablaut is that by Ferdinand de Saussure in his work, *Mémoire sur le système primitif des*

---

[1] It follows from what has been said above that the modern system of ablaut or vowel gradation must differentiate the following grades:

I. The *normal grade*, showing regularly the vowel *e*: *ei, eu, en, er, el*, etc. Greek *petomai* etc.; but also cases like Greek *rhēg-ny-mi* or *phā-mí* belong here.

II. The *o grade*: *oi, ou, on, or, ol*; Greek *pepótēmai*, also Greek *érrhōga, phōnē*.

III. The *weakened grade*: *i, u, n, r̥, l̥*; Greek *e-ptómén*, also *errhágēn, pha-tó-s*. This grade sometimes brings about the loss of a syllable, sometimes not. In addition to the normal grade *en* in Greek *génos* "race" and the *o* grade in Greek *góno-s* "offspring" we have the weakened grade as *n̥* in Greek *gé-ga-men* "we are," but as a consonant *n* in Greek *gí-gn-o-mai* "I am born, I become." We may therefore discriminate between two subgrades of the weakened grade: the reduced grade properly speaking (*gé-ga-men*) and the zero grade (*gí-gn-o-mai*).

IV. The *lengthened grade* shows a long *ē* or a long *ō*, so that we may discriminate two subgrades. Besides Latin *tegō* "I cover" (with the normal grade *e*) and *toga* (with the *o* grade) we have *tēgula* "a tile" with the lengthened grade *ē*. Besides the normal grade and the *o* grade in Greek *pétomai* "I fly," perfect *pepótēmai*, we have the lengthened grade *ō* in *pōtáomai* "I fly about."

voyelles dans les langues indo-européennes, 1879 (it actually appeared in 1878). He succeeded in explaining with great skill the vowel-alternations in which Indo-European *a* takes part (the last two sections in the table on p. 288). Although it cannot be seen from our

FERDINAND DE SAUSSURE
[After *Indogermanisches Jahrbuch*, ii]

extremely summary survey, these are the most difficult and involved of them all. After the appearance of Saussure's book Hermann Möller returned to the subject with great acumen.

The great revolution in the conception of the vowel-alternations inherited from the parent language has had much significance for our ideas about the pre-history of the parent language.

A prominent characteristic in the structure of the most ancient historical Indo-European languages is the fact that the root consists of but one syllable. Everything in the word in addition to the single root-syllable was felt by the speaker as a derivative element or an inflectional ending. This condition can be traced even in so recent a language as modern English and its dialects. In a group of related forms like *bear, bore, borne, born*, Scotch *bairn*, English *over-bear-ing, well-born, bur-den, bir-th*, the common element, the root, is monosyllabic, and everything besides is felt either as a derivative element or as an inflectional ending.

As long as Schleicher's point of view prevailed that no decay, but only development took place in prehistoric times, scholars had also to assume that this characteristic was one of the primitive features of our family of languages. The monosyllabic form of roots was assumed to have been typical of the Indo-European languages from their very beginning.

But after it had been perceived that the stage with the least volume in the vowel-alternations was due to decay, the suspicion began to dawn that in older periods roots had an entirely different appearance, and that certain elements which in historical times seemed to belong to inflectional or derivatory endings had actually been from the very first parts of the root itself. In a group of related forms like Indo-European *deiwo-s "god," Old Latin deivos, later dīvus and deus, and Indo-European *dyēu-s "heaven, the highest god," genitive *diw-os, Sanskrit dyāu-š, genitive div-ás, Greek Zeus, genitive Di-ós, we now regard both the vowels following d and w in *deiwo-s and the vowel which follows y in *dyēu-s as parts of the original kernel of the group of words, and in this way we reach a pre-Indo-European root form *deyewe- (*däyäwä-), that is, a tri-syllabic root with very simply constructed syllables. In the cases of these pre-Indo-European forms we must be even more careful than in the cases of the Indo-European forms (p. 268), not to interpret too mechanically their historical value. The vowel-alternations open to us a glimpse into the pre-history of the vowels, but we have no corresponding means for understanding the pre-history of the consonants. And these may have changed just as much as the vowels. Thus, for instance, we cannot know whether one or another of the consonants in our formula *däyäwä- (or perhaps all the consonants) had a different pronunciation from the historical one in the distant time when this root actually had three syllables.

After all the discoveries that had taken place in the course of the seventies, the view which met the eye of the scholar in the study of the old Indo-European languages was very different from the earlier one. Where before was mere irregularity, there was now the most striking regularity. The material now induced scholars to postulate complete adherence to laws in the development of sounds, and to seek an explanation for every deviation from the usual.

A contribution toward this result was made in yet another way. Certain striking irregularities were got rid of not by discoveries in the history of sounds, but by the **theoretical inquiry** which led to the recognition of the fact that these irregularities should not be considered at all from the point of view of the history of sounds.

A typical example of this sort of thing is furnished by the forms for the first person singular in the present tense of verbs:

Greek *phérō* I bear, carry	*ei-mi* I go	*dídō-mi* I give
Sanskrit *bhárā-mi*	*é-mi*	*dádā-mi*

From the point of view of the older linguistics there seemed to be, in these cases, considerable caprice in the development of sounds. The older linguistics started from the Indian forms as being the original ones, not only because of reverence for Sanskrit, but also because of the regularity it displays here: in all the forms we find the personal ending -*mi*, the relationship of which to the independent first personal pronoun (Greek *me* "me") had been recognized since the time of Rask and Bopp. But then it had to be assumed that this ending -*mi* had been dropped in some cases in Greek and preserved in others, without any perceptible rule. This apparent lack of adherence to law was disposed of by Wilhelm Scherer in his book *Zur Geschichte der deutschen Sprache* (1868), a work which was not without influence in the modern movement. One understands with some difficulty nowadays the admiration which Scherer's contemporaries (Verner and Brugmann, for instance) expressed for this book. It contains a great deal that is sheer imagination — for instance, an attempt to account for the development of sounds in the various languages on the basis of the spiritual natures of the several nations, and an equally fanciful attempt to explain the origin of inflections. There is very little in it that is usable now. But their admiration was fully justified by the intrepid energy with which Scherer liberated himself from the shackles of Schleicher's philosophy and appealed to the living source of experience. In every question involving the history of sounds he turned to phonetics, and he inveighed against Schleicher's distinction between a prehistoric period in which language was created, and an historical period of decay.[1] He recognized no other difference between prehistoric and historical than the nature of the sources themselves, and he therefore applied certain principles to the explanation of the ancient forms of language which scholars previously had avoided because they involved, for the "prehistoric" period, a recognition of that linguistic "decay" which was thought to be confined to historical times. One such principle was the assumption of transformation by analogy, or "false analogy," as it was then called. And it was precisely this principle which Scherer applied to the verb-forms just cited. He pointed out that the Greek distinction between verbs in -*ō* and verbs in -*mi* in the first person indicative occurs also in all the European languages and in the most ancient portions of the *Avesta*, and that it must therefore be a primitive feature of the Indo-European family. It follows that Sanskrit

[1] See above, p. 242.

bhárā-mi cannot be the primitive form, but must be due to the same "false analogy" which is responsible for the fact that the *-mi*-type in Old High German and in many modern Slavonic languages has developed at the expense of the *-ō*-type.

This explanation, which is certainly correct, had a liberating influence on phonology, which was no longer forced to accept an irregular and unmotivated dropping of the syllable *-mi*. And in general it is true that, in proportion as advancing scholarship recognized the significance of analogy in the development of language, the more evident did regularity in the development of sounds become. The postulation of frequent analogical changes in all linguistic periods is the logical precursor of the postulation of laws of sounds that admit of no exceptions. In *Zur Geschichte der deutschen Sprache* Scherer took only the one step. How far he was from full comprehension of regularity in development in sounds may be seen from various details in the book. But in the atmosphere of the seventies some idea of the inadmissibility of exceptions would naturally force itself upon any serious student of language, and Scherer expressed the doctrine in 1875 as follows: "The phonological changes which we can observe in documented linguistic history proceed according to fixed laws which suffer no disturbance save in accordance with other laws."

Verner had said something similar in a letter written in 1872, when he proposed to reverse the old proposition "No rule without exceptions" to "No exception without a rule"; "i.e. every exception to the rules prevailing in a language must have a cause." [1] The new ideas were in the air. Just as scholars passed from Bopp's wild treatment of sounds by way of Rask, Pott, and the others to Schleicher's period of laws with frequent, unmotivated exceptions, so one might presume that they could pass from Schleicher's treatment to our present method, which obliges a scholar to seek an explanation for every apparent irregularity. But it happened otherwise. The last step in the process was not to be taken without clamor and strife.

That this clamor and strife would come from Brugmann and his circle no one could have foreseen. A glance at the two famous articles of 1875 and 1876, Verner's and Brugmann's, will instantly show that

---

[1] This thought is repeated in a less emphatic form in Verner's famous article of 1875: "There must be a rule for irregularity; the problem is to find it."

Verner is closer, even in practice, to modern methods. Or, to put it more correctly, Verner's method is quite modern, and only some few external features recall the old period, while Brugmann's article is strongly reminiscent of the older methods of comparative linguistics. Some of his morphological explanations show a self-confidence, and a sovereign contempt for sounds, which almost remind one of Bopp. And when one reads in Brugmann that "the tendencies of sounds almost never prevail throughout," one cannot help thinking of Grimm's pronunciamento (cited on p. 262) concerning exceptions to the Germanic sound-shift. None the less, it was from Brugmann and his friends that the noisy announcement of the one saving doctrine of the new period emanated. Possibly the general rule that the new convert is the most ardent apostle worked here to some degree. At any rate, it is certain that the cataract's roar was in this case caused by efforts to hinder the progress of the stream.

It was Curtius who, with a deplorable lack of understanding, attempted to stand in the way of progress. Brugmann's epoch-making article appeared in the ninth volume of a periodical which Curtius edited, *Studien zur griechischen und lateinischen Grammatik*. With this ninth volume, Brugmann became co-editor, and Curtius was away on a journey when the issue in question was printed. His feelings when he read Brugmann's article may be inferred from a declaration that he added at the end of the volume, to the effect that because of his absence from Leipzig he had not been able to state his own opinion of his co-editor's article: "I must therefore leave to him alone the responsibility for his far-reaching conclusions." One more volume appeared with the names of Curtius and Brugmann on the title-page, but without any further contributions from Brugmann. Then Curtius decided "regretfully" to cease publication, or, rather, to replace this journal by another with which Brugmann had nothing to do. For his own part, Brugmann began to publish with his friend H. Osthoff a sort of journal, *Morphologische Untersuchungen*, which contained articles by the two editors exclusively. The first volume, which appeared in 1878, is introduced by a preface, written by Brugmann, but signed by both editors, which is in effect a programme of the new school. Much that this preface contains was theoretically justifiable, but on the whole it was an indiscreet performance. It was well enough to summon students of comparative linguistics "forth from the hypothesis-laden atmosphere where Indo-European prototypes are fabricated... into the clear air of tangible actuality of the present," [1] and it was permissible to mention Scherer as a reformer; but it was extremely imprudent of Brugmann to name himself and some of his closest friends as those alone amongst whom Scherer's words had fallen upon fruitful soil, and it was the height of imprudence to coin a special designation for the new movement thus signalized. Brugmann used the expression *die junggrammatische Richtung*, adopting a humorous nickname which had been used in Leipzig university circles of the young scholars who had rebelled against Curtius. From Brugmann's grandiose preface this term now wandered forth into the wide world, where its jocose application could not be understood; and it was of course taken as a factional name, as the name of a clique which claimed to have preëmpted trustworthy linguistic methods for itself alone. The defects in method against which the preface inveighed seemed to be regarded by its author as characteristic of all scholars who did not belong to the "Young Grammarians." The result was a strong feeling of opposition between Brugmann and Osthoff on the one hand and on the other not only scholars like Curtius who could not follow the new movement, but also scholars outside the Leipzig circle who were not inferior to the "Young Grammarians" in method — men like Schleicher's pupil Johannes Schmidt, or the school of Fick (Bezzenberger, Collitz).

The programme with which Brugmann followed his provocative introduction centered in the proposition concerning the absence of exceptions to the laws of sounds. This principle had been so long developing that there was no holding it back in the seventies: it had already been expressed more than once,[2] but Brugmann's preface was the first emphatic enunciation of it.

The vigorous theoretical discussion into the laws that govern the development of language which followed, and which as late as 1885 still called forth polemics from Curtius and Brugmann, was interesting from many points of view.[3]

---

[1] "Aus dem hypothesentrüben Dunstkreis der Werkstätte, in der man die indogermanischen Grundformen schmiedet... in die klare Luft der greifbaren Wirklichkeit und Gegenwart."

[2] See above, p. 292. In the Leipzig circle Leskien especially insisted upon it, both orally, and, in 1876, in print.

[3] An inquiry with a similar subject is to be found at a much earlier time in Jakob Hornemann Bredsdorff's *Om Aarsagerne til Sprogenes Forandringer* ("On the Causes of Change in Language"), in the programme of the Roskilde Cathedral School for 1821, republished by Vilhelm Thomsen, Copenhagen, 1886. The article anticipates many of the ideas which came up during

The most significant result of the discussions was the explanation of the influences tending to disturb the development of sounds. Such disturbing influences may be of an external nature: loans from near or distant languages or dialects, influence exerted by the written language, and so on. Loan-words, even from rather distant languages, may be so fully assimilated by the inherited vocabulary that it requires some linguistic training to distinguish them from the native stock. Such assimilated loan-words are likely to give the naïve thinker an illusion of irregular development of sounds. No doubt every English speaker will associate the noun *choice* with the verb *to choose*, and the association is quite correct. But the diphthong of the noun might seem irregular, for none of the diphthongs or vowels possible in the ablaut series of *choose* [1] could regularly yield *oi* in modern English. The explanation is that *choice* is borrowed from Old French. Such doublets as *shirt* and *skirt* do not prove that sounds may develop differently under identical conditions, for *skirt* is a Scandinavian loan-word. Nor does *vixen* beside *fox* prove any whimsicality in the development of sounds, for *vixen* is borrowed from a Southern dialect, in which *v-* from *f-* is regular.

The influence of the written language is enormous everywhere, though it is not always easy to discover. Very often it counteracts a phonetic development wholesale, so that only a few words escape it on account of their being much more frequent in the spoken than in the written language. These few words, then, may easily be mistaken for exceptions due to some dialectal influence, although in reality they represent the regular development of the spoken language. The influence of the written language becomes very evident, however, when the orthography which acts on the speakers is an abnormal one. The French noun *legs* "bequest" was written originally *lais* or *leis*, and is the verbal noun belonging to *laisser* "to leave," but the learned orthography *legs*, which was adopted because of a false etymological connection with *léguer* "to bequeathe," is gradually forcing the *g* sound into the spoken form of the word. In the French name *Lefebvre* the silent letter *b* is a learned invention de-

---

the discussions of the seventies and eighties. That it does not reach the bottom of the matter is not remarkable; and neither is it remarkable that in spite of its many correct ideas and observations it had no influence. It could have had no influence even if it had been more easily accessible, for it deals with problems which at that time were not even raised elsewhere, or which at any rate no one understood how to bring into connection with the burning questions of the day.

[1] See above, p. 282.

signed to recall Latin *faber*, but since *u* and *v* were used indiscriminately[1] the name could be written also *Lefebure*. This spelling chanced to be retained by some families until the present day, and resulted in the trisyllabic pronunciation *Le-fé-bure*. Similarly, the French loan-word *faute* was written in English *fault*, with a learned orthography which finally caused the present English pronunciation with *l*.

But however great may be the disturbing influence of these external factors, such as borrowing from various languages and the despotism of spelling, we must attach still more importance to the internal forces which may counteract regular phonetic development in the language itself. The most conspicuous of these internal forces is **analogy,** the remodelling of existing words and forms, or the formation of new words and forms, after the model of other words and forms in the language. Thus the English comparative *elder* has been remodelled into *older* after the analogy of *old*. In the preterite *I spun* the vowel *u* has crept in from other forms of the verb: the Old English paradigm was *spinnan*, preterite singular *spann*, preterite plural *spunnon*, past participle *spunnen*. Sometimes the preterite of one verb is made after the analogy of another: the preterite *flew* does not represent Old English *fléag*, but is due to analogy with *grew, blew, knew, threw*, the starting-point of the analogical influence being the coincidence in the past participles, *flown, grown, blown, known, thrown*. The result of analogy may be a wrong analysis. Thus English *an adder* instead of *a nadder* is due to the analogy of *an arm* and similar forms. The principle of analogy has played a very prominent part in the discussion of method, and scholars have endeavored to explain all its different aspects.

The indication of the great influence and extent of development by analogy, and the application of analogy as a principle of explanation even for the older periods, exercised a beneficial influence on the methods of linguistics. Much less successful was the effort to find theoretical proof for the fact that sound-development itself, after the removal of the causes of disturbance, is absolutely regular. Beside quite correct remarks to the effect that pronunciation is not learned separately for each individual word, and therefore will not shift from one word to another, one finds the wildest absurdities in the literature of linguistic theory, even in the recent literature. Again and again attempts are made to prove regularity by transferring

[1] See above, p. 239.

changes in pronunciation to the domain of physiology, or, as Scherer wished to do, by attributing them to changes in the organs of speech. This is quite as absurd as to explain the evolution of the dance as due to changes in the leg muscles. Sound-changes, quite as much as analogical formations, are of psychological origin; and, in addition, they may be due to an extremely complicated interaction of concepts. At bottom lies the concept of the auditory impression and of the movement of the organs with which the sound in question is connected. With this materiȧl operate human laziness and human haste, which seek to escape from labor as easily as possible. But two unconscious considerations always interact: that of saving labor in articulation, and that of being easily and correctly understood. The concept of the individual sound does not always occur, however, by itself. It may be connected with the concept of the sounds which precede and follow it. Hence changes in sounds are often determined by environment. Often, also, the concept of some sound at a distance plays a part. When Old Norse *lykill* "key" becomes Swedish *nyckel*, Danish *nögle*, or Latin *libella* "[carpenter's] level" is replaced by French *niveau* "[carpenter's] level, horizontal plane," it is the concept of the *l* which was shortly to be pronounced which operated upon the first *l*. Again, the concept of a given sound may not only be connected with the concept of other sounds in the immediate (or not so immediate) neighborhood, but also with the concepts of other sounds in the language, and either assimilation or dissimilation may result. This is seen, for instance, in the very frequent change of the normal pronunciation of *b*, *d*, *g* and *p*, *t*, *k*. Voiced *b*, *d*, *g* in many languages tend to unvoice almost entirely, but we find that in the same languages the sounds *p*, *t*, *k* have changed their normal pronunciation,[1] also, and have become still more aspirated than English *p*, *t*, *k*. Such is the Danish pronunciation, and such must have been the pronunciation preceding the Germanic sound-shift.[2] This coincidence of the change of *b*, *d*, *g* and the change of *p*, *t*, *k* cannot be accidental, though the causal connection may be conceived in two different ways: (1) the voiced pronunciation of *b*, *d*, *g* was slurred over because *p*, *t*, *k* had already become aspirates and were thus easily distinguishable even from slurred *b*, *d*, *g*; or (2) *vice versa*, the slurred pronunciation of *b*, *d*, *g* compelled speakers to pronounce

---

[1] The pronunciation of *p*, *t*, *k* in modern French may be regarded as "normal."

[2] But then the almost voiceless *b*, *d*, *g* became *entirely* voiceless, and therefore equivalent to *p*, *t*, *k*; and the aspirates became spirants, *f*, *þ*, *x*.

p, t, k with a very strong aspiration in order to avoid confusion. If we accept the latter formulation of the causal connection, we should have here an instance of repulsion between the two frequent classes of sounds. Inversely, we often find a sort of attraction which causes sounds which are very rare in a given language (originating in some very special phonetic development) to coincide with more frequent sounds in the same language. An instance of this occurs in such Latin words as *formīca* "ant," cf. Greek *mýrmēx*, or *formīdō* "dread," cf. Greek *mormō* "a bugbear"; here the sequence of *m-m-* has been dissimilated; but the result of the dissimilation should of course have been *v-m-*. The sound *v*, however, did not occur elsewhere in Latin (Latin *v* was *w*); therefore this very rare *v* was assimilated to the frequent sound *f*.

It has often been maintained, quite correctly, that changes in sounds as a rule take place little by little and imperceptibly, whereas analogical formations happen suddenly. English *son, sons* was in Old English *sunu, suna*. Thus in both the singular and the plural the modern form differs from the old one. In the singular, the change is due to laws which caused the dropping of the final vowel and the transition from the old pure *u* sound to the modern ʌ sound. But in the plural the change is due to the analogical influence of other plurals. In the singular the transition from *sunu* to *son* was quite gradual. Every individual shift was so slight as to be imperceptible; throughout its whole process nobody need have been conscious of any deviation from earlier pronunciation. This is true of the dropping of the final vowel, for between the full pronunciation and complete silence many intermediate stages with gradually diminishing audibility are possible. And it is true of the first vowel, for between the high round vowel *u* and the low unrounded ʌ there is a whole series of mid-positions. The analogical formation in the plural took place in quite another way. Here at one stroke the new form was substituted for the old one. But this opposition between a gradual process and a sudden change is not the essential opposition between sound-laws and analogical formations, and it is not always present. In the developments of sounds, also, jumps may take place: between *l* and *n* in Old Norse *lykill* and Swedish *nyckel*, Danish *nögle*, there was certainly no connecting link. And analogical formations may be unnoticeable, because they undoubtedly may be directed against quite imperceptible shades of sound. In the seventeenth century the two French words *grammaire* "grammar" and *grand'mère* "grandmother" were identical in pronunciation. The vowel *a* was nasal in both words, for vowels were nasal even before sounded *n* and *m*. Later they lost their nasalization in this position, and *grammaire* is therefore pronounced with a pure *a*. But in *grand'mère* the *a* is still nasal. This is due to the analogical influence of *grand* "great," and all probability points to the conclusion that in this case analogical formation did not wait for the distinct denasalization, but reacted against the first slight tendency toward it. This is a case of "conservative" or "preservative analogy."

Conservative analogy is so important a factor that one must limit in this regard the idea that the laws of sounds represent the conservative element in language and analogical formations the revolutionary element. Such a view is right to a certain extent. Laws of sounds are the result of (unconscious) efforts which in and for themselves aim at nothing save the retention of the current pronunciation. Because of laziness and haste this aim is often widely missed, but even where many successive changes have taken place, the later forms may be identified after a fashion with the older: the same elements are present, although their shape may be altered; English *son* can be identified with Old English *sunu*. Analogical formation shows itself, on the other hand, mainly as a creative factor. Where it has imposed its visible mark, the later form cannot be identified with the earlier: English *sons* is not identical with Old English *suna*. Sound-laws represent the preservation of the old along with the traces of wear and tear. Analogical formations, on the contrary, seek to level out all traces of wear and tear. The new formation *sons* had precisely the effect of eliminating the irregularity which had crept into the plural system — *eorlas*, but *suna*, etc. — and to create a clearer distinction between the singular and the plural of this particular word. But when such repairing comes at the right time, it is really more conservative than continued wear and tear would have been. Actually, both factors are preponderantly conservative. The difference between them lies only in the different materials with which they operate. And it is extremely characteristic that in languages where sound-laws have had the decided advantage over analogical formations, the morphological system and the word-system have been completely transformed, although the transformation is such that the scholar can always find traces of the older forms in the new. Such is the case in Celtic. And, vice versa, nothing can operate more conservatively upon a morphological system than a principle of analogical formation, sensitive to small differences and working quickly, though it is likely to destroy many traces of sound-changes.

The root of the matter is reached at once by saying that the psychological basis for *sound-change* is the concepts of sounds and sound-groups, while the psychological basis for *analogical formation* is the concepts of words or of other greater or smaller units of meaning. Since, however, the concepts of sounds may very well be connected with concepts of word-psychology, it is really impossible to raise a Chinese Wall between the two kinds of process. Conditions which border on both processes may and do exist. There are many cases in which concepts of words are involved in sound-laws: a sound is often treated differently at the end of a word, or at the beginning, from the way in which it is treated when it is within a word (medial); a long sound is a bit shorter in a long word than it is in a short word, and so on. In Lithuanian the word "daughter" originally had the following forms:

> *duktères* daughters
> dukterès of the daughter

But although the accent on the middle syllable was not elsewhere changed, the accent in *duktères* was shifted to the first syllable, so that the forms came to be

> dùkteres daughters
> dukterès of the daughter

Here the conception of the accent on the middle syllable was emphasized because of its opposition to *dukterès*, and this led to an exaggeration of the difference by which at first a part of the accent and finally the entire accent shifted to the first syllable. Even such sound-changes, in which motives of word-psychology participate, can be kept apart from analogical formations if the latter are defined as transformations of words or units of meaning under the influence of others with which they are connected by a bond of meaning. But the bond of meaning in analogical formations may be so slender that on this side also one may approach the border between the two. In "standard" English, r is silent in *under the tree*, but is pronounced in *under a tree*. After this analogy r has often crept in where it is not etymologically correct: thus one frequently hears such pronunciations as *Indiar ink, an idear of mine*. Here the bond of meaning between the influencing and the influenced words is so faint that one might feel tempted to see in this simply the power of drilled sound-sequences. But in reality it is not the drilled sound-sequences (for no *r* is inserted in *naïve*, for example), but the habitual word-pictures which have exercised their influence.

Yet other processes connected with word-psychology occur besides analogical formation, and thus new difficulties arise in determining a boundary. The great changes which often occur in polite formulas present a difficult case. In Spanish, *Vuestra Merced* "your grace" has become *Usted*; in Polish the corresponding *wasza miłośc* has become *waszmość* or *wmość*. In Lithuanian *tamsta* is said instead of *tavo mýlista* "thy grace." In Sanskrit *bhavān* "thou" (polite) has arisen from *bhagavān* "august," and the vocative may be further contracted to *bhōs*! In Russian, *vaše prevoschoditelstvo* "Your Excellency" may shrink to *vaše-stvo*, and the form of address *súdař* "my lord" becomes in suffixed unaccented position merely *s*: *da-s* "Oui, monsieur." All of these may be explained as pure developments in sound, if one takes into consideration all of the accelerating causes. The great length of forms of address will produce hasty pronunciation. They will often occur unaccented, and, finally, the individual sounds are of extremely little importance; understanding is assured from the situation, so that clear pronunciation is not necessary. Thus all tendencies to simplify articulation have free play. But one cannot help conjecturing that psychological causes are also present. It is common to human nature not only to devise rules of politeness, but also to treat them lightly. Just as a person in writing a letter will often involuntarily slur the characters when he writes "Yours truly" or "Yours respectfully," so there may be some feeling behind the slurring in the pronunciation of polite formulas, even though it occurs in agreement with purely phonetic tendencies. Perhaps it was a purely phonetic tendency which caused Russian *súdař* when suffixed to be pronounced voiceless or whispered, and thus to become scarcely audible, but this scarcely audible pronunciation was possibly accompanied by a certain internal satisfaction at managing the unavoidable title more easily, and at length people purposely pronounced only the *s*, the sole sound clearly audible in the voiceless pronunciation. If the process took place in this way, there is a sort of kinship between it and the spontaneous, purely psychological distortions which often occur in oaths or in words for concepts which one avoids expressing. Examples are French *parbleu* for *par Dieu* "by God," and English *gee* or *by gosh*.

The predominating view of the seventies and eighties that sound-laws (as opposed to analogical formations) are physiological in their nature, cannot be sanctioned, and all attempts to prove in this way the proposition that the laws of sounds admit of no exceptions, are idle. When the belief in this proposition made progress, such progress was due not to theoretical proof, but to experience. And no doubt the proposition is true. That the change of the sound-unit *un* to ʌ*n*, as in *son*, occurred wherever this unit was found, as, for

EDUARD SIEVERS

instance, in *sun, nun, cunning*,[1] is just as obvious as that the change of the unit of meaning *suna* to *sons* took place wherever this unit occurred — *in my sons, your sons, the king's sons*, and so on. In both cases a single fact is involved — a single fact which has the same form wherever one finds it. We use the name *law* in the one case (sound-law), but not in the other. And we can defend this usage by a reference to the fact that the units of phonology are much fewer than the units of morphology, and that therefore a statement concerning a single sound is much more significant than a statement concerning a single word. Sound-laws are actually laws to us, which

---

[1] The sound-unit *und* had a different development (*hound, bound, found, ground*), and is not included in the above statement.

we must obey *while we etymologize*. But in the evolution of language, a sound-law is merely a single fact, like an analogical formation.

If further proof is required of the proposition about the absence of exceptions to sound-laws, it must come through a systematic examination of the psychological basis of individual sound-changes. Such a study, which in the majority of cases will strengthen our

HENRY SWEET

belief in the absence of exceptions, will be nothing more than the culmination of the development which has brought the history of language and phonetics more and more closely together in the course of the century.

We find the minimum of phonetic sense in Jacob Grimm, who, even in the second edition of his *Deutsche Grammatik* could say, among other atrocities, that eight sounds were expressed by seven characters in the German word *Schrift*: he considers $f = ph$, and reckons s, c, h, r, i, p, h, t. Bopp did not distinguish himself as a phonetician, either. On the other hand, Rask, in his Danish *Orthography* (1826) showed himself to be a very respectable phonetician for his time, though by no means an infallible one. As for Germany, the level there is very much raised by Pott. He shows plainly that he has correct conceptions of the nature of sounds, even in cases where the first specialists in comparative linguistics had wandered far afield. But he defends himself with great emphasis against exaggerated claims for phonetics: "In the comparison of related languages, insight into the *etymological* agreement of sounds in related words and forms is the principal matter for us, and we must strive for it zeal-

J. A. LUNDELL

ously. Insight into the *phonetic* agreement of sounds is, on the other hand, more incidental. We accept it with thanks when it presents itself, without laying so much weight upon it as upon the former, which is quite indispensable to scholars. I have expressed myself somewhat brusquely, but I have done so purposely, in order to injure as much as possible the sound-chasers and ear-watchers among etymologists in their wretchedly petty trade."

A strong contrast to this statement is the practice of Wilhelm Scherer, who (as I have pointed out on p. 291) in all questions of the history of sounds establishes the phonetic point of view, basing his conclusions on Brücke's handbook of 1856. Scherer's method is found again in Verner, who throughout his life kept up a lively interest in phonetics. In Verner's hands this method proved most fruitful, but by a queer trick of fortune the phonetic explanation of his famous law which he gives in his principal article is hardly tenable in individual details. At least it has been seriously doubted recently, although belief in the law itself has not been shaken. Thus this case can be used to illustrate the relative correctness of Pott's point of view. Brugmann, too, was not without interest in phonetics.

OTTO JESPERSEN

Eduard Sievers, who in 1876 published the phonetics textbook [1] which superseded Brücke, was very close to the circle of young Leipzigers, and in his article on syllabic *n*, *m* (*r*, *l*), Brugmann refers to Sievers's book, which had just appeared. Thus Sievers stood sponsor, in a way, for Brugmann's famous theory. But Brugmann did not apply phonetics with the same zeal as Scherer and Verner. On the contrary, he reasserted Pott's point of view. In 1880 he said: "How many things there are which we must provisionally accept as facts in the history of sounds, without perceiving at once the connection with the physiology of sounds! First, on the basis of the phenomena of the history of language, we formulate the so-called sound-laws: the

[1] *Grundzüge der Lautphysiologie.*

explanation according to the physiology of sounds comes later." It cannot be denied that students of linguistics are often compelled to work in this way, that they must often forego an exact phonetic understanding of the laws which they establish — even the exact phonetic understanding of the sounds which they identify etymologically. But this is an extreme case. Exact phonetic understanding

OLAF BROCH

is by no means merely incidental, to be accepted if it offers itself by chance. It is most emphatically a goal toward which one must strive. The methods of linguistics will have taken a new step forward when not only the indication of sound-laws, but their phonetic explanation as well, is regarded as an imperative duty, and when the systematic investigation of known sound-laws which is necessary for their phonetic explanation has been carried out. That the tendency is in this direction there can be no doubt; it is found especially among the younger French scholars, who in this respect consider Maurice Grammont as their chief. But all this is still in its infancy.

Of the numerous phoneticians of recent times we can name (in England) Henry Sweet, (in Sweden) J. A. Lundell, (in Norway) Olaf Broch, (in Denmark) Otto Jespersen, (in France) l'abbé Rousselot.

Lately there has been no lack of would-be new methods, which sometimes have been announced in a rather noisy way. Of real importance is the principle of linguistic geography, which has been illustrated in a series of linguistic atlases and special investigations founded on them. In Germany this principle was introduced by Georg Wenker, who busied himself with linguistic geography from

PIERRE-JEAN ROUSSELOT

1876 on, and in 1881 edited a linguistic atlas of North and Central Germany. His chief work, the *Sprachatlas des deutschen Reichs*, exists in only two copies, one in Berlin, the other in Marburg: each map shows the behavior of one word in the various dialects.[1] A Danish atlas, much more modest in scope, was published during the years 1898–1912, with Marius Kristensen as linguistic guarantor; it had been in preparation since the early eighties. But in no field has linguistic geography reached greater perfection and importance than in the Romance languages. The chief work is the *Atlas linguistique de la France*, brought out (1902–08) under the direction of the Swiss Jules Gilliéron on the basis of material collected from 1897 to 1901

[1] A simplified *Deutscher Sprachatlas*, edited by Ferdinand Wrede, and based chiefly on Wenker's materials, began to appear in 1926.

by a French scholar of extraordinary ability in practical phonetics. Several other Romance atlases, and one of the Celtic dialects of Brittany, have been published or are in preparation. It is hardly necessary to remark how many-sided is the information on the his-

KARL BRUGMANN

tory of words which may be derived from these works. Among their many uses, I may mention also the possibility that they may enable us to learn something of the extinct non-Latin languages in Romance territory.

We are indebted to Brugmann for a survey of comparative Indo-European linguistics. In 1886 he began the publication of his *Grundriss der vergleichenden Grammatik der indogermanischen Sprachen*. It differs from Bopp's *Vergleichende Grammatik* and Schleicher's *Compendium* not only in that it is based upon the new conception of the history of sounds attained during the seventies, but also in that it contains a comparative treatment of the syntax of the Indo-European languages, in addition to their phonology and morphology. Brugmann did not venture to write this section himself, but turned it over to the first scholar who had devoted himself seriously to comparative syntax, Berthold Delbrück. The *Grundriss* was finished in 1900. A new edition by Brugmann alone, almost four thousand pages long, appeared during the years 1897–1916. A very condensed treatment, *Kurze vergleichende Grammatik der in-*

BERTHOLD DELBRÜCK

dogermanischen Sprachen, which includes only the more important languages, was published by Brugmann in 1904.

The two periodicals established in the first period of comparative linguistics, the *Zeitschrift für vergleichende Sprachforschung* and *Beiträge zur vergleichenden Sprachforschung* (see above, p. 277), were combined at the beginning of the new period. But this had hardly occurred when a new journal, edited from 1877 on by Adalbert Bezzenberger, the *Beiträge zur Kunde der indogermanischen Sprachen*, was founded. In 1891, Brugmann, with a co-editor, began the publication of *Indogermanische Forschungen*, which was accompanied by a bibliographical supplement, *Anzeiger für indogermanische Sprach- und Altertumskunde*. In spite of the great rapidity with which volumes of *Indogermanische Forschungen* followed one another, there was not material enough for three great linguistic journals in Germany, and after forty volumes of the *Zeitschrift* and thirty volumes of

Bezzenberger's *Beiträge* had appeared, the two were combined. The bibliographical supplement of *Indogermanische Forschungen* gave it a considerable advantage over the two older journals, but this supplement got farther and farther behind in its reports until in 1912 it was replaced by a separate periodical, the *Indogermanisches Jahrbuch*.

In addition to the German periodicals of this period I should mention also the French *Mémoires de la Société de Linguistique de Paris*, which is not confined to Indo-European, but covers the whole field. In England and America linguistic literature had to appear in the philological journals until the twentieth century, when two purely linguistic (but not exclusively Indo-European) periodicals were founded: in England, *Philologica, Journal of Comparative Philology*, which began in 1921; in America, *Language, Journal of the Linguistic Society of America*, which began in 1925, and has already printed a number of interesting contributions.

VIII

LINGUISTIC AFFINITIES OF THE INDO–EUROPEANS, HOME, AND CIVILIZATION

IN the first few chapters we have seen how the individual groups of Indo-European languages were gradually brought within the scope of comparative linguistics, Armenian and Albanian not being added until after 1870. Obviously, scholars could not remain satisfied with the mere association of all these languages in one family, but felt the need of usable subdivisions.

Schleicher set forth his view of Indo-European relations in the form of a family tree, which is reproduced on p. 312. Of this tree we retain nothing today save the final branches: we still agree with Schleicher when he arranges the upper branches so as to show an especially close connection between Indian and Iranian, between Slavonic and Baltic (Lithuanian), and between Italic and Celtic.

In the first instance, the relationship is palpable when we compare the earliest stages of the languages. Vocabulary and morphology agree to such an extent that without difficulty verses in the *Avesta* can be found which may be converted into Sanskrit by simply observing the phonological laws. If we had only the oldest forms to take into account, we should have no reason for distinguishing Indian and Iranian as separate branches. We do so only because their entire later development differs so greatly. It is characteristic that the Indians and Iranians have a common name, *Aryans*, which some scholars have unwarrantably attempted to apply to the whole Indo-European family.

The relationship between Slavonic and Baltic (Lithuanian) is not so palpable, but the investigations of their accentual system conducted by Saussure and others (see p. 66 above) have enabled the expert to detect a very peculiar development, common to both, which unites them closely and distinguishes them sharply from all other Indo-European languages. But the relationship has no practical significance: it is not close enough to make mutual understanding easy, and translation from one language into the other by a mere observance of the phonological laws would be quite impossible, unless fragments devoid of content were prepared expressly for the purpose. But, on the other hand, it is very difficult to find parallel texts of any length which fail to show special similarity, at least in some words; and if we could follow Slavonic and Baltic as far back as we can Indian and Iranian, it is not impossible that the resem-

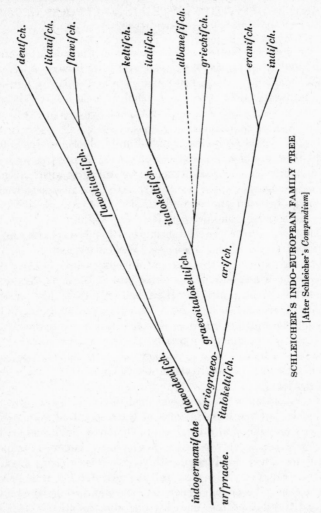

SCHLEICHER'S INDO-EUROPEAN FAMILY TREE
[After Schleicher's *Compendium*]

blances would be just as striking. The two branches certainly had a period in common, but afterward there followed a geographical separation which lasted up to the time when the Baltic and Slavonic peoples made their first appearance in history. The wide dissemination of the Slavs brought these peoples again into contact, but only as neighbors who were unaware of any special kinship.

We also recognize unconditionally the relationship between Celtic and Italic. Between these two branches special similarities, which cannot be accidental, exist in certain inflectional endings and in some details of the verb-system. A "common" period must be postulated, but it must have been long ago. While we need go back only to 600 B.C. for the unity of Indian and Iranian, and perhaps no farther for the unity of Slavonic and Baltic, we know definitely that the Italo-Celtic period of unity was much more remote. At the time when the two Aryan branches were separated only as dialects, there was already a vast difference between Italic and Celtic: and indeed, even within each of these branches there was a split which was already wide. Thus in any case we must go back several centuries, perhaps a thousand years, from 600 B.C. to reach a point where unity between Celtic and Italic could still be perceived. This result agrees very well with the lack of similarity between the two branches in historical times. It is no great feat to find Celtic and Italic parallel texts which betray no special agreement whatever.

Schleicher himself separates Italic and Celtic more widely than Indian and Iranian or Baltic and Slavonic, and hence he is correct so far as the upper branches of the family tree are concerned. But the rest of his scheme is objectionable. We should not blame him overmuch for putting Albanian in the wrong place or for tacitly including Armenian with Iranian, although other scholars of the older period saw more clearly. But his arrangement of the languages which had already been brought into the clear light of comparative linguistics leaves much to be desired, and cannot be taken as representing opinions which were ever undisputed. The idea that Greek and Italic come from the same common source — a notion that accorded more or less with the views of the ancients themselves — was for a long time the general opinion. Yet Grassmann, in 1862, asserted that the Greeks and the Aryans had a period in common after separating from the rest of the family; and, as a matter of fact, it is not more difficult to cite special points of agreement between Greek and the eastern languages than between Greek and the western languages. The theory of a special kinship between Balto-Slavonic and Germanic (which Schleicher, following Grimm, is still pleased to call *deutsch*) is also very old, and arguments of considerable weight can be used to support it. But in 1853 Bopp had freed himself from this opinion, and with no less good reason had asserted a special unity between Aryan (Indo-Iranian) and Balto-Slavonic. This would lead to an initial division of the family into a western and an eastern group, rather than the northern and southern division adopted in Schleicher's genealogical tree. Finally Curtius and Fick [1] accepted, though on grounds which are no longer tenable, an initial division into an Aryan and a European group.

JOHANNES SCHMIDT

The new period dispelled the opinion of Curtius and Fick, but greatly strengthened Bopp's. This was taken over in a rejuvenated form by Schleicher's pupil Johannes Schmidt in *Die Verwandt-schaftsverhältnisse der indogermanischen Sprachen*, 1872 (*The Relationships of the Indo-European Languages*), but at the same time he acknowledged that Schleicher had good reason for favoring a special relationship between Balto-Slavonic and German. In other cases Schmidt likewise determined that a given Indo-European branch showed special similarities with more than one other branch, and from this he inferred that the relationship among the Indo-European

[1] See above, pp. 265, 273 ff.

languages could not be portrayed by means of a family tree. Indeed, he proposed the theory of a wave-like dissemination of various dialectal peculiarities within the Indo-European family while it was still united. Such dialect-waves rolled forth in all directions from different centers, in such a way that territories are often found which have characteristics in common with a neighboring group on one side and with another neighboring group on the other side. In this way it is possible to explain why the Indo-European branches constitute, in a way, an unbroken chain. Balto-Slavonic provides the natural link between Indo-Iranian and Germanic; some dialect-waves united Balto-Slavonic with Aryan, others united Balto-Slavonic with Germanic; and, continuing the reasoning of Johannes Schmidt, one may regard Greek and Armenian as two links between Indo-Iranian and Italo-Celtic. Italo-Celtic in turn forms a link between Greek and Germanic, possibly in such a way that there is a slight preponderance of evidence for similarities with Greek as against similarities with Germanic (this is the only remaining relic of the old belief in a special Græco-Italic group). Thus the chain is closed. But waves may have crossed one another in more than one direction, and it would be quite possible to consider Albanian as a link between Armenian and Balto-Slavonic, and then to take these three groups together as a link between the branches farther east (Indo-Iranian) and the western branches.

It is true, nevertheless, that we do not find mere continuous transitions within the Indo-European family, but on the contrary discover sharply defined boundaries between the branches. Schmidt's explanation of this is that a series of intermediate forms have disappeared. In a dialect series $a\ b\ c\ d\ e\ f\ g\ h\ i\ j\ k$ with only continuous, unnoticeable transitions, it might happen that a single dialect, for instance f, became more highly regarded than its neighbors, for one reason or another (because it belonged to a political or religious center, and so on), and gradually submerged them until further progress was stopped by the influence of some other political or religious center. If f submerged $b\ c\ d\ e$ and $g\ h\ i\ j$ in this way, a new series $a\ f\ k$ would come into existence, with such great differences between a and f and between f and k that the case would be no longer one of shifting variations in dialects, but would become one of distinct languages, which from that time on lived their own lives independently of one another and developed new dialects which had nothing to do with the old dialectal variations.

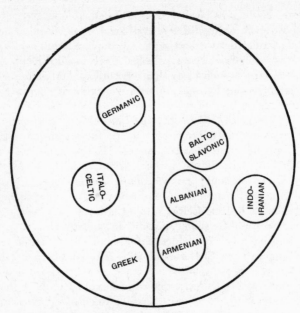

THE RELATIONSHIP OF THE INDO-EUROPEAN
LANGUAGES TO ONE ANOTHER

Johannes Schmidt's book called forth a reply from Fick: *The Former Linguistic Unity of the Indo-Europeans in Europe.*[1] Fick naturally felt called upon to defend the family tree, which was essential to his reconstruction of all the intermediate units between the original Indo-European language and the individual languages (the European linguistic unit, the Balto-Slavonic unit, and so on).[2] In particular, he felt obliged to combat Schmidt's adoption of Bopp's idea of the connection between Balto-Slavonic and Indo-Iranian, for this idea ruined his initial division of the family into Aryan and European groups. But Fick fought in vain. Today, if we admit a two-way division of the family we draw the boundaries where Bopp drew them. On the one hand we have the eastern languages: Indo-Iranian, Armenian, Albanian, Balto-Slavonic. On the other hand we have the western languages: Greek, Italo-Celtic, Germanic. It seems impossible to doubt that the line of division between these

[1] *Die ehemalige Spracheinheit der Indogermanen Europas.*
[2] See pp. 273 ff.

two groups is the boundary of one of the oldest Indo-European dialect-waves. It was the pronunciation of the Indo-European *k* sounds which fixed the boundary.[1] But even this very ancient wave-boundary is nothing more than just a wave-boundary which was crossed by many other waves. In addition to the special similarities between Germanic and Balto-Slavonic, which it is impossible to explain away, we must also recognize a series of special similarities between Greek and the eastern languages, especially Armenian. Schmidt's wave-theory has won the day, and we can fittingly set forth our present understanding of the relationship among the ten Indo-European branches by drawing them as small circles within a larger circle, the vacant parts of which represent the Indo-European dialects which have passed out of existence without leaving a trace.[2]

This table differs very little in arrangement from the geographical positions of the ten groups of languages in historical times. The natural inference is that the dissemination of the Indo-European languages came about through quiet expansion, without violent dislocations or distant wanderings.

There is no *a priori* reason, however, why the picture should be drawn in just this way. Even though dialectal waves are the most natural and common source of language differences, it is not to be doubted that sudden divisions occur very often, especially as the result of migrations. Not infrequently the linguistic consequences of migration are completely obliterated by the national disintegration of a people in foreign surroundings. Such was the case with the Germanic Vandals in Northern Africa, and with the Galatians in Asia Minor. But it is possible, also, for a wandering people to maintain its nationality: witness the Magyars, in the Finno-Ugrian family of languages.

By no means, then, can we assert that the dissemination of the Indo-Europeans proceeded exclusively by regular and quiet expansion, as is suggested by the drawing that shows the ten living Indo-European branches of the family. All traces of a great many migrations and violent separations may have vanished because the migrating or separated part of the family gave up its language. But all that was known until near the close of the nineteenth century of the remnants of dead Indo-European languages not belonging to any of

---

[1] Recently the two groups have been called *satem* and *centum* languages after the Avesta and Latin forms of the numeral *hundred*.

[2] See figure, p. 316.

the ten living groups — that is to say, all that was known of Venetic and Messapic (in Italy) and Phrygian (in Asia Minor) — did not change the general impression made by the living languages, but seemed to fit very well in the accepted scheme. It was the discovery of Tokharian that first tended to disturb our circles, for this language from the extreme eastern boundary of the Indo-European family was manifestly nearer akin to the western branches than to the eastern (it is a *centum* language), and was certainly more closely related to Italo-Celtic, the westernmost branch, than to any other member of the Indo-European family. This is sufficiently striking in itself, although it is an isolated phenomenon. But if it should turn out — and there is no little probability that it will — that Hittite is in very much the same situation as Tokharian, then our map of the dialects will be completely changed. Instead of a mere Italo-Celtic unit, which could not be much more remarkable than the Balto-Slavonic unit or the Indo-Iranian, we should then have a linguistic group of such vast extent as to force upon us the question whether we must not recognize here the action of one of the oldest of all Indo-European "dialect-waves" — a wave at least as old as that which divided the family into *satem* and *centum* languages. And the members of this huge linguistic group would be so situated geographically as to make the whole map of the Indo-European family of languages quite as dislocated in its appearance as, for example, the map of the ancient Greek dialects.[1] But this very comparison shows that the dislocated appearance of the new map would be no argument against its probability. The division of the Italo-Celtic-Hittite-Tokharian group of languages into a western, middle, and eastern section, of which the middle was the most changed, would not be more remarkable than the division of the southern Greek group into three sections, of which likewise the middle was the most changed. A final judgment, however, cannot be formulated until we have a better knowledge of the ancient languages of Asia Minor.

The question of the age of the Indo-European languages can be answered only by a guess. We must first surmise how far back the individual history of the various branches goes. It is the current view that the Indo-European migration to India took place about 2000 B.C., and that Indian literature begins about 1500 B.C. What chronological inference one should draw from the traces of Indian

[1] See above, p. 84.

influence which have come to light in the Mitanni and Hittite cuneiform inscriptions of the second millennium before Christ is still not
clear. It can be confidently assumed that the Greeks also were
already settled in their historical country in the second millennium
before Christ. The peculiar relationship between Celtic and Italic
compels us to reckon this group's separate existence from a point of
time not much later than 2000 B.C. As to the earliest date of the
presence of the Germanic tribes in their historical homes not much
can be determined. Yet it may be worth noticing that the Norwegian scholar Magnus Olsen has explained some Norwegian place-
names as referring to conditions which were hardly existent much
later than the third millennium before Christ. If Hittite is a pure
Indo-European language, and not merely a language related to Indo-
European, we must admit that as early as 1500 B.C. it had passed
through a very long and very strange development. There is little
doubt that the Indo-European family of languages was widely separated and divergently developed by 2000 B.C. But how long a period
this divergent development required, we cannot tell, even if we seek
a standard of measurement by observing how long it has taken in
more recent times to bring about a similarly divergent development
in other instances. The most probable guess is about two thousand
years, so that we must go back to 4000 B.C. before we reach an undivided Indo-European language.

The location of the home of the parent language is no less difficult,
and it has been the subject of a number of widely different conjectures. One of the newest treatments is by P. Kretschmer (1896).
From the most ancient historical homes of the Indo-European peoples
he deducts quite simply the regions where it seems certain to him
(for definite reasons) that they arrived late; the remaining region he
takes to be the home of the parent language. Partly on good and
obvious grounds, partly without discussion or by the use of questionable arguments, he eliminates India, Asia Minor, the Balkan Peninsula and Italy, Ireland and Great Britain, Scandinavia and Northern
Germany. There remains as the original territory of the Indo-
Europeans a relatively narrow stretch of country from France across
the whole of Central Europe and the Kirghiz Steppes of Asia to
Persia. There is some obvious truth in this reasoning. In some
period the Indo-Europeans must certainly have inhabited a very
large territory as a people who varied dialectally but were not

separated by definite linguistic boundaries; and the territory that
Kretschmer marks out is no larger than that occupied by many
homogeneous languages in historical times. But it may be doubted
whether the map should be drawn in some of its details as Kretschmer
drew it; and anyhow the map is no solution of the problem as to the
home of the parent language. Latin, which by classical times had
spread throughout the majority of the Mediterranean countries, and
even had sent out offshoots still farther, originated in a small and
narrowly limited home in the province of Latium; [1] and the contemporary world language English had its original home in a small
district in or near a part of modern Friesland. For the Indo-European
language also we would fain know the particular province which was
its original point of departure.

The question has generally been put in this way, but the reply
has varied. In the oldest period of comparative linguistics, the current opinion was that the home of the primitive Indo-European
family must be sought in Asia, which was regarded as the cradle of
the human race. It was in that portion of the world that the oldest
and most primitive Indo-European language, Sanskrit, was found.
Where the cradle of the human race may have been is a matter of no
importance in this connection. The Indo-European parent language
does not take us back to the childhood of man, but only to a period in
which we must reckon with popular migrations and disseminations of
language from Europe to Asia as well as from Asia to Europe, exactly
as we do in historical times. Nor have we any right to suppose that
the language which has preserved the most ancient appearance,
Sanskrit, is the closest geographically to the original home. In historical times we see now and then examples of the contrary, as in the
case of Icelandic, in the Scandinavian group. Hence nothing can be
objected *a priori* to the point of view first advanced by the Englishman R. G. Latham, [2] that the home of the Indo-Europeans must be
sought in Europe. Moreover, this was an opinion likely to be regarded with sympathy on account of the impression of a seemingly
quiet dissemination which the ten branches give, for there can be no
doubt that this dissemination had its center of gravity in Europe.
Benfey, among others, supported Latham. He selected a region very
close to Asia, north of the Black Sea, from the mouth of the Danube
to the Caspian. The European theory has been much favored, and

---

[1] See above, p. 92.

[2] In *Elements of Comparative Philology* in 1862, and in earlier works from 1851 on.

for a time it has been the prevailing one, although adverse criticism
has not ceased.

In the course of the inquiry some arguments have been used which
cannot be justified. Thus the question of the home of the language
has often been confused with the question of race. But Indo-
European is purely a linguistic conception. To what extent the Indo-
Europeans in their limited home had any special characteristics that
distinguished them from surrounding races we do not know. Most
probably the formation of races is much older than the dissemination
of the Indo-European languages. And if the Indo-Europeans in their
larger territory (that sketched by Kretschmer, or a similar one) had
certain predominating racial peculiarities — tall stature, for instance, or blond hair — this does not necessarily mean that these
racial peculiarities were disseminated along with language. On the
contrary, it may just as well mean that the language made its way
to a series of peoples who already showed these racial peculiarities.
Possibly the first speakers of the language did not show them, or if
they did, perhaps they were not the first link in the racial chain,
but the last. Any attempt to seek the home of the language by trac-
ing back the development and expansion of the tall blond race is
therefore mistaken.

Scholars have sought quite rightly to utilize certain linguistic facts:
Common Indo-European plant names, animal names, expressions of
climatic and geographical conditions. But it must be borne in mind
that inferences can be drawn only from the words that occur.
Nothing can be inferred from the absence of certain terms. There
is no Common Indo-European name for *tiger* or *camel*, but this fact
would not constitute a refutation of the idea that the original home
might have been in a region where tigers or camels existed, for the
names must necessarily have been forgotten by tribes which later
came to dwell in a land where the animals themselves were not found.
Highly significant, on the other hand, is the Common Indo-European
word for *bear*: Sanskrit *ṛkša-s*, Greek *árktos*, Latin *ursus* are identical,
the various forms correspond according to incontrovertible laws,[1] and
the same word is found again in Iranian, Armenian, Albanian, and
Celtic — that is, in so many branches remote from one another that
there cannot be the least doubt that the word is inherited from the
parent language. It is strange, indeed, that this ancient word has
faded into oblivion in Germanic and Balto-Slavonic, among just

[1] One of these is pointed out above on p. 284.

those tribes which perhaps had most to do with bears. Possibly this was due to a sort of name taboo — an aversion to calling the bear by its own name. At all events, the folk has substituted various "pet" names: the Germanic peoples called the bear "the brown one," [1] the Slavonic peoples called him *honey-eater*, and the Baltic peoples gave him a third name which is no longer comprehensible. Other animals which had a Common Indo-European name are *wolf* [2] and *hare*. A tree which the Indo-Europeans knew is the *birch*. Whether they knew the *beech* is very doubtful, however. Old Norse *bók*, Old English *bóc-tréow* are certainly the same word as Latin *fāgus* "beech" and Greek *phēgos* "oak"; [3] but since the word occurs in but a small group of languages which are neighbors — attempts to find it in more remote regions have not succeeded — we must consider the possibility that it never had more than a dialectal dissemination within the larger territory occupied by the Indo-Europeans, [4] and we cannot use it for conclusions involving more than those branches of the family where it occurs. For these three branches, the possession of the word points to a prehistoric home in regions where the beech grew, i.e., west of a line drawn from Königsberg to the Crimea. Whether the sea was known to the Indo-Europeans in their original home is likewise uncertain. Several neighboring branches have a word in common for "sea": Old Norse *marr*, Old English *mere*, Old High German *mari*, Modern High German *Meer*, Latin *mare* (also in Celtic and Balto-Slavonic), but this word also is convincing for only a part of the family, and we do not know what sort of sea it was these Indo-Europeans knew and named. Two of the words that were certainly Indo-European property are terms for *snow* and *winter*, and these give us a hint as to the climate of the original home. All in all, we can infer very little from such an examination of the vocabulary; yet it gives us the impression that the original home of the family is not to be sought too far south.

Johannes Schmidt adopted another method when (in 1890) he attempted to prove that the Indo-European folk when still undivided were influenced by the Sumerians. The necessary consequence of this influence would be that their home was to be looked

---

[1] This is the original meaning of English *bear*, German *Bär*, Danish *Björn*.

[2] See p. 284.

[3] The word no doubt shifted in meaning among the Greeks in the course of their migration to the Balkan Peninsula, where the beech becomes rarer and rarer toward the south.

[4] Cf. above, p. 276.

for in Asia. Very ancient influence upon Indo-European from Babylonian cultural centers cannot be denied. Sanskrit *paraśu-ṣ* "axe," Greek *pélekys*, is plainly enough the same word as Assyrian *pilakku*, which in turn may have a Sumerian origin; and it must have been borrowed at a time before Sanskrit had come into existence, at a time when the principal characteristics of the Aryan branches had not been formed, at a time when the *centum* and *satem* languages hardly existed — in short, at a time before the great Indo-European unity of languages was broken. But since the word occurs in only Aryan and Greek, we have no assurance that it ever had more than dialectal currency. Hence it need not have been borrowed in the original home of the Indo-Europeans, but may have been borrowed by some tribe or division after the Indo-Europeans as a whole had become distributed over the great "empire." The case is different with Sumerian *urudu* "copper," which apparently can be traced throughout the entire Indo-European family: Middle Persian *rōd*, Modern Persian *rō* "copper, bell metal, smelted metal," Latin *raudus* "a piece of unformed ore used as a coin," Old Norse *rauδi* "bog-iron ore." In spite of manifold doubts, it is probable that all these words belong together. But it does not follow that the Sumerian word was taken over in the original home of the family. It may have been accepted by one of the remote members of the expanded Indo-European family, and may then have wandered from tribe to tribe through the entire "empire" of the related languages. It is not only in our own times that new discoveries and their names have been transplanted from people to people throughout the whole length and breadth of a given civilization; the process took place earlier also. It would be convincing if Johannes Schmidt had been right in asserting that throughout our entire family of languages certain traces persist of the extraordinary Babylonian system of counting in sixties, which was presumably formed on an astronomical basis; [1] but everything that Schmidt interpreted as a trace of this system among the Indo-Europeans (for instance, the "great hundred" = 120, with which all the Germanic peoples counted) can be explained in other ways, without disturbing the Sumerians.

A third kind of argument has reference to the foreign groups of

---

[1] This system is shown in writing in that the numerals 60 and 1 are designated by the same vertical wedge in different places, or supplemented by different sound-characters. Linguistically it is shown in the special names for 60 and some multiples of 60: *šuššu* 60, *nēru* 600, *šar* 3600, rendered by the Greeks as *sōssos*, *nēros*, *saros*.

languages with which the Indo-European family is related. Among the living languages, Indo-European is first of all related on the one hand to Finno-Ugrian, on the other to Semitic, but possibly it has had a still closer relationship with the extinct non-Indo-European languages of Asia Minor. Yet we cannot draw very definite inferences; our knowledge of the languages of Asia Minor is still too uncertain. And even though the relations with Finno-Ugrian and Semitic point toward the east, and might direct us to a district in the neighborhood of the Caucasus, we are in no position to determine for what period this criterion is valid. We must keep in mind the possibility that the connection with these foreign groups may have been broken long before the distinct dialect was formed which became the parent language of the Indo-European family. Great migrations and processes of expansion may have taken place in the mean time, and it may have been a dialect at a very great distance from Finno-Ugrian and Semitic which submerged the intermediate ones and became the parent of the Indo-European family of languages. In such a case it would not be the direct mother language of our family, but a distant ancestor of this mother language, which we could conceivably locate in the neighborhood of the Caucasus.

The cultural stage of the undivided Indo-European folk was apparently that of the Later Stone Age. Of the names of metals in which agreement can be pointed out among several branches, most give the impression of being either wandering loan-words or Indo-European dialect words.

For *gold* there are two names which are distributed throughout the field of more than one branch. One of these is our word *gold* itself, Gothic *gulþ*, which is identical with the Slavonic name for *gold*, Russian *zóloto*, and with the name of the same metal in one of the three Baltic languages, Lettish *zelt-s*. Since Germanic and Balto-Slavonic have elsewhere various special points of similarity, we have no right to attribute to this word a greater age than is consistent with its being a dialectal word within the greater territory of the Indo-Europeans. It seems, moreover, to be etymologically transparent and to mean "the yellow [metal]." That Indian and Iranian also designate *gold* by color terms which belong to the same root as the Germanic and Balto-Slavonic (but with other formative endings) cannot disturb our determination of the age of the word, but at most leads us to regard it as a wanderer which in connection with this or that product of civilization passed from one Indo-European tribe to another, being transposed or adapted according to the needs of the various dialects. More remarkable, and presumably older, is another name for *gold*: Latin *aurum*, earlier (in the ancient grammarians) *ausum*, Lithuanian *auksa-s*, Old Prussian *ausis*. Yet we have no right to believe that this word, either, was taken as a heritage from the original home of the Indo-Europeans. We have already noted that Latin and Baltic agree in the word for *sea* (p. 322), to which nevertheless we can ascribe only dialectal age; the same may be the case with *aurum*. Yet it must be admitted that since Italic and Baltic are not conterminous, the word once had a wider distribution, perhaps quite similar to that of the word for *sea*. Then it must have been lost in part of its original territory. In this there is nothing remarkable, for we have instances enough of the loss of inherited names of metals. Perhaps the ancient **auso-m* in Germanic and Balto-Slavonic found a competitor in the word meaning "the yellow metal" (brought into the district by some cultural stream or other) which superseded it among the Germanic and Slavonic tribes, while the Baltic languages preserved both. If the Celts also had **auso-m*, the reason for its disappearance from their language might possibly be different: when, with the Celtic dropping of medial *-s-* it became an inconvenient form to pronounce, it may have given way before the Latin *aurum*, which the superior culture of the Romans imposed upon the Celts. At any rate, it is the Latin word by which the Celts nowadays designate the precious metal. Recently it has become known that the Tokharian for *gold* belongs with Latin *aurum* and Lithuanian *auksa-s*; but, since the existence of special points of similarity between Tokharian and Italic (-Celtic) cannot be doubted, this discovery does not raise the term above dialectal age.

For *silver* most of the Indo-European languages have names related to Greek *árgyros*, Latin *argentum*. But the endings vary, only Latin and Celtic having the same form, and the word is certainly a wanderer which originally meant "the white [metal]," and in the course of its wanderings was translated and adapted at need. Germanic and Balto-Slavonic have another word: Old Norse *silfr*, Gothic *silubr*, Old Slavic *sĭrebro*, Lithuanian *sidabras*. The original form, like the Slavonic, no doubt contained the two *r* sounds, which became dissimilated in Germanic and Baltic.

For *copper* we have discussed a wandering name whose ultimate source is Sumerian *urudu* (pp. 323 ff.). It appears, however, that the

Indo-Europeans had also a name which they brought with them from their original home. This ancient word occurs clearly only in the two Aryan branches, and in Latin and Germanic: Sanskrit *ayas* "copper" (later "iron"), Latin *aes* "copper, ore," Gothic *aiz*, Old Norse *eir* "copper," Old English *ár*, Modern English *ore*. But here branches are involved which are quite remote from one another and have no special similarities. From a purely geographical point of view, it is not inconceivable that the word was borrowed from a foreign language, say somewhere in Asia Minor. Here the two Aryan branches could have taken it over, before the migration to India. On the other hand, it could have reached Italy overseas in commercial relations, and from Italy it could have found its way to the Germanic peoples. But no one has succeeded in indicating a probable source for such a loan. It does not look like a wanderer or a loan-word, either; the agreement between the Latin and Sanskrit forms extends to inflection and gender, and such agreement is not to be expected in the case of parallel loans from a foreign language. Hence we can scarcely help recognizing the word as inherited from the undivided parent language.

But it is, then, the only Common Indo-European name of a metal. *Iron* has neither Common Indo-European nor even Indo-European dialectal names. And there is no Common Indo-European word for *smith* or for any metal trade.

The general impression one gets from all this is that the Indo-Europeans knew very little of metals in their original home, and still less of metal work. Reminiscences of a time when some of the most important tools were of stone are to be found in such cases as

Lithuanian *akmuõ* stone	Greek	*ákmōn* anvil
Old Slavic *kamy* stone	Old Norse	*hamarr* hammer

We get a very incomplete conception of the technical skill of the Indo-Europeans from linguistic comparison. In the case of many names of utensils and weapons it is almost impossible to make out whether they originated in the original home or in the dialectally divided "empire." Among the many ancient names for *axe*, that in widest use is Greek *aksínē*, Latin *ascia*, Old English *æx*. But because the branches in which these forms occur adjoin one another so closely, we cannot prove that this term is more than a dialect word. The case is somewhat better for a name for *sword*, though this occurs in only two branches, for they happen to be very distant from each other: Sanskrit *asi-š* (*a* from *n̥*), Latin *ensis*. Certainly an Indo-European word held in common is Sanskrit *śaru-š* "spear," Gothic *hairus* (pronounced *herus*) "sword," Old English *heoru*. But there might be some doubt of the original meaning, since the two branches do not agree. Fortunately, however, there is a Greek derivative, *keraunós* "thunderbolt" (the dread weapon of Zeus), which settles the matter: the original meaning was "spear, javelin," as in Sanskrit, and it is Germanic which changed the sense.

That the Indo-Europeans used the bow and arrow could hardly be doubted, but it is very difficult to find linguistic proof. The two Aryan groups and Greek have names in common for *bow* and *arrow*, but this proves no more than dialectal age. *Arcus*, the Latin for "bow," is common to that language and Germanic: Latin *arcus* (*arqui-tenens* "bow-bearing"), Gothic *arhvazna* "arrow," Old Norse *or* "arrow" (plural *o̥rvar*), Modern English *arrow*, but this also proves only dialectal age. However, it may well be that the languages are silent even where there is something to tell. We must always beware of drawing inferences from the absence of testimony.

Of terms pertaining to the potter's art, one must here suffice — the word for *kettle*, certainly a Common Indo-European word: Sanskrit *čaru-š* (from *$k^u eru$-s*), Old English *hwer* (also in Celtic). The verb by which the act of making pottery was designated was undoubtedly the same as that which still has this application in Latin: *fi-n-gō* "to form, mold, shape" (from clay, wax, dough), from which comes *figulus* "potter," and *figūra* "shape, figure." [1] It occurs in so many branches of the family that there can be no doubt of its Indo-European age. We can cite, for instance, Gothic *deigan* "mold from clay," *daig-s* "dough," Old Norse *deig*, Old English *dāh*. The original meaning is certain, but it is worthy of note that the verb was used not only of the potter's work in clay, but also of the construction of walls and the like. The agreement among Iranian, Greek, and Oscan is evidence of this.

We can also determine the ancient words for the builder and his trade. His name was Sanskrit *takšā*, Greek *téktōn* "carpenter." Greek *téchnē* "art," is a derivative; but the laws involved are somewhat complex. His trade involved, of course, the use of the axe: the verb *takša-ti* means in Sanskrit "he hews, fashions by hewing"; a corresponding word with the same meaning occurs in Slavonic and

---

[1] Latin *f* here comes from Indo-European *dh* and corresponds to Greek *th*, etc. See the table on p. 252.

Baltic, and a derivative meaning "axe" is found in Slavonic, Germanic (Old High Germanic *dehsala*), and Celtic. But it was also his job to do the plaiting or weaving necessary in the construction of walls and doors; the skilful joining of wood, whether in the large or in little, was his trade. This is reflected in the semasiological development of the word in Latin. *Texere* is very rarely used of joining great timbers, and then it is most frequently used of ship-building (*textrīnum* is "wharf, shipyard"), but it is very common in the sense of "weave" — a willow basket, for instance, a fence, a gabion, a parapet. Even woven walls did not belong to a period too far distant for the memory of the Romans: the poet Ovid tells us that the walls of a temple in ancient days were woven of tough willow withes (*et paries lento vimine textus erat*). The constant use of *texere* of the more delicate kinds of plaiting caused it to take on the meaning *to weave* [cloth], which it could not possibly have had in the parent language, where "to weave" was expressed by an entirely different word. This new meaning gradually obscured the old one.

Several Common Indo-European words are evidence of the carpenter's and weaver's products. We have particularly well-documented names for the house and its parts (*door, doorframe*), for *ship, oar, wagon, wheel, axle, yoke*.

We have also linguistic proof of the production of clothing by the Indo-Europeans. There are certain Indo-European words for *to spin, to weave cloth, to sew*. The last two are the words which we use in English today. We have also traces of one and the same verb meaning *to dress, clothe oneself*. One derivative of this last is Latin *vestis* "clothing."

From the numerous words in common for *ox*, we infer that the Indo-Europeans raised cattle in their original home. Among these are English *ox*, Sanskrit *ukšā* (also in Celtic and Tokharian), and English *cow*, which occurs in all the Indo-European branches save Albanian. That these numerous names cannot be explained as due to the hunter's interest in the animal, but must be ascribed to the activity of the cattle-breeder, appears quite certain from the existence of a Common Indo-European word for *to milk*:

Greek *amelgō*, Latin *mulgeō* "I milk," Old English *meolcan*, Old Norse *mjolka* "to milk" (also in Celtic, Baltic, Slavonic, Albanian).

It is true that the conclusiveness of the last series of comparisons is somewhat diminished because no corresponding words can be found in Armenian and in the two Aryan branches, but the only natural explanation is that these two languages have lost the word, not that they never had it.

An Indo-European word meaning *cattle* is Sanskrit *paśu-š*, Latin *pecus, pecu*, Old Norse *fé*, Old English *feoh*. The corresponding Gothic *faihu*, pronounced *fehu*, we know by chance only in the meaning *property, money*; cf. English *fee* and Latin *pecūnia* "money."

Besides cattle, the Indo-Europeans certainly had sheep as domestic animals, to judge from the Common Indo-European words for *sheep* (Latin *ovis*, etc.) and for *wool*. As to other domestic animals, we can make sure that they knew animals like pigs, horses, dogs, geese, and probably ducks. For *goat* only partial agreements can be pointed out, as between Latin and Germanic, between Greek and Armenian, and between Indian and Balto-Slavonic — similarities which permit no conclusion as to conditions in the "common" home of the Indo-Europeans. But we have no means of determining by linguistic methods whether these creatures were domesticated. We can seek for help in the general history of domestic animals, and thus reach the conclusion that horses and dogs are the most likely to have been domesticated, fowls the least likely. But here we go outside the field of linguistics.

The as yet undivided Indo-European folk also carried on agriculture. A convincing argument is the existence of words in common meaning *to plow* and *a plow*. These occur throughout Germanic, Celtic, Latin, Greek, Baltic, Slavonic, and Armenian:

Old English *erian*,   archaic Modern English *to ear*.

The word, to be sure, does not appear in the two Aryan branches. This holds good for certain other agricultural expressions, and some scholars have been disposed to utilize this situation to bolster up the theory of an initial division of the Indo-European family into an Aryan and a European branch, a theory which can no longer be supported by grammatical arguments.[1] These scholars have inferred that the Indo-Europeans first began to till the soil after the Aryans had become separated from them. But this whole line of reasoning has a double weakness. In the first place, an inference is drawn from the *absence* of the words concerned — an obvious fallacy. Their

[1] Cf. above, pp. 265, 285.

absence does not necessarily mean that the words were never present; it can be explained by the assumption that after having inherited these words from the parent language as did the other Indo-European tribes, the Aryans later lost them in the course of their own special cultural development. Many reasons can be imagined for such a loss of ancient words. For instance, one cannot dismiss arbitrarily the possibility that the loss may have been due, not to a lowering of culture, but to an advance in culture involving new methods of agriculture, improved implements, new varieties of cultivated plants, and, as a consequence of all these, new names. In the second place, the real state of things is falsely described when it is asserted that there is a line of cleavage (with respect to agricultural expressions) between the rest of the family and the two Aryan branches. As a matter of fact, we have here the same sort of intersecting dialect-waves as those which are characteristic of the Indo-European family in general. Greek and Armenian, as well as Indo-Iranian, often lack agricultural terms which are common to the other branches. Thus we find a word in common for "to grind (grain)" in Italic, Celtic, Germanic, Baltic, and Slavonic:

Latin *molō* I grind,   Old Norse *mala* to grind.

From this verb the noun for *meal* was formed in Celtic, Baltic, Germanic, Slavonic, and Albanian (Old Norse *mjǫl*, dative *mjǫlvi*, Russian *mélevo*, Albanian *miellttɛ*), and a derivative meaning *mill* is found in Greek *mýlē*. In connection with these words, which clearly indicate an old heritage in common, some scholars have emphasized the fact that the two Aryan branches lack these technical expressions, while on the other hand the verb occurs in Sanskrit in the non-technical meaning of *crush*. If one adopts the opinion that the non-technical meaning is older than the technical, then these facts accord very well with the theory that agriculture was first developed after the separation of the Aryans from the rest of the Indo-European family. But the theory is shaken when we observe that Armenian behaves almost exactly like Aryan: the technical terms are absent, while the verb exists in a non-technical meaning — *malem* "I crush," used of everything possible, but only exceptionally of grain. Still more significant is the fact that the Greeks had no verb corresponding to the Latin *molō*, although *mýlē* "mill" proves that such a verb must once have existed. It disappeared, no doubt, because it was superseded by another, *aléō* "I grind" — a verb which occurs also in Armenian (*alam* "I grind"), and of which there are traces in the two Aryan branches. The only probable inference is that Latin *molō* is an ancient Common Indo-European technical term which was forced out, in a group of Eastern languages, by a new word (perhaps disseminated in connection with some technical advance) and has maintained itself there in the non-technical meaning only, just as nowadays we know the English *botch* (an old tailoring term) only in the non-technical sense.

The situation is similar in other cases. A word for *to sow* and for *grain, seed* occurs in common in Germanic, Celtic, Italic, and Slavonic:

Old English *sáwan*, Old Norse *sá* to sow, Latin *sē-vi* I sowed, *sa-tus* sowed (participle), Old High German *sámo* seed, Latin *sēmen*, etc.

The dissemination of this word is the same as that of the word *sea* (p. 322) and is certainly insufficient to prove that the word is of Indo-European age. If it were a dialectal term, however, not only Indian and Iranian, but Greek, Armenian, and Albanian also would lie outside the path of the dialectal wave in question. There is, however, a word in Sanskrit which seems to be a derivative of the reduplicated root *sē-* : *sasyá-m* "seed," which in any case is an ancient word, since it occurs in Celtic also. Thus it becomes probable that the branches which lack the verb *sē-* once had it. Its loss may be due to a dialect-wave which included several eastern Indo-European tribes.

There are also many cases in which Aryan itself has preserved an ancient agricultural expression. For instance, we have the word which is reflected in Middle English *quern* "mill-stone," Sanskrit *grāvā*, accusative *grāvāṇ-am* "pressing-stone" (also in Armenian, Slavonic, Baltic, and Celtic), or the following name applied to cereals: Sanskrit *yava-s* "grain, barley," Lithuanian *javaí* (plural) "grain" (also in Greek in the meaning "spelt"). Thus there seems to be no doubt that the Indo-Europeans carried on agriculture in their original home, though perhaps under primitive conditions.

With regard to the more spiritual side of life, language affords us various bits of information — first of all as to the make-up of the family, which B. Delbrück made the subject of a classic investigation in 1889.

There is no doubt of the existence in Common Indo-European of words for *father, mother, son, daughter, brother, sister* — and these are exactly the words which are reflected in the English terms. So also for *grandchild*: Sanskrit *napāt*, Latin *nepōs* (feminine forms, Sanskrit *naptī*, Latin *nepti-s*). From the first, this word was possibly a little elastic in meaning, for it shows a tendency to pass over to the sense of *nephew* (or *niece*). Such is the meaning of the modern survivors of the Latin word — French *neveu, nièce* — and German *Neffe* and *Nichte* have the same meanings. A word in common for "widow" is Sanskrit *vidhávā*, Latin *vidua*, Gothic *widuwō*, Old English *widewe* (also in Celtic and Slavonic). Most interesting of all are the designations of affinity. There is a word in common for *daughter-in-law*: Sanskrit *snušā*, Greek *nyós*, Latin *nurus*, Old High German *snur*, Old English *snoru*, etc. On the other hand, there is no Common Indo-European word for *son-in-law*; here and there we find a trace of similarity between the two branches of languages, but there is no consistent agreement among a large number of branches. There are certain words in common for *parents-in-law* (that is to say, the *husband's* parents):

Sanskrit *śvaśura-s* "father-in-law," Greek *hekyrós*, Latin *socer*, Old High German *swehur*, Old English *swéor*.
Sanskrit *śvaśrū-š* "mother-in-law," Latin *socrus*, Old High German *swigar*, Old English *sweger*.

These are documented in all ten branches of the Indo-European family, and it is clear from the agreement among Armenian, Greek, Slavonic, and Baltic, as well as among the oldest monuments of the Indian language, that they applied only to the husband's parents. The wife's parents had different names, which do not agree in any two branches: *wife's father* in Greek is *pentherós*, Lithuanian *úošvis*, Old Slavic *tĭstĭ*, Armenian *aner*. For the relationship of brother-in-law and sister-in-law we have Latin *lēvir* "husband's brother," *glōs* "husband's sister," and *janitrīcēs* "brother's wives," all ancient Indo-European names. On the other hand, there is no general Indo-European name for the wife's brother or sister, for the sister's husband, and so on.

It can scarcely be accidental that we have general words for all the -in-law relationships which would have been in daily use if the family was regulated as it is today among the Southern Slavs, where adult married sons still live in their father's house. In this family arrangement there is daily use for the forms of address to and from daughters-in-law, while there is no such use for the corresponding forms of address to and from sons-in-law; hence in the latter case the terminology has been less fixed, and each of the branches has taken its own path.

We need not linger on the general word for *king*, Latin *rēx* (also in Indian and Celtic). Even wild tribes have their chiefs. Here language teaches nothing that we did not know already.

More interesting are the traces of the ancient religion of the Indo-Europeans. The word for *god* was Sanskrit *dēva-s*, Latin *dīvus, deus*, Irish *dia*, Old Norse plural *tívar* (the singular *Tý-r* is the name of a particular god), Lithuanian *diēvas*; Greek *dîos* "divine" also belongs here. This term for *god* is a derivative of the word for *heaven*, which also designated the highest god: Sanskrit *dyāu-š* (*dyāu-š pitā* "father heaven"), Greek *Zeus* (*Zeus patēr* "Father Zeus"), Latin *Jū-piter* (where the divine name is combined with the word for *father*).

The Indo-Europeans could count at least as far as one hundred. We can reconstruct with certainty in Indo-European the numerals from 2 to 10 and for 100, and indicate how the multiples of ten were formed. For one thousand we have a name common to Greek and Aryan, but it need not be more than an Indo-European dialect-word. Our own word for one thousand, Old English *púsend*, is found again in Baltic and Slavonic, but it is doubtful whether it is an Indo-European word or merely a wanderer. In any case it is very old.

This is approximately all we can say of the "enlightenment" of the Indo-Europeans in their original home. One scholar, however, has maintained that they had also the art of writing; and it is interesting to discuss this question in some detail, since it affords an excellent example of the difficulties and uncertainties that beset the reconstruction of cultural facts on the basis of linguistic material. In this case, that material is as follows:

Old Persian *ni-piš-tanaiy* "to write," Modern Persian *ni-viš-tan*, Old Slavic *pisa-ti* "to write," Runic stone from Einang, Norway (*ca.* A.D. 400: primitive Old Norse), *dagaR ÞaR runo faihido* "(*I*) *Dag* wrote these runes"; Tokharian *paiyka-tsi* "to write."

Undoubtedly these are one and the same verb, and this verb occurs in so many branches that its Indo-European age cannot be doubted. But its earliest meaning cannot have been "to write" if by that term we intend to designate anything systematic. The utmost that can be conjectured is that the word applied to narrative pictures or marks and symbols of various kinds; and even of that we cannot be sure. The verb may have had a meaning that lay still farther from any idea of communication, and nearer to that of the Latin *pic-tu-s* "painted," or the Greek *poik-ílos* "variegated." From such an original sense it might have been accidentally specialized in the same way in different groups of languages.

The effort to reconstruct the civilization of the Indo-Europeans in the far distant past by means of linguistic evidence is about as old as the science of comparative linguistics.

As early as 1818 Rask, in his *Undersögelse*, arranged the Indo-European vocabulary according to categories of meaning, not with the purpose of reconstructing the civilization of a buried age, but in order to prove that the words common to the different branches belonged to the central part of the vocabulary. But soon after Rask, works appeared which directly and expressly contemplated the history of Indo-European civilization. The first relatively thorough attempt was made by Adalbert Kuhn in 1845. Adolphe Pictet published a very complete treatment in 1859–63; and I might add a long series of works by various authors, among them many of the best-known scholars of the older period. But the older school was altogether too uncritical, and the result of their efforts was to depict the culture of our oldest linguistic forefathers in far too brilliant colors. Vigorous opposition manifested itself in Victor Hehn's *Culturpflanzen und Hausthiere in ihrem Übergang aus Asien nach Griechenland und Italien sowie in das übrige Europa* (1870. "Cultivated Plants and Domestic Animals in their Journey from Asia to Greece, Italy, and the Rest of Europe"). With pitiless scepticism he dispelled the romantic glamour with which the distant past had been surrounded. He perceived that the scholar must be on his guard against the temptation to associate modern cultural ideas with the ancient terms. He saw — and even exaggerated — the danger of mistaking wandering loan-words for words inherited from the ancient stock. His conception of the primitive culture of the Indo-Europeans rests first of all upon concrete facts and historical information concerning the less developed Indo-European peoples. And although he was unquestionably too cautious at times in drawing inferences from the linguistic material, his methods have exerted a powerful influence upon subsequent investigation. Among the many since 1870 who have attacked the problem of Indo-European civilization, it must suffice to name Otto Schrader and his *Sprachvergleichung und Urgeschichte* (1883), and *Reallexikon der indogermanischen Altertumskunde* (1901, new edition 1917–29).

The question of the relationship among the Indo-European and foreign families of languages came up in the first period of comparative linguistics. Relationship between Semitic and Indo-European was asserted by Rudolf von Raumer, beginning in 1863, and by Ascoli from 1864 on. But convincing proof could not be expected at that time. Resemblances in the morphology of the two families are extremely few, and proof by means of vocabulary and the laws of sounds was not then understood. Schleicher denied most positively any relationship between the two, pointing to the great dissimilarity in the forms of the roots: in Semitic the roots consist of three syllables of very simple and uniform structure, as in Arabic *katala* (root form and preterite of the verb "to kill"), while in Indo-European the roots are monosyllabic and of widely varying — partly heavily compounded — form, as in Latin *ī-re* "to go," *stā-re* "to stand," *lub-et* "it pleases," *vert-ō* "I turn," *ed-ō* "I eat," and so on. At that time nobody could weaken this argument. And it might have been added, although Schleicher did not do so, that the phonetic systems of the two families are extremely different, as may be seen from a single example: in Semitic there is an abundance of gutturals, whereas in Indo-European there is not one, not even the (to us) ordinary *h*. With this in view, one might feel tempted to assent to Schleicher's exclamation, "What weight have the few similarities in roots in the two families against these sharp contrasts?" And one might well be disposed to neglect "the few similarities" which one could not help observing.

Nothing was changed in the problem by the first step in a systematic examination of the vocabulary which Friedrich Delitzsch took in his *Studien über indogermanisch-semitische Wurzelverwandtschaft* (1873). But the development of Indo-European linguistics changed the problem greatly. The monosyllabic form of Indo-European roots turned out to be an entirely secondary phenomenon: in historical times the roots of the words for *heaven*, *god*, or *heart* may appear to be *diw-* or *kerd-*, but we have good reason to believe that in a period older than that of the Indo-European parent language these roots had forms like *däyäwä-*, or *kärädä* (see above, p. 290), and that the phonological system in this older period had quite a different appearance from that which we attribute to the Indo-European language.

HERMANN MÖLLER

With this background, there appeared in 1906 an extraordinarily important work by the Danish scholar Hermann Möller, *Semitisch und Indogermanisch*. This is a splendid attempt to discover the laws controlling the relationship between Indo-European and Semitic consonants — a successful attempt, although only the main lines of development are traced. Time alone will show how far we can advance by Möller's method. Certain it is, however, that the comparison of the two families can never be carried out so completely and in such detail as the comparison within the fields of the individual languages of one family.

But Indo-European has been brought into connection with other families besides Semitic. Vilhelm Thomsen, as early as 1869, indicated the possibility of a relationship with Finno-Ugrian, but he did not pursue the subject very far. In 1879 the Esthonian Nicolai Anderson published an extensive work on the subject, the value of which is considerably impaired by its many errors. Great interest was awakened when the English scholar Henry Sweet advocated the relationship somewhat passionately in a little popular book, *The History of Language* (1900). However, among the individual similarities which Sweet mentions, some are incorrect, and his space was too limited to permit of actual proof. Trustworthy studies of some length by K. B. Wiklund and H. Paasonen appeared in 1906 and 1908. After these works it seems unnecessary to doubt the relationship further.

Moreover, the inflectional systems show much greater relationships than in the case of Semitic. The original ending of the accusative case in Finno-Ugrian was -*m*, which in Finnish has changed to -*n*. The same ending is Indo-European:

	Finnish		Cheremissian	Latin	Greek
Nominative	*käsi*	hand	*kit*	*vespera* evening	*hespérā*
Accusative	*käde-n*		*kiδ-əm*	*vespera-m*	*hespérā-n*

The similarities in the personal endings of verbs are especially striking:

	Finnish	Cheremissian	Greek		Sanskrit
1st person sg.	*kuolen*	I die *kole-m*	*é-phero-n*	I carried	*a-bhara-m*
1st person pl.	*kuole-mme*	we die	*e-phéromen*	we carried	
2d person pl.	*kuole-tte*	you die	*e-phére-te*	you carried	

Furthermore, there is an unmistakable similarity between the two families in a series of pronouns and in the negation "not":

	Finnish	Latin
minä	I (Lappish *mon*)	*mē* me
sinä	thou (*s* from *t*; Lapp. *don*)	*tē* thee
		Sanskrit
tä-mä	this	*ta-*
jo-ka	who, which (relative)	*ya-*
ku-ka	who? (interrogative)	*ka-*

	Hungarian	Old Norse
	ne not	*ne* not

It is impossible to regard all this as the result of accident. It is noteworthy, however, that the similarities hitherto pointed out in the more concrete part of the vocabulary are very few, although some of them are as striking as Finnish *nimi* "name," Latin *nōmen*. Consideration of the problem whether sound-laws still unknown to us, or morphological developments not yet understood, have obliterated the originally more numerous points of similarity, or whether the vocabulary in one of the families was largely renewed after the period in common, we must postpone until later. But to deny relationship between the families would be overbold.

If we accept relationship, we are led yet farther afield, not only to Samoyed, which cannot be separated from Finno-Ugrian, but throughout all of Northern Asia and across Bering Strait, because similar, though fainter, resemblances like those here cited are found also in Turkish, Mongolian and Manchu, in Yukaghir, and even in Eskimo. If, on the other hand, we agree in the matter of relationship with Semitic, then we must also accept relationship with the far-flung Hamitic family, and perhaps with Basque. And squarely in the midst between our supposed Northern and Southern relatives stand the Caucasian languages, which we cannot ignore, and various extinct languages in Asia Minor and thereabout. It is not impossible that some of the non-Indo-European languages of antiquity in Asia Minor were once the most closely related of all to the Indo-European family.[1]

As a comprehensive designation for the families of languages which are related to Indo-European, we may employ the expression *Nostratian Languages* (from Latin *nostrās* "our countryman"). The boundaries for the Nostratian world of languages cannot yet be determined, but the area is enormous, and includes such widely divergent races that one becomes almost dizzy at the thought. It includes the world's most highly civilized nations together with degraded polar races and perhaps negroes. If, however, one considers the racial opposites and the widely varying stages of culture which are occasionally included within one and the same linguistic family (for instance, Finno-Ugrian and Turkish), or the enormous distribution which a single language has at times attained in the historical period (Latin, Arabic, English, Russian), one's principal misgivings on the score of this far-reaching inclusion will fade away. The question remains simply whether sufficient material can be collected to give this inclusion flesh and blood and a good clear outline.

[1] See above, p. 150.

Or will it all resolve itself into a suspicion that all the languages of the earth.are related one to another — a doctrine which, in spite of Trombetti's eloquent plea,[1] we still have no prospect of proving, or even of beginning to prove?

[1] *Lunità d'origine del linguaggio* (1905), and *Elementi di glottologia* (1922).

INDICES

GENERAL INDEX *

$\ddot{u} = ue;\ \alpha,\ \ddot{o} = oe;\quad \alpha,\ \ddot{a} = ae;\ \dot{d}$ after $z;\ \acute{s} = s$

Abkhasian 114
ablaut 23, 39 ff., 244, 272, 285 ff.
absence of a word does not permit of sure cultural inferences 321, 327, 329
Abu Simbel inscriptions 213
Accadian 116 note
accent 66, 283
Achæmenides 23, 159, 162
Adelung, Johann Christoph (*1732–1806*) 10, 65, 100
Æneas 3
Æolic 3, 85 (2), 88
Æquians 92
affricate 132
Afghans 24
agglutinative languages 99 f.
Ahiram inscription 177 and note 1
Ahrens, H. L. (*1808–81*) 89
Ainu 134–35
Alaska, language of 137
Albanian 12, 64, 77 ff., 188, 247, 276, 311 ff., 316
Alemannic 34 f.
Aleut 136
Alexandrian period 80
Almkvist, H. (*1839–1904*) 123
alphabet 142, 145, 146, 148, 173, 176–239
——, Albanian 71 f., 239
——, Anglo-Saxon 239
——, Arabian 111, 130, 180, 187
——, ——, South 181
——, Armenian 74, 115, 208
——, Avestan 27, 185
——, Berber 121, 188, 200
——, Coptic 176, 208–09
——, Ethiopian 180
——, Etruscan 216
——, Georgian 115, 208
——, Gothic 31, 32, 208, 235
——, "Gothic" 239
——, Greek 88, 142, 145–46, 148, 203 ff., 228
——, Iberian 124
——, Indian 145, 188 ff.
——, Ionian 207, 223
——, Irish 57, 238
——, Kalmuk 112, 113
——, Korean 147
——, Latin 209, 226, 238
——, Lemnian 220, 221

alphabet, Libyan 121, 188
——, Manchu 112, 186
——, Mongolian 112, 113, 186
——, North Etruscan 225, 226, 227
——, Nubian (Christian) 176
——, "Old Nubian" 122, 176
——, Oscan 228
——, Pehlevi 185
——, Permian 104
——, Phrygian 221
——, Semitic 118, 142, 145, 146, 148, 153, 176–88
——, Slavonic 45, 47, 208
——, Sogdian 111, 186, 199
——, Tuareg 121, 200
——, Turkish 110, 188, 196 ff.
——, Uighurian 112, 186
——, Umbrian 227
Altaic 107, 111 ff., 186, 248
Amarna tablets 164, 181
Amathus inscriptions 170
American languages 136–37
American script 137, 142–43, 148
analogy, principle of 291 ff.
Andaman Islands, language of 139–40
Anderson, Nicolai (*1845–1905*) 336
Andreas, F. C. (*1846–1930*) 186 note 1
Anglian 33
Annam 145
Annamite 131
Anquetil du Pérron (*1731–1805*) 24 f., 159
Anzeiger für indogermanische Sprachund Altertumskunde 309
Aquitanians 53, 124
Arabia, Southern 178
Arabian geographers 139
Arabic 39, 116–19, 146, 180, 187, 205, 241, 338
Aramaic 116–19, 184–85, 190, 199, 205, 220
Arcadian 85
Archimedes 85–86
Archiv für slavische Philologie 53
Arkiv för nordisk filologi 43
Armenian 12, 64, 73 ff., 79, 100, 149, 208, 223, 246, 247, 276, 311, 313, 315, 317
Armorica 55
Aryan 311 ff., 314, 316, 329 f.
Arzawa 165
Ascoli, Graziadio Isaia (*1829–1907*) 60, 97, 279 ff., 284, 335

* Prepared by the Author.

INDEX OF WORDS

(Order of the Latin alphabet except for Sanskrit and Greek)

kyn 252
leifa 243
lykill 297, 298
magr 253, 261
mala 330
marr 322
mik 253
mjolka 328
mjǫl, mjǫlvi 330

ne 337
nefi 261
ǫr 327

port 253
rauði 323
reita 253
sá 331
sik 253
silfr 325
slá 282
synir 30 note
tamr 252
tár 261
titra 253, and note
tívar 333
tryggr 30 note
tveggja 30 note
Týr 333
þegja 253
þrír 252
vatn 30 note
verða 286
víkja 253

Swedish
kind 281
kön 281
nyckel 297,298
son, söner 38

Danish
ældre 268
barn 8
björn 322 note
horn 268
nögle 297, 298
pige 260 note
sende 268
sky 251 note 2
sönner 30 note

Old and Middle English
æx 326
ár 326
béodan 286
bídan 286
bóc-tréow 322

bróþor 261
bycgean (bohte) 38
céosan, coren 282
dáh 327
M.E. ei 30 note
eofor 261
eoh 267
eorlas 299
erian 329
etan 39, 265
fæder 261
feoh 329
findan 286
fléag 296
getréowe 30 note
giest 30 note
helpan 286
heoru 327
hwá 281
hwer 327
meolcan 328
mere 322
M.E. nadder 296
nefa 261
M.E. quern 331
sáwan 331
sellan (sealde) 38
séoþan 282
sléan, slegen 282
sníþan 282
snoru 332
soden 282
spinnan 296
stígan 271
sunu, suna 298, 299, 302
sweger, swéor 332
téon, togen 282
þúsend 333
uncúþ 284
wæter 30 note
weorþan 286
widewe 332

Modern English *
adder 296
angel 26
arrow 327
axe 326
axle 328
bad 263
Scotch bairn 289
to be 30 note
bear 321, 322 note
to bear 38, 100, 289

* Here are included the English words used in the last chapter as translations of cultural terms in the older Germanic languages if they are etymologically identical

MIDLAND BOOKS